Promise You Won't Forget Us

STORIES FROM AFRICA

Belinda Evans

All of the events and people in this book are real; some names have been changed to protect privacy

Copyright © 2013 Belinda Evans. All rights reserved.

ISBN 978-1-291-35594-9

Many people touched my life during my journey in Kenya. From the beautiful friendships I formed to the heartbreaking tragedies I witnessed, these are the stories of my friends.
I dedicate this book to my African family.
Mungu akubariki – God bless you.

AFRICA

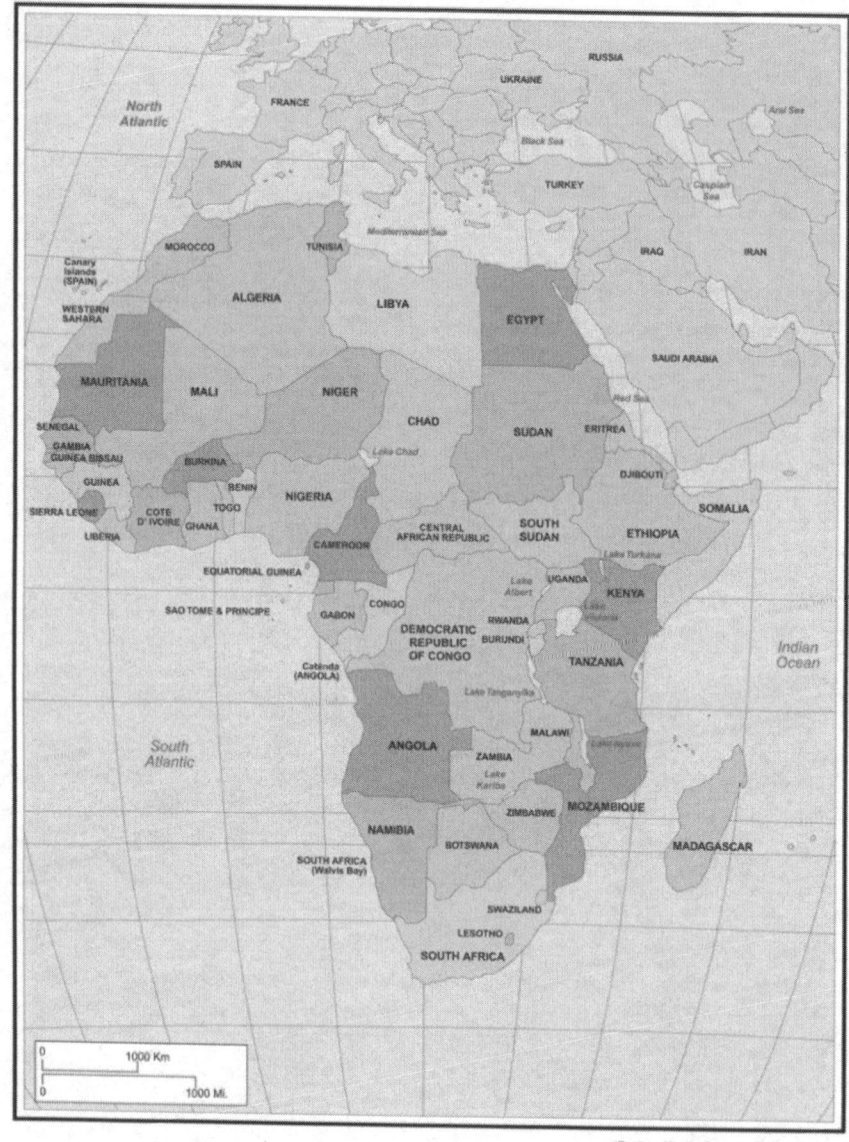

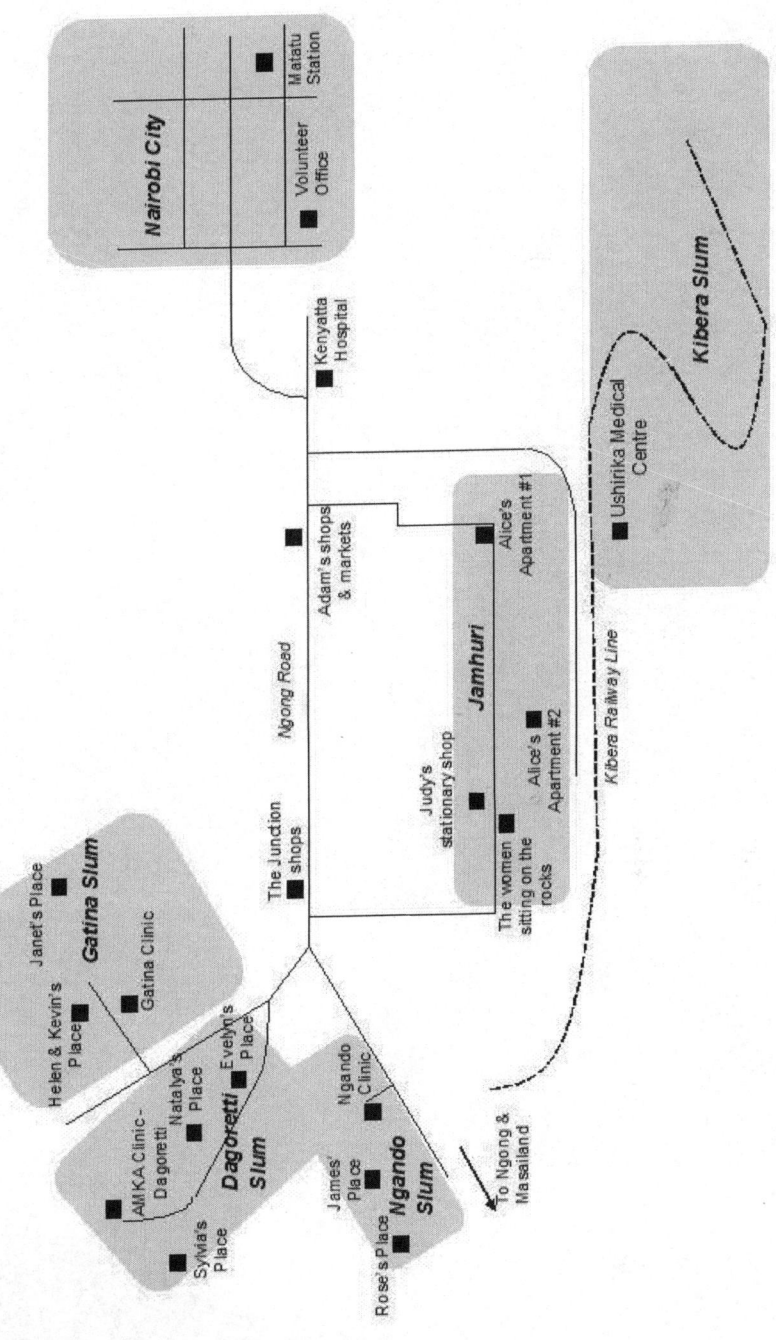

The world is a book and those who do not travel
read only one page - St. Augustine

Belinda Evans

Prologue

Adelaide, Australia

I've been camping once. I was in Year 8 and the weekend before we left for camp I spent a whole afternoon practising putting up the tent with my friend Claire in my family's backyard. I'm a city girl, born and raised. I've backpacked around Europe on my own, climbed the Eiffel tower in Paris and eaten gelati outside the Colosseum in Rome. But I've never been to an underdeveloped country. I've never seen poverty or famine, or lived without certain luxuries or securities. I've never been to Africa; but it has always been a dream.

Now it is all about to happen. Following months of preparation, fundraising activities, vaccinations, training courses and arranging time off work, it's finally here. My bags are packed with everything I can think of, from first aid supplies, anti-malaria pills and a mosquito net to a beginner's guide to Swahili, my handbooks on HIV education and some Australian souvenirs. I've left behind my make-up bag, gym membership and laptop. Visiting Africa and working as a volunteer has been a vision of mine for a long time. Up until now I've been working as a Radiation Therapist in a large oncology centre helping patients in their battle against cancer. I'm about to extend this job of caring for others in more ways and with more experiences than I could have ever imagined.

Promise You Won't Forget Us

Belinda Evans

Chapter 1 - Changes

The key to change..... is to let go of fear – Rosanne Cash

April 2006 – Johannesburg, South Africa

I step outside Johannesburg International Airport, wary and wide-eyed, in search of my hotel shuttle bus. There are dozens of unfamiliar faces crowding in around me, men of all ages and races, offering to take me where I need to go. I watch their hands waving me towards their cars and their eyes engaging with mine, the young white woman dressed in her brand new hiking boots and trying to balance a 20kg pack on her back. I'm on my own and feel overwhelmed with my very first decision.

I was given some advice before leaving about not trusting people. Friends told me their stories of people travelling through these parts of the world. It's a long way from the calm and secure neighbourhoods of Adelaide in South Australia. And now recalling this advice, I'm paranoid about doing anything. So here I am, stalled outside the arrivals gate, watching everybody else coming and going in the chaos that surrounds me. I pull myself together, choosing to ignore my friends' advice as I realise that I have to trust somebody if I want my African dream to go beyond this airport.

A young man in shorts and a reassuring (or am I mistaking it for convincing) smile ushers me away from the congestion around the airport.

'Where to?' he asks me.

'The Southern.'

He says he knows it and that he'll take me there. I follow the boy into the isolated, moonlit car park of the airport. We keep walking until soon there is no longer anybody around me. He insists it's not much farther. It is completely dark outside and I am jet lagged from the long flight. Not to mention completely unfamiliar with this part of the world. At this point, paranoid and naive, I'm convinced that I've let myself be led into a trap and that any moment now somebody will pull out a knife and take all my bags. That is, after all, what happens to every traveller on their first day in Africa isn't it? We keep walking. Finally I see the shuttle and in great relief jump on board with my bags, delighted to leave the airport and its seediness behind me. I've already learnt my first lesson in this African journey: *Sometimes you just have to trust people.*

I arrive shortly after at the hotel and make the most of a big double bed with an abundance of white fluffy pillows, clean towels, satellite television and drinkable tap water for one last night. Who knows when the next time I'll have such luxuries will be, or what conditions I'll be living in at all. Already, I know that I'm in for an adventure here like nothing I've experienced in my lifetime. I'm in Africa and tomorrow I'll arrive at my destination - Kenya.

Chapter 2 – At first sight

One's destination is never a place, but a new way of seeing things
– Henry Miller

April 2006 – Nairobi, Kenya

There are people everywhere. Many are walking alongside the streets, some sitting by their road-side stalls, others riding bikes with containers of water strapped to the backs. Dozens more are crammed into overfilled vehicles that speed along the pot-holed bitumen roads. Outside the air is dusty and polluted with the smell of diesel fumes. It is warm and this African sky is fiercely lit up by the glowing afternoon sun. All my senses are switched on with excitement at this first glimpse of Nairobi.

I'm met at the arrivals section of Jomo Kenyatta Airport by Eric, a member of the volunteer organisation I'll be working with. I put to use some of my well-rehearsed beginners Swahili.

'Habari, bwana. Jina langu ni Belinda.' *Hello sir, my name is Belinda.*

Much to my amazement Eric replies in fluent English. Oh well, I'm still glad to have made the effort. Our driver arrives and we take the journey through Nairobi towards my home stay where I will be living for the duration of my placement.

The drive is fascinating. My eyes are wide open and my face is glued to the dirty windows of the white minivan, a common vehicle in these parts of Africa. I see many *matatus*, which are the shared mini buses that serve as public transport in Kenya. These sometimes colourfully painted cars, decked out with impressive audio systems and sub-woofers, swerve recklessly in and out of traffic along the city roads. Some are painted in bright hippy patterns; others are decorated with large stickers of popular singers like Nelly, Beyoncé or 2Pac. There are so many people walking along the sides of the roads. I wonder where they're all going. People are selling their fruits and vegetables at small stalls made of timber sheets set up by the roadside. As we attack the first roundabout at great speed I quickly learn there are not too many road rules here in Nairobi. In the back of the van I hold onto my dusty seat as we head closer to the suburb of Jamhuri.

I will be staying in host-family accommodation arranged by the volunteer organisation. I will be living with Alice, who is a local Kenyan lady in her early thirties and works as a nutritionist at Kenyatta Hospital. She's unmarried and lives on her own. This is all the information I know on my arrival in Kenya. I can't wait to find out more details, I have so many questions. I want to ask Eric about Alice, where she lives, are there any other volunteers staying with her, does her place have electricity and running water, do you know where I will be working, is it far from Alice's house, what happens tomorrow, what time will I get picked up, what does our orientation session involve? I have the eager inquisitiveness of a twenty-three year old westerner. Instead I quietly take everything in through the windows of our van as we approach Jamhuri. Everything is captivating to my innocent eyes.

Alice lives in Jamhuri, which is a suburb south west of Nairobi city near the Ngong forest. We turn off the main Ngong road and onto a bumpy dirt road as we approach her place. Little stalls selling food, fabrics and hardware products line the streets as well as small hairdressing salons and tailors sitting inside tiny wooden shops. Chickens and stray dogs wander around aimlessly. We pass big rubbish dumps by the roadside and I can see open sewage running alongside the street.

Jamhuri is a newer residential area in Nairobi. There is a mix of built-up and half-finished houses and apartment blocks lining the main road. Some of the homes, complete with driveway and car, are impressive compared to the underdeveloped surroundings they have been built within and are enclosed by large steel security gates. It is a vision of contrasts, as nearby building works are taking place and teams of young men are busily working on top of the half-built apartment blocks. I watch a group of small children playing soccer out in the dusty street with a ball made of old plastic bags bundled together. There are few cars along the street. As we drive down the main road, the locals step out of our way and look inside the van which weaves around the big potholes on the uneven dirt road, interested to see who's passing by.

Alice lives in a block of four apartments along the main street in Jamhuri. As our van pulls in outside the apartment, we greet the young security guard out the front who lets us through the front gates and Eric leads me into Alice's place. I am greeted by Molly at the front door; she's a young volunteer from New York also staying at Alice's apartment. Inside, the apartment is well furnished and welcoming. Having prepared for living in any condition, I'm surprised there is electricity, running water, a toilet, and even a television here. Although she's just two weeks into her placement, Molly is a wealth of information and advice as a fellow newcomer to this vastly different part of the world. Her bubbly personality and relaxed attitude are an immediate source of reassurance for me, as I step into the unknown. Molly is a medical student at the University of New York and is volunteering in one of the medical clinics in Kibera, right behind where we are living.

Kibera is the largest slum in East Africa, and one of the most populated areas of substandard housing and living conditions in the world. It is located just five minutes' walk across the railway line from Alice's apartment in Jamhuri, on the outskirts of Nairobi. I can't wait to see Kibera. I've seen pictures and read many stories about this slum which is home to about one million people living in a 2.5km^2 area; a population density of about 300,000 people per square kilometre. This massive slum is considered by the government to be an illegal settlement, having been established on government land. They therefore offer zero assistance to these millions of people living in poverty in Kibera. The poverty is severe, with no running water or electricity in many parts, no toilets or waste collection and an open sewage system. These conditions promote poor hygiene and the spread of infections and disease. HIV has been estimated to affect up to 20% of the people living in Kibera. I suspect it is here where a lot of my work will be done.

Molly shows me around Alice's apartment. From the main living area, where there are two couches and a colourful rug on the floor, we walk into the kitchen area which is modern looking. There are cupboards, all of which are empty as Alice has not been in the apartment long. As I will also learn, food is only bought as it is needed, on a meal-to-meal basis. Other than a bag of sliced bread, some butter, tea bags and a few kitchen utensils, the kitchen is otherwise bare. There are two other rooms, one of which is Alice's bedroom and the other I will share with Molly. A bunk bed has been set up inside and there are some small drawers for our belongings. Molly is already well settled in, with a row of large water bottles lined up along the bedroom wall and her mosquito net attached to the ceiling. Next to the bedroom, there is a toilet and a separate shower. It's a nice simple apartment, equipped with facilities that I hadn't been sure to find.

Molly invites me to play a game of cards with her in the living room while we wait for Alice to come home from work. I can't remember the last time I played cards, but it feels great. It's nice to have such a friendly and helpful roommate and Molly tells me all about Alice, life in Nairobi and her volunteer work at the clinic.

Alice arrives home later that evening after work. As she steps inside her apartment, dressed smartly in a beige western style suit, with her hair beautifully braided, she is wearing a big smile and shows great warmth.

'Hello Belinda!' she beams, and she gives me a traditional Kenyan hug, leaning in on either side of my shoulders. I immediately love Alice and feel at home with her here. She is very friendly and welcoming and so happy to have guests stay in her house. We sit down immediately with Molly in the living room and get to know each other.

Alice was born in Nyeri, a town in the central highlands of Kenya. She completed her studies in Nutrition at Egerton University, Njoro, in the nearby Rift Valley Province, before moving to Nairobi a few years ago to find work, like many Kenyans are forced to do. Alice tells me she's a Kikuyu, which is the largest ethnic group in Kenya typically inhabiting the central highland region. As well as speaking fluent English and Swahili, Alice also speaks Kikuyu, the native language of her tribe. I have so much to learn about this country, its races, traditions and culture.

Alice prepares some traditional chai– an extra sweet tea prepared with black Kenyan tea, steamed milk, a little water and plenty of sugar. *Chai*, in Swahili, means tea. I love it all.... drinking tea with Alice and Molly in my new home, sharing stories of Australia, Kenya, America and our families. Alice has no fridge or stove and cooks over a small kerosene cooker on her kitchen floor. She prepares an amazing dinner of minced beef with spices of cinnamon, cumin and coriander, served with vegetables and *chapatti*, the traditional tortilla that Alice makes herself. I watch her roll the dough out into flat circles and then spin them around on the heavy steel chapatti plate over the cooker, like she does every day. We share another mug of chai each before heading to bed. I can't believe that I'm finally here, in my new home, with a new family. I feel excited with the anticipation and uncertainty of what lies ahead.

Chapter 3 – Hakuna Matata

Life is a succession of lessons, which must be lived to be understood
– Ralph Waldo Emerson

I wake up early on Saturday morning, put on my jeans, long sleeved shirt and hiking boots, drink some chai for breakfast and then sit waiting on the couch in Alice's apartment at 9 o'clock sharp. I'm waiting for a driver to collect me to go to today's orientation session for the new volunteers in Nairobi. I'm excited about meeting other volunteers and learning more about what my role will be in my project. It's now 10:30 a.m. Sitting, waiting eagerly on the couch inside the apartment, I learn my next two lessons in this African journey. *Lesson 2* is the concept of *African time*. There is little understanding of punctuality here. People come when they're ready, there is no point stressing about being late because things happen when they're ready to. I notice already that there is no clock inside the house. My next lesson and perhaps the most useful for my transition into this different culture is *lesson 3: Hakuna matata*. It's a popular Swahili expression that means 'no worries'. As Westerners, we want to and have to know everything. Our days function around our schedule in our day planners or phones. Today I learn to pack away my planner and my watch as I adjust to this new culture. Don't worry; everything will happen in its own time. African time.

My ride eventually arrives and I climb into the back of the van. I greet the driver and Eric, who smiles and introduces himself to me in Swahili, mimicking my performance at the airport yesterday. I laugh with him and feel glad to see a familiar face. We head off down the main dirt road of Jamhuri and before we know it the driver is revving the engine but we've stopped moving. The car has broken down right in the middle of the road. People walking by stop and stare, not so much at the broken down vehicle because apparently this is a common affair, but at me. The *mzungu* – the white person. I feel like a celebrity spotted amongst hundreds of people. There are few mzungus in Kenya, especially in these parts of Nairobi where I'm staying and will be working.

The only white people are usually other volunteers working in these areas close to the slums.

Our vehicle is not moving and smoke is now coming from the engine. I'm amazed to watch the locals come from everywhere to offer their help, assisting in whatever way they can. That is something we no longer see all the time back home. The community here is very united. Men with containers of water help the driver by filling up the tanks. Before I know it, sitting alone in the back of this van, I'm being pushed along the road by seven complete strangers and I've become a spectacle on the main road of Jamhuri. Of course knowing nothing about cars I'm in no position to offer my help so I continue to enjoy my newfound popularity. I refrain from waving like the Queen, realising that it's not quite the same sitting in the back of a dusty minivan in Jamhuri as it is travelling down Buckingham Palace Road in a Rolls-Royce. Our vehicle eventually starts again and we're once again on our way. I've just had my *fourth lesson* in Kenya - *Every day is an adventure*, painted by unexpected events that add to the thrill of this experience.

On the way into Nairobi city we stop to pick up five other volunteers from their home stays. First is Gaby a pale redhead from Ireland who, in her first two days in Kenya, has managed to be scolded with second degree burns around her neck and chest from the African sun. Staying with Gaby is Sarah, a young school leaver from New York, whose parents thought it would be a worthwhile experience to send their daughter to volunteer in Africa. She's here firstly because of them, and secondly for herself. We then stop at another home stay where Susan, a young bubbly real-estate agent from London joins us, alongside her is, Suen a quietly spoken girl from Hong Kong. Finally we collect Claire who is French and has come directly from a similar volunteer project in South Africa. She appears the expert next to all of us amateurs in her Khaki shorts, boots and special purifying water bottle dangling by her side. We all silently wonder if we should have added this attire to our pre-packing list, feeling clueless about the ventures that are in store for us. Well it's too late we're here now.

Nairobi city is hectic. There are people, buses and cars everywhere, and it is noisy. Black diesel pollution stings my eyes and pick-pocketers lurk about. I find no other way to describe Nairobi than shady. It is even known to be nicknamed '*Nairobbery*'. Thousands of people wander the streets with or without a mission and as mzungus we stand out. Money pouch on and bag gripped tight, I'm alert and extremely cautious.

The city skyline is framed by modern-looking skyscrapers, many belonging to an increasing number of international companies that contribute to a growing expatriate community. Nairobi is the capital of the Republic of Kenya and the largest city in East Africa. It has the strongest economy of all cities in East and Central Africa. The city's population is about 3 million people, of which an estimated 60% live in slum settlements around the city. Kenya's population of 39 million is composed of different races, tribes and cultures. Its British colonial history dates back to the late 19th century when it was known as British East Africa up until 1920. The Mau Mau rebellion which saw conflicts between Africans and British rule dominated the 1950s, and paved the way for Kenyan Independence in December 1963. One year later, on the 12th December 1964 the Republic of Kenya was proclaimed and Jomo Kenyatta was named the first president. Subsequent presidential leaders have been Daniel arap Moi and current day President Mwai Kibaki.

Today, Kenya's economy is largely fuelled by its strong tourism industry. Many of the best safari parks in Africa are located in Kenya, including the Masai Mara, which showcases natural environments and the popular African wildlife. Kenya also boasts strong exports in agriculture and horticulture, with flower exports, tea and coffee contributing substantially to their economy. Despite its significant growth and development, Nairobi still has high levels of crime and poverty. The majority of the population continues to live below the poverty line and the slums surrounding the city are growing bigger and bigger. These create an obvious divide between middle and lower classes in a city that is modernising but affected by ongoing political and ethnic differences.

Our van of enthusiastic volunteers arrives outside an office building in the city centre, and one by one we walk up the steps to the volunteer organisation's office. Our orientation session involves meeting the co-ordinator and staff at the volunteer office. I meet Irene, who is Alice's sister and the head co-ordinator of all of the volunteer projects, placements and home stays in the Kenya program. Her big smile and laugh are infectious and I immediately warm to Irene's friendliness and carefree manner.

I have come to volunteer for Global Volunteer Network (GVN), a New-Zealand based non-government organisation that has volunteer projects all around the world, including countries in Africa, Asia and the Americas. Their key vision is to support the work of local volunteer organisations operating within the community through the placement of international volunteers. The projects requiring support in Kenya include teaching roles in schools, working in orphanages, helping in the HIV/AIDS outreach programs, working in medical clinics and in rural Masailand. All the volunteers have come from diverse backgrounds and experiences and will be staying for different periods of time, ranging from a couple of weeks to a year.

Throughout the morning Irene conducts the orientation session, providing an introduction to life in Kenya, including important aspects of the culture and lifestyle that we might experience living and working here as volunteers. We all participate in a short language lesson in Swahili and are given the opportunity to finally ask the dozens of questions that we've all jumped off the airplane wanting desperately to ask.

We all need to change our money into Kenyan shillings and to buy mobile phones so we're led into the nearby covered markets by Eric who tells us he knows somebody who can offer us a good deal. One by one we step behind this private curtain in a hidden corner of the market place and sit down at a table to change our money with a man. He is sitting at a small table with a calculator and money box and is accompanied by a friend standing next to him. I take my Kenyan shillings and get out of that room as quickly as possible. Standing outside the small booth with the other new volunteers, we chat amongst ourselves about how dodgy the secretive money exchange is, especially having walked past a few proper exchange booths on the streets. We've all instantly bonded during the morning's session, having been brought together as new arrivals in this different and exciting country.

After eating a lunch of rice and beans in a small city diner, we're all driven back to our home stays in the afternoon. One by one, our driver drops off Sarah, Suen, Susan, Sarah, Gaby and finally myself back into the Jamhuri neighbourhood. We say goodbye to each other, knowing we'll be seeing each other soon. Despite coming from different countries, families, careers and age-groups, we feel so similar in our mission here in Kenya. Today we've found out about our projects and where we'll be living, some staying in Nairobi like myself, others about to travel into rural placements, where the conditions are much different again. We'll start our volunteer projects on Monday. Gaby, Sarah, Claire and Suen will all be working as teachers in a local primary school; while Susan will be in an orphanage on the outskirts of Nairobi. Irene told me during the orientation that there's a lot of work waiting for me to do in my project. I can't wait.

Chapter 4 – Ushirika

One person's slum is another person's community – May Hobbs

It's my first day at work and I'm ready to go. My job is to work as a part of the HIV project and I've been placed at Ushirika Medical Clinic in Kibera. Molly, my housemate, has already been working in this clinic for the past few weeks in the medical program so I'm relieved to have somebody by my side.

Ushirika Medical Clinic is a small private clinic, just five minutes' walk from our apartment in Jamhuri. As we leave Alice's place, the walk into the slums of Kibera is incredible. Dressed in jeans, my hiking boots, a long sleeved khaki shirt and my backpack, I walk through the dirt paths and cross the main Kibera railway line that separates the slums of Kibera from the more civilised, yet still under-privileged streets of Jamhuri. Once over the train tracks, the picture is amazing. Fruit and vegetable stands are set up one after the other on old wooden displays. Women sit on the ground stringing beans which are heaped onto canvas sacks for sale. Next to them are their children turning fresh chapattis on a hot plate one by one, stacking them onto a big pile for sale. The air is filled with this smell of chapatti being cooked as well as the dusty African air. This is Kibera. Chickens and stray dogs roam about and the air is alive with the sounds of people singing, talking and preaching. The light of a new day brings a fresh hope for goodness. Gospel music booms from a small music shack, giving a loud positive feel to the poverty I see before me. I walk along the main path lined by many different stalls, conscious of everybody staring at us as we head to work. '*Jambo*' they call out, the common Swahili word for hi. I say 'Jambo' back, delighted to be spoken to and to interact with the locals. This community feels so welcoming and united. Walking into these slums I experience feelings of discovery for a place and culture that are new to me, and at the same time feel strangely at home.

Ushirika means *fellowship* in Swahili. The clinic is an outpatient centre where locals from all around Kibera present with any type of medical problem, ranging from malaria and typhoid, to infections, injuries and wounds, to HIV. It is also a maternity clinic where many pregnant women living in the slums come in for their check-ups and to give birth. The clinic consists of one main building, containing several smaller rooms inside that include a pharmacy for dispensing medications, a laboratory for testing, three consulting rooms and an adjoined maternity ward and delivery room for maternity patients. The facilities are very basic and limited, and the clinic is very much overrun by the growing poverty-stricken population around these slums. My role is to help start up the HIV program in the clinic following the recent construction of some new rooms that will form a HIV unit and ward. This role will encompass counselling programs, testing facilities, treatment and education. There is a lot to be organised and I will be starting from scratch.

There are an estimated 2.2 million people in Kenya living with HIV. This represents an adult prevalence rate of about 6.3%. HIV (Human Immunodeficiency Virus) is a virus that mutates readily and exists in two types: HIV-1 and HIV-2 and many subtypes. HIV attacks the body's immune system and at its most advanced stage of infection is known as AIDS (Acquired Immune Deficiency Syndrome). It is at this stage that a patient becomes susceptible to infections and other serious illnesses. In comparison to other African countries, the highest rates of HIV are in Swaziland (25.9%), Botswana (24.8%), Lesotho (23.6%) and South Africa (17.8%). Worldwide, at the end of 2009, it was estimated that 22.5 million people were living with HIV in Sub-Saharan Africa.

In East Africa, Uganda is regarded as a role model for other African countries for its success in reducing HIV rates in the 1990s. Due to a strong government campaign and public education program (the ABC campaign; Abstain, Be faithful, Condoms) their rates dropped from 15% to as low as 5%, which has since been stabilised and used as a role model for Kenya. HIV prevalence in Kenya peaked in 2000 at 13.4%, and this decline has been attributed to increased education through government campaigns in the 1990s, and the increase in the availability of Antiretroviral drugs (ARVs). These are drugs that treat HIV and AIDS. There is no cure for HIV or AIDS. But taking ARVs can lower the amount of HIV in a person's body and allow them to live for a long time without being affected by their illness. These drugs have only recently become available to patients in many developing countries such as Kenya, despite the high incidence of HIV and AIDS. They can significantly improve the quality and lifespan of a

HIV infected person. The most common ARV treatment is combination therapy, where two or more antiretroviral drugs are taken every day.

Despite the progress in Kenya there is still a very long way to go. An estimated 80,000 people died in 2009 in Kenya from AIDS related illnesses. With 70% of the Kenyan population being under 30 years old, the younger generations have been significantly impacted upon. An AIDS orphan is defined as a child who has lost one parent or both parents due to AIDS. At the end of 2009, there were an estimated 1.2 million AIDS orphans n Kenya. A large percentage of Nairobi's population living with HIV are from Kibera, with up to 1 in 5 people estimated to be affected, a much higher incidence than in outside areas. High crime rates, the practice of polygamy in many of the ethnic groups, a lack of education and extremely challenging living conditions are amongst the factors contributing to the high prevalence of HIV in these slums. In Kenya, as for the rest of sub-Saharan Africa, heterosexual sex is the main route of transmission for HIV. Homosexual intercourse and intravenous drug use account for a very small number of cases of transmission. In Kibera there are no government clinics or hospitals. The only centres available are charitable organisations, missionary clinics or private centres such as Ushirika. It is impossible to reach out to most of the population and the services are severely under-resourced.

Ushirika is surrounded by white steel gates and as we walk through Molly and I are greeted by the caretaker Anna. Her kind and gentle smile is welcoming and she embraces me with the traditional greeting. I am introduced to all the other staff members. In the little hut out the front of the clinic is Ruth, the cook. She sits on her stool on a dirt floor warming up some chai tea for the staff to drink. Plastic plates and cups are hung from hooks on the wooden walls of her little kitchen which is without running water or electricity. Inside the clinic there is running water and intermittent supplies of electricity. Patients are seated next to each other on long benches in the common waiting area, patiently waiting their turn to be seen. This is not a free clinic. Patients must register then pay when they arrive before being seen by a doctor. A typical visit will cost 200kSh (about $Au2). The average Kenyan living in Kibera earns less than 50ksh ($Au1) a day. The clinic is obliged to ask a fee from patients to cover its running expenses since there is no government assistance in Kibera.

I meet Judson, a handsome dark young man who works in the pharmacy dispensing medications to the patients. Like all the medical staff, he is dressed smartly in black leather shoes, with his white lab coat over his trousers and shirt. Judson is 28 years old, and has a young daughter who lives away from him, whom he works to support. In the pharmacy all the drugs are kept in little containers in an old wooden cabinet and counted out by hand by Judson. He places them in tiny paper envelopes which he labels by hand with directions for the patients to collect. Paracetamol, Ibuprofen and Diclofenac (NSAIDs), Amoxicillin (antibiotic), Amodiaquine (anti malarial) and Tinidazole (anti parasitic) are the commonest drugs dispensed here. The clinic is not yet a recognised centre to distribute ARVs but they are available to patients at several nearby nominated centres in Kibera.

David is the technician who works alone in the laboratory, a small room located behind the reception area. Here blood tests are taken, rapid HIV tests are run and many other common diseases such as malaria, typhoid and diphtheria are diagnosed. David separates blood samples in the centrifuge, looks at blood cultures on slides under his microscope on his small work bench. He alone determines if patients have a positive or negative test result. I observe somebody spitting into a sample cup outside and passing in through the open windows to David in the laboratory to be tested for tuberculosis. It really is basic third world medicine.

The nutritionist working at Ushirika is a delightful young man with the happiest smile of anybody I've met. His name is Daniel he informs me as he shakes my hand enthusiastically, his white teeth shining against his dark black complexion. Immediately I adore Daniel. He's fun to be around and he jokes a lot. He's from the Kalenjin tribe, which Daniel tells me is known as the tribe of the marathon runners, where most of Kenya's top athletes come from. He says this proudly with a hint of charm. There are many different tribes in Kenya, each one having their own dialects, customs, beliefs and regions of origin. Tribal differences contribute to the great diversity across Kenya but have also been responsible for violence and fighting throughout the country's history.

The most populous ethnic group in Kenya is the Kikuyus (Alice's tribe), accounting for 17% of the population. This tribe is considered to dominate politically as well as economically in Kenya.

Many of Kenya's politicians including presidents Kibaki and Kenyatta and their governments come from this tribe.

I am quickly noticing the pride in introducing one's tribe when people introduce themselves here in Kenya. Other tribes that follow in dominance are the Luhya (accounting for 14% and originating from western Kenya), Luo (10% of the population), Kalenjin (Daniel's tribe centred around the Great Rift Valley, 13% of the population), Kabma (from east central Kenya, 10%), Kisil (from the western corner of Kenya, around Lake Victoria, 6%), Mijikenda (heavily forested areas inland from the coast, 5%), Meru (north eastern Kenya, 4%), Turkana (2.5%, along with the Masai tribe known to have kept their traditional lifestyles) and the Masai (2.1% the most famous tribe, extending into Tanzania).

Finally I meet Debra, a recent graduate from nursing school who is another of the 'doctors', *daktari*, here at Ushirika. I've quickly learnt that all of the staff examining patients are nurses. There are no doctors working here at Ushirika, though the nurses seem to be able to do everything a doctor would normally do. Debra is a beautiful, tall, slim young Kenyan woman from the Luo tribe with lovely long dark braids that fall midway down her back. She arrives at work in bright coloured dresses and manages to deliver babies in her black strappy sandals without a single stain on her white lab coat. Molly and I nickname Debra *Super nurse*. She can do and diagnose anything and delivers babies in a facility with no extra support like she's been doing it all of her life. She's 22 years old. The conditions in this clinic really are extremely primitive. Walking through the clinic and seeing the facilities for the first time, I feel like I'm in a different era, like the set of a war-time film. The 'delivery room' is a bed set up in the back room, at the end of the maternity ward with lino covered floors that I find Ruth scrubbing and hosing down following a delivery. Blood stains the walls next to the bed which the ladies have used to push against during their delivery. The most modern piece of equipment they have to use here would be the stethoscope. While equipment and supplies are limited, the practices I observe are always sterile and safe. Gloves are found in every small consulting room along with a small sink and soap and the boxes of supplies contain sterile syringes and dressings.

On my first day at Ushirika I spend time observing the running of the outpatient's clinic. While Molly is paired up with Super nurse Debra, I am accompanying Martin, another of the nurses in the clinic. We see a number of patients come through, quite a few women at different stages in their pregnancies. They have a special card and come by the clinic for regular check-up appointments to have their blood pressure taken as well as the position of the foetus measured by palpating the abdomen. A number of other patients come in with flu-like symptoms, all are tested for malaria, and all are positive. They are then sent to see Judson in the pharmacy for medication. The diagnosis of malaria here is as frequent as the winter flu back home. We also treat a few patients for infected wounds caused from falls or accidents which have not been kept clean or attended to for many days and have therefore developed into infections. One young boy presents with a bandage wrapped around his head, he fell from a timber roof and split his head open. We stitch his wound and prescribe some antibiotics. In just one afternoon in the clinic I've seen trauma cases, maternity patients and a variety of infectious diseases and yet this is just a glimpse of the range of patients that walk through the gates into Ushirika.

Tea time arrives and we go outside to join Ruth in the small wooden kitchen where she has prepared a large pot of chai tea. I see all the patients lined up in the waiting room on our way out and wonder if we should be taking a break with so many more cases to see. Then I remember the lessons I've learnt in *African time* and *Hakuna matata* and realise that they will be seen when we get to them. Incredibly, the patients are so orderly in that waiting room considering the severity of their health problems. They are grateful to be seen regardless of the number of hours they wait. For many, to be seen at all is a privilege.

We all regroup out the front of the clinic: Debra, Molly, Daniel, David, Judson, Martin and I. Outside I observe the people coming and going around us in Kibera as life goes on in this community. We listen to the reggae music coming from a small run down shack near the clinic called the World Music shop. It sells a whole range of music and has a loud speaker system setup that brings the nearby area alive. Nearby, buses come and go, transporting locals into Nairobi city. Incredibly, despite its 'non-existence' according to the Kenyan government, Kibera is well served by the city's public transport service, with many residents going into the city to work, and others coming from the city to look for work.

The chickens are wandering around out the front of the clinic and more patients walk through the gates to be seen. As the mzungu doctors, Molly and I continue to receive a lot of looks from passersby. Daniel spends some time trying to teach me the common greeting used amongst Kenyan friends. It is similar to a handshake where the palms of each person's hands touch before clenching the fists together followed by leaning in at the shoulders in an embrace. We finish up our mugs of chai which taste delicious. Suddenly so many simple things here are tasting better than ever before. I'm aware of my surroundings and where I am at right now and completely embracing this experience. We finish our mugs of tea before heading back inside to continue our clinics.

I pass on lunch today, having observed Ruth cleaning the blood from the delivery room walls not long before she took to preparing the lamb stew and ugali for the staff members to eat for lunch. The staff don't always have lunch provided, it just depends on the day and whether Ruth is given a small amount of money from the boss to buy some rice and vegetables. Today there is food so the staff take it in turns to be plated up by Ruth and sit at the tiny wooden table in Ruth's tiny wooden kitchen. The lunch is cabbage and *ugali*. Ugali is one of the most common staple foods eaten in Kenya; it's made from a maize flour and water and has a sticky floury consistency and bland taste. It is often eaten by hand accompanying meat, fish or vegetables. Today, Molly and I politely decline lunch, still unsure about what we should and shouldn't be eating - another typical western mentality and cautiousness that we have yet to shake off in this transition.

In the afternoon a man called Peter arrives at the clinic to meet me and take me on a short tour around Kibera. Peter is a local Kiberan from the Kikuyu tribe. He helps out with some of the volunteer organisation's programs in Kibera and takes pride in showing new volunteers around his community. Short and solidly built, Peter has a cheeky smile that reveals a set of teeth which are crooked and half-missing. He is extremely friendly, full of life and known by many people in Kibera for all the good work he does. I haven't yet ventured beyond Ushirika into the depths of this slum so am interested to see how things really are and I've been told that Peter is the best guide. He knows everybody and everywhere to go.

Not long into our walk, Peter starts to tell me about his claim to fame. He was photographed in an issue of the National

Geographic magazine for a story written about Kibera. Peter has lived in Kibera most of his life. Like most Kenyans, he is dressed very respectably in trousers, black lace-up shoes, and a smart collared shirt. Since arriving I have been surprised and impressed by the dignity and self-respect that Kenyans demonstrate, particularly in the way they present themselves. Even people with just enough money to see through one day from the next take pride in their appearance, with women wearing nice brightly coloured traditional shawls with their hair neatly combed or braided and men wearing clean trousers and polished lace-up shoes. It is not the image of people dressed in rags and tatty clothing I had somehow expected.

In my blue denim jeans, brown hiking boots and orange chequered shirt, I feel substantially less stylish than the locals. Style and colour were not what came to mind when I selected my wardrobe for Kenya from the two dollar rack at the Salvation Army charity clothing store before leaving. My intentions had been to dress down so as not to portray myself as a wealthy foreigner and to be able to fit into my new surroundings. While formulating this plan, I somehow failed to consider the fact that my white skin, regardless of how I am dressed, seems to tell all. I have realised since day one that my long sleeved shirts and dark denim jeans make no difference whatsoever because to the people here I am firstly a mzungu. It is the colour of my skin that defines my identity.

With Peter I walk the busy streets of Kibera. We set out on the main street around the outskirts of the slums which is bitumen, looking further into the depths of the slums, is a series of small dusty dirt paths meandering around the hundreds of timber matchbox shacks that so many of the residents here call their home. Joined together, the timber sheets that form the roofs of these shacks create one continuous plateau of different shades of brown. I'm yet to see just what lies beneath this cover. Cars and buses circulate through these parts of the slum, swerving around the many people walking in all directions. One man cycles past us with at least five large crates filled with bananas and other fruits stacked perilously on the back of his bike. Other men tow large wooden carts filled with fruits and vegetables on their way to their shops. By the side of the street there are women cooking maize over small cookers and others with large boxes of dried tilapi fish for sale. It is always noisy with car horns being tooted, people yelling out the prices of their fruits for sale and talking in the streets. But it is a reassuring noise; the noise that there is life and optimism in this community.

There are also the sounds of children running around in the streets. Kenyan children are adorable. Before we even see them they have spotted us, and all I can hear is the familiar *'How are you!' 'How are you?' 'How are you?'* being screamed out over and over again, as one-by-one somebody else joins in until there is a chorus of children singing at me. It's the widely recognised chant for greeting the mzungu within the community, as this is an English expression that is learnt and spoken only to the mzungus. Incredibly, children as young as two even seem to be able to manage an 'owwwwaarrrrrroouuuu'.

The first experience I have with these Kenyan children is when Peter and I walk past a local primary school. First of all I hear the 'How are you!' chants then suddenly I can see nearly 20 kids running in my direction. More like stampeding as the little ones get run down by the older ones in competition for who can get to me sooner. It is the most incredible experience to be bombarded by this entire class, or maybe it is actually the whole school of children. They are so ecstatic to see a white person and want to touch me just to see how I am different from them. I play a game with them by asking them how they are, 'Habari', to which they instantly respond 'Mzuri' (fine). 'Habari?' 'Mzuri'. 'Habari?' 'Mzuri'. I switch back to English, asking 'How are you?' 'Fine' is their common response. 'How are you?' 'Fine'.

The kids grab my hands, pull at my shirt and block me in so that I cannot go anywhere. I see one little boy look at the colour of his hand after touching mine, checking to see if the colour has rubbed onto him. They are beautiful. Their small dark bodies dressed in the common royal blue school uniform, wearing shoes that are often too big or worn on the wrong feet. Some have no shoes at all. Many of the young girls have their hair braided. The boys have short, often shaved heads. The sea of little faces standing around me is a mixture of big toothless grins and shy inquisitive stares. Runny noses and filthy hands aside, I want to hug them all.

Peter manages to weasel me out and tells the kids to go back to school, their teachers having long been left behind in an empty classroom. We continue our walk through Kibera. In contrast to the high of seeing the bright and happy children, Kibera is marked by grave signs of poverty. We're now walking off the main road and into the centre of this massive slum. The narrow paths mean you can only access these parts of the slums by foot. Open sewage consisting of filthy water, animal and human faeces and other waste, streams around the timber shacks. It is greenish in colour and unbearable in odour. My eyes are on the ground beneath me watching every step I take. Peter glides along like a pro while I balance on the little wooden planks forming bridges over the sewage like I'm an elephant on the tightrope, risking a lot if I take a wrong step. The muddy paths are littered with rubbish and thousands of plastic bags. Peter asks me if I've heard of the *flying toilets* of Kibera. Due to the lack of access to proper toilet facilities people are forced to defecate into plastic bags which are then thrown onto the roofs of their tiny shacks, left on the paths where people walk and found in the expanding dumps in the slums. I think of all the plastic bags I have walked over so far. There are thousands of them littered everywhere in the slums. Peter describes the effects when the rains arrive, when water runs through these extensive piles of waste creating an unbearable stench and an even worse haven for disease.

  The shacks all around us that they call their homes are tiny timber sheds. Peter explains how often families of up to eight people will live in these spaces of no more than 10 square metres. Inside the shacks, the single room is often divided into a sleeping area and a small space for cooking. Several family members will often share a bed (in the case where they are lucky enough to have one) with the others sleeping on the dirt floor. This is why so many people are out and about all the time as their tiny homes, without electricity and running water, are not somewhere to stay cooped up in all day long.

  As we walk through Kibera everybody knows Peter. He seems to walk into friends he knows every five minutes or so. They stop to greet him with the cool handshake that Daniel has been trying to teach me at Ushirika, and then they chat for awhile. It's also an opportunity for Peter's friends to introduce themselves to me too, as I am clearly a new face in the community. Along the walk we visit a group of youths from Kibera who run a volunteer group called Kibera Youth. This is an example of one of the many positive initiatives within Kibera that has been formed to keep the youths busy and helping their community. One of the projects they have created is to provide a rubbish collection within the slums; they use a big truck to collect unwanted waste that is otherwise polluting the area. Because Kibera is considered an illegal and non-existent settlement by the government, such services are not otherwise provided. The boys allocate one day a week to serving parts of their community. They are all friendly and delighted to have a visitor show interest in their work. They ask me to write in their visitor's book. They also describe a role-play to me that was performed recently within the community, in conjunction with their church, dispelling myths about HIV and AIDS and teaching others about how it is transmitted and prevented. It's great to see that despite being unemployed, these young people are so passionate about being part of something, especially helping the greater community. Their work is inspiring.

Peter leads me deeper into a clustered area of shacks and I ask him where we're going now. I am completely dependent on him as I have no idea where we are. As we walk in front of the hundreds of small homes, I see women out the front doing their washing on the littered paths. They stare at me. I feel like an intruder, having a nosy into their living situations. Yet they all seem content to have visitors and wave at me as we walk past and the children often follow me for awhile with the familiar 'How are you?' before returning to their mothers and siblings. I'm led inside one of these timber homes as Peter announces to me that we're at his place. I really don't know anything about him and now here we are inside his home. Peter sits me down on his couch and proudly shows me his photograph in National Geographic. It's a lovely shot capturing the immenseness of Kibera, with the brown sea of timber roof, and a photo of Peter standing to one side. I can see he is so proud of this.

I have to admit I am surprised to see that Peter lives in this slum. When he met me at Ushirika, I imagined him as a man of higher wealth, with a good job and income. It just goes to show that you can never tell. Or more importantly, that one should never judge. Peter tells me that a number of key Kenyan politicians live in Kibera themselves. These people, including Peter, are proud of their community and wish to remain a part of it, irrespective of their financial or social position. I commend this, as I begin to witness the diversity and complexity of this politically non-existent slum.

Peter pops his head into another of the rooms in his large shack, which unlike some of the surrounding homes we've walked past, is decked out with modern electronics (a television) and has an electricity supply and running water. It is decorated nicely with crocheted rugs and the walls have a few pictures of the President Kibaki as well as some symbols of Christianity. I'm introduced to a lady who comes into the room and a young boy. These are Peter's wife and son. His wife is very quiet, she mostly speaks Swahili. His son is very shy too, about 7 years old, and I observe Peter's paternal instincts with his young son as he strokes his head and holds him closely. I introduce myself to his wife and son and we sit together for a little while before Peter and I head outside again to continue our tour of Kibera.

Just when I think I've seen the worst of Kibera in the rivers of open sewage and the thousands of tiny timber shacks, a whole new picture of poverty stretches before my eyes. We've walked quite far, almost through to the other side of the slum, and I start to witness the real level of poverty affecting the inner core of Kibera. There are people sifting through massive rubbish dumps covering an area of more than $50m^2$ which contains anything and everything from discarded plastic bottles and clothing to food, metal scraps and human waste. There are flies everywhere, stray dogs sniffing about and people rummaging through the rubbish with their bare hands. I even see young girls holding water bottles in small ponds of sewage, collecting water for drinking. It is sickening to imagine what diseases are breading and being transmitted in these areas. Seeing these pitiful scenes I feel like I'm in one of those World Vision television commercials. And yet there really is no comparison at all with the two-dimensional images I've seen from my living room, as I stand here amongst the flies hovering around the dumps, the air filled with the stench of sewage and decomposing rubbish and a picture of poverty that continues indefinitely all around me,. These living conditions are horrendous and these people who know no better life continue with such strength and pride.

Peter and I walk through Olympic, a slightly improved area of Kibera that is less cluttered and polluted. There are a number of good schools in this area as well as better quality roads and properly built houses and shops. However the improvement doesn't last for long, as we approach the railway line running through Kibera again, we have a panoramic view overlooking the poorest part of these slums. The view is a mosaic of timber-roofed sheds overlapping and sprawling outwards in a radial pattern, reflecting the progressive expansion of this poverty-stricken community. I am able to see all those plastic bags, the flying toilets, littered across the thousands of timber roofed shacks of this slum. Peter informs me that this is where the film The Constant Gardner was filmed, and points out different locations chosen for scenes in this movie. I recognise the bridge that arches over a river of revolting sewage. The director of this film, Fernando Meirelles, built a school, a set of public toilets (which have *Donated by the Constant Gardner* painted across them) and a water tank in the centre of this community. Apart from the fact that I see today that somebody is now charging 10ksh to use the toilets (which I am sure was not a part of the original donation) Kibera has really become visible to the outside world thanks to the production of this movie.

Nearby, Peter shows me one of the larger and well-established HIV clinics in Kibera, run by the big, international humanitarian organisation Médecins Sans Frontières (Doctors without Borders). It is modern looking and as we walk through I pass numerous young women, many younger than myself, collecting their supplies of antiretrovirals distributed by the clinic. I'm pleased to see there are clinics such as this one serving the community and to hear from Peter that at present there is a good supply of antiretrovirals available to the community. The problems being faced lie much deeper, in the challenge of reaching the thousands of people living with this virus in the slums, including those who may not even know about it or are affected by the stigma of HIV/AIDS, or unaware of the help that is available. The reasons are extensive as to why the fight against HIV is ongoing in these environments but it is a positive sight for me today to see women confidently visiting an outreach centre in the slums and walking away with their free ARV treatment.

I have been walking with Peter now for over two hours and feel emotionally and physically fatigued. There is just so much to take in that is unlike anything I've ever seen. We pass a lot of factories where men are hard at work outside welding steel, sparks flying everywhere, and wooden crates being nailed together by hand. I can only imagine the lack of safety procedures.. We pass a man stirring large pots of ugali and vegetables outside, next to big stacks of chapatti, with people eating at the small wooden chairs and tables he has set up around his kitchen. The man is another friend of Peter's who insists we eat something here and he heads over to select something for me.

I have a plate of cooked mashed plantains, a type of banana used for cooking, and kidney beans. This is quite a traditional dish known as *matoke*. Having been the cautious mzungu in Nairobi for the past few days today I take my *fifth lesson* in Kenya - *Just do it*. At some point or other risks have to be taken, and I cannot insult Peter and his friend by refusing to eat the yellow and red mixture before me prepared in the slums of Kibera, so I dig in. It's an interesting combination and extremely tasty. I have no problem in finishing my plate. The people passing by seem to appreciate that I have embraced their food and culture as they watch me eat a traditional dish. Or could they just be thinking how awkward I look eating with a fork rather than with my hands as Peter and everybody else is doing? That will have to be another day's lesson.

After our meal Peter tells me we're going to Sango for a soda. Sango, I discover, is a small bar in Kibera. Like any other shop or home it is made of timber sheets and as we arrive I see the rusty Sango sign hanging outside the front door, or rather the entrance, since the door has fallen off and it is just an open entrance. Inside, it is just like the local pub. Behind the front bar there appears to be a wide selection of drinks and Kenyan beers. As they say in Australia, the definition of a town is somewhere with a pub, and maybe a few shops. I have now seen how complete Kibera is. Listening to the local reggae music coming through their sound system, we order two Fantas and have a seat at one of the wooden tables. Being mid-afternoon it is quiet except for one drunken customer who looks as though he hasn't left this bar in a couple of days. As I drink my refreshing cold Fanta out of the recycled glass bottle, I really appreciate having Peter as my guide and showing me the depths of the Kibera slum. I am overwhelmed by the reality of what I have seen but equally comfortable in this welcoming community. I can see I'll be back at Sango again for another Fanta which is of course a real luxury in these surroundings. It's only when the time comes to pay that I realise Peter doesn't have any money on him and although we have spent the day walking through Kibera as equals it is these little things that show me again we're not. The meal we shared and soda we had at Sanga are a real treat for him and it is my pleasure to offer him that.

Finally Peter walks me back to Ushirika clinic, to where we started this insightful journey into life in Kibera. We meet up with Molly, Debra, David and Daniel at the front of the clinic as I share my tales of the afternoon's walk with them. I soon realise that most of the staff working at Ushirika live in Kibera too. Despite being educated and employed, life is still really difficult for them. I work in the same clinic as Daniel, David and Judson and in many ways am not as experienced or competent at my work as they are. And yet at the end of the day some of them go home to one of these small shacks that we walked past today in the slums and others go on to work the evening in another job and I can't help but feel guilty adjusting to this. Despite these difference, as people we are all together and united and we laugh about my eating of the plantains and beans with a fork, and I share more stories with them about Australia. This is just my first day but I leave Ushirika with Molly feeling like I already have a family here.

Chapter 5 – Settling in

Home is where one starts from – T.S.Eliot

The next morning I wake up to an amazing breakfast of chai tea, eggs fried over the kerosene cooker, toast and fresh fruit. Alice has been busy preparing this treat for us and we all sit down to drink our morning chai together. I am now settling into the morning routine, which starts with climbing out of my mosquito net, remembering to take my anti-malaria tablet, sharing breakfast with Alice and Molly, brushing my teeth with the water from my water bottle, applying my high level sunscreen and DEET insect repellent. Next to the front door I have my boots which are the final step in this process before venturing out into the lively streets of Jamhuri and beyond into Kibera.

Our daily walk into Ushirika from Jamhuri sees Molly and I take the short-cut path through the grass fields behind Alice's apartment up to the railway line where we cross over. We once again see the chickens wandering about and all the women sitting next to their sacks of fruit and vegetables, set up since dawn. I greet them all with '*Habari*' and they respond '*Mzuri*' like we've known each other for a long time. We take the main path between the stands of food and I embrace the feeling of independence and freedom.. As we turn the corner to where the white gates of Ushirika are open, I see Anna at the entrance who sings out 'Molly! Belinda!' And we are welcomed into her arms. New tunes resonate from the World Music store across the square from the clinic. Today they're playing Bob Marley – No Woman No Cry. Nearby, a big yellow and green City Hopper bus takes off from the depot headed for Nairobi city. We say hello to Ruth who is already busy washing dishes from her little wooden stool in the kitchen. Inside the clinic I see David in the laboratory and Judson in the pharmacy, and I greet them both with the cool handshake I've been working on with Daniel, which they're very impressed by! Debra comes out from the maternity ward where she says she has already delivered two babies this morning.

'Easy', she smiles confidently. 'No complications'.

Molly and I take our white lab coats and fill our pockets with pens, notepad and alcohol hand gel. Molly will be working alongside Debra in the maternity clinic while I will be helping Daniel the nutritionist in the tuberculosis (TB) clinic today. He has already set up the boxes of medications in the back room and I can see a queue of patients waiting inside the room. My job is to check their cards which document their course of treatment. I'm guided by the patients themselves, who help me out where I'm unsure, knowing exactly what medications they require. For many, this is not their first course of treatment for TB.

Tuberculosis is a bacterial disease that most commonly occurs in the lungs. If left untreated it can be contagious and fatal. TB is the leading cause of death among HIV infected people in Africa. It is classified as one of the HIV-related opportunistic infections. An opportunistic infection is one of a number of defined infections and malignancies that HIV positive patients are vulnerable to due to a weakened immune system. A HIV positive patient who has any one of the opportunistic infections including TB is defined as having AIDS, the advanced stage of HIV.

The rates of TB in Kenya are amongst the highest in Africa. In 2009 there were more than 132,000 new cases diagnosed. Nearly 48% of newly diagnosed TB patients in Kenya are co-infected with HIV. So it is even more critical to diagnose and treat the disease to prevent the spread of TB and to maintain the patient's state of health. Daniel tells me that many of these patients presenting for treatment at Ushirika may be HIV positive, but as we are still working to establish the HIV program at the clinic they have to go elsewhere to receive their treatment for this. So today is just TB medication. The standard course of treatment is 6-8 months of antibiotics taken in the form of combination therapy. Phase 1 consists of a certain drug combination for the first two months and then phase 2 continues with different drugs for the next four to six months. Our patients at Ushirika return to the clinic every two weeks to report on their health and to collect their medications which are provided for free.

Ruth serves us our morning cup of chai through the barred windows today, which we drink in the clinic room. Daniel keeps me entertained with his jokes and before I know it I've acquired a new job of recordkeeping in the books. He admits he hates this part of the job and is happy to allow the new volunteers to do it for him. He flashes his cheeky big smile, how can I refuse? The task of recordkeeping consists of each patient having a card with their outpatient visits recorded on it and the dates. For the TB clinic, we have one big book where we record each patient's name, the date of their visit, the week they're at in their treatment and what medications are dispensed.

In the afternoon, I spend some time helping David in the laboratory. He shows me the malaria parasites on a stained slide under the microscope from a patient's recent blood test. The presence of parasites is the indication that it is a positive diagnosis for malaria. Almost every day we have patients or staff members or friends of theirs presenting with symptoms of malaria. Following a simple needle prick on the finger, the slide is stained and studied under the microscope for the visible parasites. A positive diagnosis is treated immediately by the nurse with a two week course of drug therapy. Most cases which are diagnosed and treated early will recover. Following the malaria slide, David prepares another blood sample for a typhoid blood culture test, another illness that is frequently seen at the clinic.

Our next patient is a lady who has been referred from one of the outpatient's clinics for an HIV test. David tests for HIV everyday in his small laboratory. This is done via a blood test that is taken from the patient's veins in her arm. The young lady looks scared and shy. David starts to take the blood sample. HIV can be transmitted in three main ways: through sexual contact, blood-to-blood and from mother-to-child. In this region of Africa heterosexual transmission through unprotected sex followed by mother-to-child transmission account for the majority of new cases of HIV. Mother-to-child-transmission occurs when an HIV positive woman passes the virus to her baby during pregnancy, labour and delivery, or breastfeeding. Most of these babies, without treatment, will not live to be adults. Treatment, however, is now available to the mothers and babies which will significantly reduce the chance of HIV being transmitted to the child.

The young lady goes back to the waiting room while David performs the Rapid HIV test. It's a type of HIV antibody screening that is simple, highly sensitive, and inexpensive, requires minimal resources and training, and provides a result within 15 minutes. A big advantage is that patients can wait for their results, avoiding the common problem of them never returning to the clinic for their diagnosis. All results are confirmed by a second type of rapid testing, in this case the Bioline test, to avoid false positives. There is also a third type of test, Unigold, if needed. In all cases a small sample of the patient's blood is placed on the testing device.

The test process is rapid and accurate. Fortunately for this young lady the result is negative. This is passed back to the nurse who explains the results to the patient. She's one of the lucky ones. Many patients receive a positive diagnosis for HIV. Even more are living with the virus in the slums, unaware of their status and continuing the spread of HIV. Before the patient leaves, my job is to make sure she is well informed about the importance of having protected sex to prevent the transmission of the virus. Although it has been traditionally taboo to discuss sexual relationships and activities amongst many of the tribal cultures, it has now become fundamental to speak openly about such topics in this fight to prevent HIV and AIDS.

Molly and I finish at Ushirika and leave Kibera feeling like we've once again seen and done so much today. We walk towards the nearest group of shops, known as Adam's, on the busy Ngong Road. Here there is a supermarket for supplies, a cafe, hairdresser, some small restaurants and tourist shops. We each buy a couple of big water bottles for our room and have a look around the shops. Molly is meeting up with some other volunteers later so I decide to walk back home for a much needed shower and rest. I'm slowly getting more confident about finding my way around. The main street that heads back from Ngong road to Jamhuri is lined with many market shops. I've always been one to love markets and the atmosphere is very lively. There is everything from second hand clothes and shoes, hand-made jewellery, fresh fruit and vegetables, spices, to books and pots and pans. I spend some time looking through the stalls until it becomes too overwhelming as the market vendors see me, the mzungu, as good business and pressure me into buying everything my eyes fall upon.

As I near closer to Jamhuri, I'm back on the dirt road where our vehicle broke down on my orientation day. That was just a week ago but already feels like so much longer! Now here I am finding my way around by myself already, feeling as safe as ever. There are always people wandering around and I can feel them staring at me. They know I'm not from around here. Quite often the locals who pass me stop to say hello and to introduce themselves, in a simple yet kind-hearted and humbling gesture. They make me feel welcome in this incredible community.

Amongst all the little shops lining the sides of the road as I arrive in our neighbourhood of Jamhuri, one small fruit and vegetable stand grabs my attention. Standing out the front is a young boy who looks about 15 years old with a happy smiling face. I stop to look at the fresh pineapples, bananas and mangoes that he has arranged neatly on his small wooden stand. All of these fruits look amazing. I introduce myself. The young boy's name is Stanley and he tells me he sells the best fruit and vegetables in Nairobi. He's a bright young man, fluent in English, who spends his whole days at this stand from the earliest hours of the morning until well after sunset. I decide to buy a few bananas to share with Alice and Molly. I ask how much the bananas cost, *'ni bei gani?'* They only cost 5ksh each. I give him a few extra shillings. We say goodbye, *kwaheri*, and I head back to Alice's apartment in a positive mood. I'm becoming a local here, working all day at the clinic, walking through the markets and now buying fresh fruit from the local street vendor in Jamhuri. It's been yet another big day to reflect upon.

Chapter 6 – New friends

Life is partly what we make it, and partly what it is made by the friends we choose – Tennessee Williams

It's my last day at work for the week at Ushirika, tomorrow I'm going on a weekend safari with a group of the other new volunteers. Over the next three days we'll be visiting the Masai Mara, Lake Naivasha and seeing more of Kenya beyond its capital of Nairobi, including the famous Big Five animals in the game parks.

I'm working with Daniel today in the baby immunisation clinic. Held once a week, this is where all the young babies are weighed, vaccinated and assessed by Daniel on their nutritional needs. Not one to be especially clucky over children, least of all babies, I'm confronted by a waiting room packed full of mothers and babies. I can't help but notice how well behaved and adorable they all are. These babies receive a lot of physical contact with their mothers in their early years, often being carried in a sling over their backs, accompanying their mothers on their long journeys to collect water and down to the markets to buy fruits and vegetables. They grow up in the reality of a harsh environment, never being the centre of attention or spoilt with an abundance of fashionable toys. These African women are naturally brilliant mothers and their babies and young children are so obedient.

Daniel has set up the baby scales where I am to weigh each baby and he grins as he shows me where I'll be recording all the patients' names, ages, weight and the medications we'll be giving them. Looks like I'll be doing the documentation yet again I tease him sarcastically. I have a pile of appointment cards in front of me with each baby's name on the front.

'Priscilla Nnngggooorroooo....' Immediately I struggle with their African names and before long I find myself as the source of entertainment in front of all of these women in the waiting room. They wait for me, the white doctor, to attempt the pronunciation of the next baby's name which is often nowhere near correct. They laugh at my attempts and now and then one of the women gets up to help me read the name on the card and to point to where the patient is seated. Well at least I'm keeping them amused. Not only am I unfamiliar with the names but the babies don't seem to be overly familiar or reassured with the sight of me, the mzungu, as I take them from their mother's arms to weigh them. I remember Molly's story on the walk into work today about having babies pee on her when she started out in the immunisation clinic, so I try to hold them at full arm's length to avoid getting in the firing line.

Almost all the babies seen at Ushirika are below the desired weight for their age. Daniel tells me that although they are otherwise healthy, they are often malnourished. This is a significant problem across Africa, contributing to a large number of infantile deaths. Daniel's job as nutritionist is to talk with the mothers as I weigh their babies, to see what feeding routines they are following. All newborns (with the exception of those born to a HIV positive mother) are encouraged to be exclusively breastfed for the first six months. This regime is important in preventing infections and illness in young babies. Due to the mother-to-child transmission of HIV through breast milk, all HIV positive mothers are strictly advised against breastfeeding and in this case a commercial formula is recommended. Not only does Daniel check about the child's feeding but it is equally important to enquire about the mother's health, as they too are often malnourished and low in iron. The mothers are provided with a free multi-vitamin tablet at each visit. Following our consultation with each patient I check to see if the baby is due for a vaccination (Measles, Polio, and Tetanus) and refer the mothers to the doctors who are giving the injections. Today it is David, the laboratory technician, who is delivering the vaccinations. I continue to be surprised at everybody's diverse skills and jobs in this clinic. I'm told that Ruth, our cook and cleaner, has even done it before!

After the clinic is finished, I catch up on some documentation which Daniel instructs me needs completing.

'You're so lazy', I tell him.

'I know, that's what you're here to help me with', he responds with his cheeky smile.

Afterwards I head into the waiting room where I hear a familiar tune on the television that is surprisingly working today. *That's when good neighbours, become, goood friendsssss.*

'It's Neighbours!' I share excitedly with Daniel. 'This program is Australian!'

It is unbelievable that I am working in the slums on Kibera and yet Neighbours has made its way onto the semi-functioning television on a day that the electricity supply has been working at Ushirika. It never ceases to amaze me what technological advances make it through to these parts of the world, whether it is mobile phone networks, high-speed internet connections or television programs, while they still struggle behind in so many other areas.

On my way home from the clinic I pass Stanley at his small fruit and vegetable stand in Jamhuri. He tells me he has a delicious pineapple for me today which he has been keeping for me. He's a good salesman. I can't resist. I negotiate the price with him, buying a few more bananas too, and we settle for 40ksh. That is the average daily wage for a Kenyan. Stanley is young and full of life. We talk for a little while as I explain that I am working at a clinic in Kibera. He's naturally interested to know what a young Australian girl is doing living in Jamhuri, well away from the touristy parts of the city. Stanley has finished school and is supporting his father by working in this shop. I try to find out what he'd like to do one day but he seems unsure, clouded by the harsh reality of his family responsibilities. I head home to Alice's to eat my pineapple which looks delicious. I've made a friend in Stanley and everyday feel more and more a part of this warm and welcoming community.

Chapter 7 – An African safari
It is a rough road that leads to the heights of greatness – Seneca

I'm picked up early Friday morning and meet the other seven volunteers whom I'll be joining on this weekend safari. The volunteer organisation has organised this trip for us to see some more of this incredible country. The word *safari* is Swahili and means journey. Our driver is called Ringo and we're also accompanied by a cook for the first night of camping, which will be spent just outside the Masai Mara. We're all filled with excitement for our weekend adventure. Besides me there is Susan (the Brit), Galvia (the Irish), Monika (French), Chris (the sole man, a teacher from the U.S), Suen (from Hong Kong) and Sarah (the young New Yorker). We're all seated in a white mini-van that will take us around the game parks we'll be visiting over the next few days.

As we head out of Nairobi, we exchange stories and experiences about our first few weeks in our projects. Sarah and Gaby witnessed somebody being stoned outside their nursery school, apparently for stealing a piece of fruit at a nearby market. Chris is living like a Masai in rural Kenya and getting along magically with all of his students. Susan is volunteering at an orphanage where she has fallen in love with all of the adorable children living there.

Not long into the drive we stop at a lookout with a view over the Rift Valley. It's green, mountainous and picturesque, and suddenly we're no longer in the polluted and busy city of Nairobi. The roads are bitumen so far but covered in pot-holes, so it's a very bumpy drive. As we head farther out, the roads change to a dirt surface which is actually better to drive on than the poor quality bitumen roads. We start to spot impalas and zebras by the side of the roads. Ringo also points out some Masai warriors walking in the distance with their cattle. They are easily identified from their red clothing wrapped around their tall slender black figures bodies which glide through the fields. This is it, the real countryside of Kenya.

After a few hours of driving we arrive at Acacia camp in the Masai Mara which is where our overnight stay will be. It's comfort camping, with running water and a shower and toilet facilities. There are several large tents set up with mosquito nets and mattresses inside. I'm sharing with Susan who I get along with really well. We unzip our sleeping bags and organise our gear for the evening. There's still enough light to head out for an evening safari drive so we all jump on board with our cameras and Ringo takes us into the game park.

The Masai Mara is Kenya's largest game reserve. It is located in the southwest corner of Kenya at the northern border of Tanzania where it is the continuation of the Serengeti National Park - home to the Masai tribe. It's a popular tourist destination for its abundance of African wildlife and classic African savannah landscape. The Masai Mara has a dense animal population, including all of the African 'big five'; which are the five most difficult animals in Africa to hunt: the lion, elephant, buffalo, leopard and rhinoceros. But there are also many many more: zebras, impalas, gazelles, giraffes, wildebeests, hyenas and ostriches... The Masai Mara is the site of the annual migration of millions of wildebeest from the Serengeti.

The entrance to the park is marked by a big gate for cars to enter and to read the rules and regulations, but no actual fence encases these large game parks. The animals know their limit -; well at least I'm hoping so for tonight's camping in the tents. The environment is green, picturesque and peaceful and it's a relief to breathe some fresh unpolluted air. It amuses me to see a car load of tourists on our drive wearing masks over their mouth; to protect them from what? The air couldn't be more pure in this untouched part of the world.

The rolling green hills, a perfect blue sky and beautifully structured acacia trees provide a picture perfect image of this savannah landscape. Immediately we spot the zebras, impalas and giraffes in their natural environment. Ringo is connected to other drivers within the park via radio transmitter and knows the best spots. We have the roof of the van popped up, so we can stand up with a 360 degree view. There is always something to see. Chris spots the elephants from a distance and we're all ecstatic as we approach them. It's a family, the mother closely protecting her little baby. We sit stationary watching them move around and cleaning each other in the pond. I can't believe I'm finally here, in Africa, watching the elephants up close and personal! But there's more to come.

Ringo receives a call over his radio that some lions and their cubs have come out for a play. We speed along the path and head in the direction of the other white vans. The park itself is huge, covering over 1,500km², so everything is very spread out. There they are, a female lioness with her seven cubs. Our cameras are being worked overtime and the lioness wanders towards our van. She comes right up close and two of the cubs follow her. She's beautiful. Her big eyes are a glowing brown as she confidently glides forward, followed by her family of young cubs, running around playfully under the supervision of their mother's watchful eyes. The males are nowhere to be seen. Being nocturnal creatures, they are more than likely sleeping.

We've had just a taste of what's to come on this late afternoon game drive. We return to the campsite and entertain ourselves with a game of hook, using the sticks and an old drink bottle to improvise as best we can, before dinner is ready. We spot some baboons in the trees around our tents who are keeping an eye on us. Our cook serves us a feast: mushroom soup, pasta, cabbage and meat, with mango for dessert. This is the best meal most volunteers have had since their home stays. Meat, especially, is a rare treat. Later, we sit around a big campfire together, embracing the experience. In the distance stands our Masai night watchman, tall and upright with his wooden stick in his hand. He will keep an eye on the camp overnight. It's only natural to wonder what we need protecting from, but perhaps that question is best left unanswered. We find ourselves singing campfire song such as '*In the jungle, the mighty jungle, the lion sleeps tonight*'....and '*Row row row your boat gently down the stream....*'. Shortly after, Chris gets us started on sharing our life's accomplishments and biggest regrets in front of the campfire. Quickly we find ourselves knowing each other a whole lot better than when we came together in the van several hours earlier.

Chris, Susan, Monika and I take a walk out under the night stars and stare at the view. The sky is a plethora of bright stars that can only be seen in a place as remote as this. Chris, the science teacher, points out the Milky Way galaxy which he is excited to be able to see. Coming from the city, being able to stand under a blanket of stars with only the sounds of nature around is something extraordinary. I feel my spirit being set free in these moments in Africa. We make a vow to wake up early for sunrise the next morning, hoping for something spectacular. We return to the campsite and say good night, *alamsiki*, as we retreat to our tents. The sounds of the night are intriguing. I can hear the hyenas in close proximity. They are known to roam the camp grounds in the evening, scavenging for food. I am putting all my faith in the young Masai watchman to get us through the night.

Chapter 8 – Meeting the Masai

A sweeping pink and orange backdrop to the silhouette of an acacia tree is the picture at sunrise. It is worth every minute of sleep we sacrifice this morning in the Masai Mara. This sunrise is as peaceful as the evening stars of the night before but with the added anticipation of a full day ahead.

In the morning we tour a local Masai village. The village is remote and consists of a few families, their animals and their traditional house, *the manyatta*. As we arrive, a few young Masai men come out to greet us. In the distance we can see the women working outside the houses and looking after the young children. Although less populated than Kenya's other main tribal groups, the Masai are widely recognised and known for their nomadic lifestyle, tribal customs and their unique dress and style.

Looking around me, the Masai people in their traditional village are a picture of beauty. The men, tall, dark and slim, are dressed in their traditional striped and chequered fabrics, mostly bright red that is draped around their bodies and over their shoulders. They walk either barefoot or wearing a black strappy sandal often made from disused car tyres and symmetrical in shape so their walking tracks cannot be traced. Their earlobes have been pierced and the holes stretched. Brightly coloured beaded earrings hang from their lobes and layers of necklaces, beaded collars, bracelets and anklets can also be seen. Next to each other, the Masai men all stand alike, one foot behind the other and arms resting behind them, bodies leaning over the wooden stick that they can always be seen walking with, used to muster the cattle and for self defence. They call this stick the *eng'udi*. The Masai men have an inner confidence and grace about them. Their faces are welcoming and not intimidated by our curious and even interrogating looks. We have never seen the Masai up close like this before.

Behind our Masai greeters, the Masai women are wearing brightly coloured *kangas*, a piece of colourfully designed cotton fabric often bearing a written message that is traditionally worn by the women of East Africa. The bright yellows, purples, greens, blues, reds and oranges provide a spectrum of colours, particularly against the beautifully dark Masai bodies. Some of the Masai women are also dressed more traditionally in a sky blue dress with the red and orange patterned fabrics draped over their shoulders. Like the men, the women are stylishly accessorised with beaded jewellery, but in much greater quantities. Beautifully handmade necklaces are layered around their necks, and long heavy earrings dangle from their ears. Their heads are shaved, as are the children's, and many of the Masai have one or two of the front teeth removed, a custom performed during infancy.

One of the young Masai men introduces himself as Joseph and leads us through the village. The Masai speak a tribal language, *Maa*, amongst themselves but many are able to communicate in Swahili and English, particularly in these areas frequented by tourists. Joseph explains the role of the male Masai as being responsible for the cattle which the Masai lifestyle centres around. The number of cattle represents a man's wealth and social position in the Masai community. They must also find suitable land for grazing and water, and the men slaughter animals when required. The women take responsibility for many of the domestic duties: looking after the children, cooking, cleaning, making crafts and all the jewellery, collecting water, milking the cows, as well as building and repairing their mud huts, *the manyatta*. The manyatta is made with interlaced branches and is plastered together with a mixture of mud and cow dung. Inside the manyatta is where a family cooks, eats, sleeps, socialises, stores food, and shelters small animals.

One by one we enter a manyatta with Joseph. It is dark inside and the smoke from the fire where the women have been cooking makes my eyes water and sting. There is a bed made from interwoven sticks and covered with a large cow hide and this is where all the family will sleep. I stay inside a few minutes before stepping outside; the smoke becomes too intense and I can no longer see inside. Several people will often squeeze into each manyatta, many of them sharing the one bed. We observe a young girl repairing one of the manyattas, mixing the cow dung mixture with water and moulding it with her hands onto the outside of the structure. Flies are in abundance but the Masai are so used to them that the children sit content and unbothered outside their houses with dozens of black flies over their faces, undeterred.

Joseph leads us into an area in the Masai village where all of the women have come together with their children to perform a traditional Masai dance for us. I can't wait as I've always been fascinated by tribal music and dance. The colours of red, green, white, blue, black and yellow are beautiful against the brown manyattas and the green fields of the Masai Mara beyond. These popular colours are each said to represent important aspects to the Masai culture. The women begin to sing in Maa and sway their bodies in perfect rhythm. Their voices are delightfully tuned and in harmony with one another, even the children demonstrate their natural ability and gift in singing. We all start to clap along with the women as they move their bodies forwards and backwards in a traditional dance, their arms moving from side to side with the music. It is an amazing performance and we applaud enthusiastically at the end.

We are then treated to a performance by the young Masai men. In a performance that is quite different to that of the women, the Masai men bob their heads back and forth as they project a low deep sound from the back of their throats, resembling a warrior cry. Their beaded jewellery jingles rhythmically with the movement of their bodies. Then comes the most entertaining part of their display, the jumping. Aligned in a semi-circle, one by one the men have their turn at standing in the middle of the circle and doing a vertical jump, as high as they can. With their naturally slim and athletic bodies, these men are elastic and jump well beyond our height.

These traditions are a part of the Masai tribe's rich culture and history. The practice of female and male circumcision, polygamy and their social and living conditions are what make this ethnic group so intriguing and widely studied. While some of the ancient rituals are being phased out of practice, many are still performed today and hold a significant importance to the people and their communities.

As we continue to walk around the village, many of us notice a number of animal bones scattered randomly around the fields. When Chris asks Joseph about the cow skull we walk by, he explains that this is another Masai tradition. The Masai do not bury their dead animals. They are left to die in their environment. The bones are considered sacred and must remain where they lie. The Masai have their own religion, believing that they are the centre of the universe. Their god, *Enkai*, is believed to be present in many forms, in the mountains, colours and the moon.

The visit to this village is captivating. We are given the opportunity to hold the baby lambs, to try on the Masai lion mane and finally the women lead us to a large market area displaying all their jewellery for sale. We take a look around at some of the amazing hand-made necklaces and earrings and some of the volunteers buy a few pieces to take back home. Finally the group leader requests a small fee for our visit to the village which we obligingly hand over. With the increasing number of tourists visiting safari parks, many Masai villages have these types of tours to benefit from their Western visitors and to make some money for themselves, in a culture where money was historically of no value.

We spend the rest of the day driving through the Masai Mara Park in search of the Big Five. We see the zebras, giraffes and elephants again, but today we venture farther into the park, beyond the green fields of yesterday, to parts that are more dry and brown. The vegetation is still sparse. We stop and get out of the van when we get to the Mara River. This is the very site I have associated with Africa from my days of watching documentaries on television on the annual migration of the animals from the Masai Mara across the Mara River and into the Serengeti River. This is it. The migration is due to start within the next month when some animals make it across and many others do not in the stampede of wildebeests through these crocodile infested waters. I still can't believe I am here. I think back to watching *Africa: the Serengeti* at the IMAX as a child and dreaming of being a park ranger in Africa. Ringo points out the hippopotamus footprints near where we are standing by the banks of the river. After taking it all in, we reboard the van and briefly cross the invisible border of the Masai Mara and the Serengeti, into Tanzania.

As we cross back, we continue to explore the different environments and animals spread throughout this enormous park. There are wildebeest everywhere and beautiful impalas that elegantly prance across the rolling hills. I spot some ostriches and many other beautiful species of bird in the park. Ringo parks our van under a large acacia tree and we all jump out of the van to stretch our legs and to eat our packed picnic lunch in the glorious sunshine and peacefulness of the Masai Mara. We don't forget for a second that we're still inside the park with the big cats and many other animals lurking about.

After lunch we head back through the park. We spot a cheetah lying down by the road, its slender body stretched out as it basks in the afternoon sun. I'm desperate to see some action and the cheetah's incredible speed in real life. By this stage the batteries are running out and memory cards filling up quickly from the hundreds of photos we've been taking. Ringo slows down the vehicle and we're all looking around to see what is there. The large golden mane is hidden amongst the long grass under the shade of a tree. It's a male lion, well camouflaged and sleeping. We observe him for some time before quietly continuing on our journey, reluctant to disturb the sleep of this nocturnal beast. That just leaves the leopard and the black rhinoceros as the two remaining animals of the Big Five that we haven't yet seen. It looks like we'll have to wait for another day to see them.

After another night under the stars in the Masai Mara, we head out the next day towards Lake Nakuru. We have a long drive ahead of us on these extremely bumpy, dirt tracks. And it proves to be a rocky start with two emergency road-side stops, one for car sickness and the other for the toilet, in the first 30 minutes. It's all a part of the true African safari! We pool all of our emergency medicine supplies together to help each other out and pray that it doesn't hit the rest of us.

The traffic is hectic and roads dusty as we continue on our drive towards Lake Nakuru. After several hours we arrive, much to everybody's relief. Tonight we're staying in the budget Waterbuck hotel in the town of Nakuru. There are real beds with real towels and a television in the rooms. 'And soap!' I can hear Susan say excitedly as she explores our bathroom. We join everybody else that evening at the bar for a drink before dinner. Chris and Susan enjoy a cold Kenyan Tusker Beer by the poolside and we unwind after our long day of travelling. While some of the others head out to a local disco in the evening, all I feel like doing is taking a shower and making the most of real pillows and my hotel bed.

The next morning we set out in the van with Ringo to visit Lake Nakuru National Park. It's the last day of our safari, as we'll be heading back into Nairobi in the evening. The park is quite different to the Masai Mara; it is lush and green with dense vegetation around the main lake. Lake Nakuru is beautiful and the blueness of the lake is complemented beautifully with the thousands of large pink flamingos herded together. We get out of the van and walk around the lake which is a sea of pink. The flamingos are stunning. In the distance, we can see herds of water buffalo standing around the lake. We drive further into the park, around the bending roads where we're enclosed by the dark foliage of the trees. We try to peer through the trees to see some animals.

Suddenly, standing right before us in the middle of the road is a rare black rhino. His immense body is poised confidently, with a long, strong horn pointing into the air. Ringo informs us that there are now very few of these incredible animals left in the wild, having been illegally poached for their horns. They are now listed as a critically endangered species. The rhino is blocking our route and does not appear to be going anywhere. We approach slowly in the vehicle until we are within several metres. The rhino turns its head and lowers its horn which is its way of saying not any closer please. We start to get a little nervous as it takes a few steps closer our way, eyes engaged with the vehicle. A few nervous cries escape the vehicle. Ringo reassures us we're fine but that we might just have to wait here until the Rhino wants to move. So we wait. Eventually it moves slowly off the road into the bushes where it stays hidden, this rare beauty, in its native environment.

The time arrives for us to leave Lake Nakuru and take the busy route back into Nairobi, which means more bumpy roads and vulnerable stomachs. The journey goes by quickly and before we know it we have left the tranquil serenity of rural Kenya with its spectacular animals and surroundings behind us and we're back into the polluted busyness of Nairobi's outskirts. Ringo drives us back to the volunteer office in central Nairobi from where everybody finds their own way home. Susan promises to arrange a weekend when I can join her at the orphanage and meet the children. Chris has completed his stay in Kenya now and this safari was his last trip before heading back to his job in Canada. Gaby, Sarah and Suen all live close to me in Jamhuri so I know I'll be seeing them all again soon. We promise to all keep in touch.

I take the City Hopper bus back to Jamhuri were I find Alice and Molly at home, eager to hear all about my weekend.

'It was amazing', I tell them enthusiastically. 'It was so nice to step outside of Nairobi and to see another part of Kenya'. Alice, like most Kenyans, has never been to a game reserve and is eager to hear my stories, as I describe the animals we saw and my fascination with the Masai tribe. Returning home to my family of Alice and Molly is the perfect way to end an amazing weekend.

Chapter 9 – Guilt
Guilt is universal – Tennessee Williams

Returning to Ushirika after my time away in the Masai Mara, I am greeted excitedly by Anna, Daniel and Ruth as I walk through the gates to the clinic. I've almost mastered the cool handshake with Daniel now which visibly impresses him. All my colleagues ask about my safari and I share the details with them. Today I have brought my camera with me with some of my photos and the others come out from the clinic to gather around my small screen to see the pictures of the animals. The digital camera is fascinating to everyone I've met so far in Kenya. Especially here in Kibera. They all try to pull my camera out of my hands, wanting to get in close to have a look. Everybody laughs when they see me, the mzungu, dressed up in the Masai jewellery and with the lion mane on my head. Daniel points his finger at me in the photo, laughing his head off, as only a good friend can do.

I learn that none of my colleagues at Ushirika have ever been on safari or visited the famous African animals. It's a tourist attraction and unaffordable to the majority of Kenyans. I feel like I'm rubbing it in their faces a little, showing them somewhere I've been in my first couple of weeks in Kenya, where they might not have the opportunity to go in their lifetime. But there is no animosity or envy, just happiness for me and my travels and we are all pleased to be reunited again at Ushirika.

This morning there are important government officials visiting Ushirika to inspect the facilities for the new HIV patient block. The clinic is hoping to gain permission to have an ARV dispensary for its HIV patients. The representatives are shown around the clinic and its facilities and we learn that the approval will be granted, providing a few small changes are made to the new rooms. It's interesting how things can happen quickly here if they want them to. By mid-afternoon a team of workmen have already arrived and they demolish one of the windows in the building to put an extra doorway in, as instructed in the report by the officials. Hopefully this all means that my role in establishing the HIV/AIDS program at Ushirika will kick off very soon.

I bring out some photos at lunch time that I have brought from Australia of my family, friends, our house, the beach and Adelaide city. With my colleagues' obsession with photos, everybody wants to see the pictures. They're the same photos I showed to Alice when I first arrived in Nairobi. Everybody loves seeing my parents, my sisters, the modern city and the beauty of the Australian beaches. But today, along with the episode of sharing my safari stories, I experience another lesson in my Kenyan journey. *Lesson 6: Guilt.*

When I look at the photos of myself with my family seated at our dining room table on Christmas day with an over-abundance of food, or where I am dressed as Xena the Warrior Princess on Halloween, or out at bars with my friends with a drink in hand, it suddenly feels inappropriate to show these photos from my life of luxury to my friends who live in the slums of Kibera. I'd chosen the photos before I left to reflect some of the highlights of my life in Australia. I now see them through different eyes. I'm embarrassed to let Ruth see all that food on the table on Christmas day. Oblivious to my shame, they love my photos. Daniel wants to know if my younger sister is married, seeing a potential opportunity. Ruth announces that I'm going to take her home to Australia with me so she can walk on the beach. They all speak of dreams. I'm quickly learning that I come from a paradise that I have never truly appreciated.

Chapter 10 – Babies

A new baby is like the beginning of all things-wonder, hope, a dream of possibilities – Eda. J. Le Shan

The mornings are my favourite part of the day. Waking up, having breakfast in Alice's apartment, and then taking the daily walk across the railway line into Kibera. I greet the women at their fruit and vegetable stands and the old grandma, *bibi*, who is always sitting in the same spot next to her sack and peeling her beans. We exchange our daily 'Jambo' with a smile. I pass other locals who, like me, are off to work. We're the lucky ones to have a job to go to. Many more set off early hoping today will be the day they find work. The chickens run around freely near the railway line, and as I approach Ushirika I can hear the welcoming sounds of morning gospel music coming from the World Music shop. I can smell the breakfast chapattis being cooked on the hot plates. Everybody walking around is bright and cheerful, filled with optimism and hope for this new day ahead.

This has become my daily routine and I feel like I've already found my place here. Kibera really is an incredible community. It feels like home to me, and yet it couldn't be farther from my living conditions back home. Kibera is one of the biggest slums in the world, and yet it boasts an incredible sense of community. I embrace the feeling of unity with my colleagues when I come into work. In Kibera, the people have their faith and the support of each other. They live through one day without worrying beyond the next. I can't help but compare the life here to the complexity and obsession of western life back home where we strive to have every material object we desire and still want something more. When did the compulsive pursuit of things become so consuming that we can no longer appreciate what we have?

Nearing Ushirika I see the local rooster perched on the top of its little hill acknowledging the start of the day. It's Wednesday which is the weekly TB clinic. I am now familiar with the running of the clinic and get straight to work with Daniel. The patients arrive early, well before we do, and are sitting patiently with their treatment cards. We work our way through the waiting room, checking the patients' cards and dispensing their medications. I am beginning to recognise faces and names of patients we have met already. There is Bernard, Grace, Charlie and Collin. Most of the patients are quietly spoken and shy, just waiting to collect their prescription and then head off. Daniel and I manage to get through all the patients before lunch and complete the daily documentation.

Today Molly has bravely agreed to taste the ugali that Ruth has been preparing in her small wooden kitchen out the front of the clinic. Kenyans rave about their cooking, in particular the taste and privilege of eating ugali, which is a mix of flour and water. They love to see us partake in their culture, including drinking the chai and eating their traditional foods. Molly takes the ugali with spinach. It has been prepared in a big pot and Ruth lumps a big spoonful onto her plate, solid and white. David, Daniel, Judson, Ruth and even my eyes are on Molly, waiting for a reaction to see what she thinks. She screws her nose up and does her best to finish her mouthful.

'It's too bland, it needs more flavour', she says. 'Like some sugar'. You can always rely on an American to add sugar to something to make it taste better. Ruth watches in horror as Molly covers the ugali, a staple food eaten for lunch or dinner, with a couple of tablespoons of sugar. She then proceeds to taste it, managing better this time around. Meanwhile I think our colleagues feel like we have insulted their national dish.

I spend the first part of the afternoon working alongside Amos in the outpatient's clinic. He is one of the new nurses working at Ushirika. Short, with a dark beard and very well-spoken, Amos has had several years experience in nursing and I quickly learn that he knows what he is doing. He teaches me a lot as we see our patients, each presenting with a range of different symptoms. As usual there are a few patients who present with symptoms of malaria and Amos sends them to be tested with David in the laboratory.

Next, a father and his young son enter the clinic room. The boy's father proceeds to describe how his son, Timothy, ran away from home and they did not see him for six months. He became involved in a gang with older boys, living on the streets. Since returning, the father has wanted to put his son Timothy in a children's home. Timothy has a number of physical and psychological symptoms. It is likely that he has a urinary tract infection or sexually transmitted disease which Amos arranges tests for. The boy is just 11 years old. He is shy, withdrawn and uncomfortable inside the clinic room. I admire Amos' professional manner and his rapport with Timothy, who is too traumatised to even talk to us. I can only wonder what he has been through at such a young age.

During the morning I ask Amos about some of the posters I've seen inside the consulting rooms and the patient waiting areas at the clinic. Amongst the common educational messages on hand-washing and immunisations, I've noticed a series of posters on HIV displaying the ABC method of prevention: 'Abstinence, Be faithful and Condoms'. Except on many of these posters the C for Condoms has been crossed out by somebody with a thick pen. I ask Amos about this and he explains that many people are still opposed to using condoms as a contraceptive, in many cases for religious reasons. It is for this reason that some staff advise patients against the use of condoms, despite their extremely important role in preventing HIV transmission. As I look at the posters and the misleading message they're conveying to patients at the clinic, I struggle with the challenge of overcoming these different beliefs and understandings within the community in our fight to prevent HIV and AIDS. Even some of my trained and educated colleagues are not helping the fight.

The outpatient clinic quietens down in the late afternoon so I move into the maternity ward to help Debra. The maternity section of the clinic consists of a small room with ten beds, closed off from the consulting rooms with a cotton curtain. With no medical supplies or equipment it is more like a dormitory than a hospital ward. I walk past a young girl who is sleeping in one of the beds. She looks to be no more than 14 years old. Debra informs me that she gave birth last night. Once born, the babies share the bed with their mothers. Their families bring in food for them to eat. She will go home later today, once rested. There are three other women here today, all due to give birth at any time. Two young ladies walk up and down the room, clearly in their early stages of contractions. No pain relief is available here. The women generally know how to manage their contractions and pain. They are incredibly strong and admirable. Another lady is lying in bed on her side, trying to relieve the discomfort. Debra keeps checking on her, but after doing an internal check informs me that the cervix is not yet dilated enough, so we just have to wait.

A couple of hours later and the two women are still walking about with contractions. Debra has checked on the older lady, Mary, and says she is ready to move into the delivery room. It looks like I'm going to see a baby delivered. Or wait, I'm going to deliver this baby? Debra, aka super nurse, tells me it is easy, and this is Mary's seventh child. She is almost 40 years old which is considered old for childbirth in Kenya.

'You can deliver the baby Belinda; it will not be a difficult birth for Mary. She knows what to do'.

Despite the generous offer, I say I'd rather watch. And from a distance, if possible. I'm fascinated to see a real childbirth but also reluctant to jump into a procedure that I have no experience with, particularly with the medical risks of working in a clinic in these slums. At least let me watch the first time I tell Debra, after that I might be able to help out.

Mary starts to push with her contractions, not even screaming a word. She is completely in control. Debra puts a wet flannel over Mary's forehead and brings over a lightly stocked trolley, containing the forceps, some sterile equipment and gloves. I look over at Debra who, as usual, is wearing beaded thongs and a pretty knee length skirt under her white lab coat. After awhile the baby's head starts to crown and I can see it. Mary pushes against the wall, next to her bed, and without much effort the tiny baby slides out and into the world. There is minimal blood and as Debra lifts this little boy up we can see the length of the umbilical cord. Holding the baby upside down by his feet, Debra lightly taps his lungs, making sure any fluids are voided from his tiny body. She cuts the cord and then I measure the newborn's ABGAR score (Activity, Pulse, Grimace, Appearance, Respiration) within the first minute of birth, and again at 5 minutes. The baby weighs 2.5kg. Small, of course, but standard for babies born here. Mary seems to be doing alright. She is in awe of her tiny new baby boy.

I have never seen any of the pregnant women in the matnerinty ward of Ushirika accompanied or visited by a partner. Debra informs me that some of the women are on their own and for the others with husbands it is not customary for the husband to be involved in the birthing process. That's the woman's business and responsibility, and they will be helped out by their family members and friends. The men will be waiting at home.

We wait for the placenta to be discharged and then Mary and baby are quickly cleaned and returned to the ward to rest. We do another set of observations on the baby who seems to be perfectly healthy. I'm then given the pleasure of seeing where the placenta is disposed. Outside, around the back of the clinic is a large tin structure next to a water tank, labelled 'septic tank'. I open the hatch, turn my head away and hear the splash of the placenta as it hits the deep bottom of the pit. What a day.

Chapter 11 – Amos

Anywhere is walking distance, if you've got the time – Stephen Wright

It's Thursday again, which is the baby immunisation clinic at Ushirika. Daniel and I have to relocate our normal clinic into a smaller room today due to construction work that is going on in the usual clinic room. We find ourselves crammed into the tiniest space which is usually used as a small supply room. It feels like we're working out of a cupboard! At one point, there are at least ten mothers with their babies, all waiting to be weighed and immunised, plus myself and Daniel in a room no larger than 15m². As usual, I am responsible for weighing the babies and recording the data in the documentation book, while Daniel looks after the nutritional aspects and refers the babies needing vaccinations into another room where a nurse has set-up a vaccination station. The clinic is crazy, there is no system or organisation whatsoever and I can only wonder how each baby will receive the correct vaccination.

By the end of the morning clinic we are exhausted. I decide that Daniel and I deserve a treat, so I venture out into Kibera to the lady I see every morning cooking her fresh chapatti on the hot plate. There has to be a stack of about 100 chapattis for sale. At 10ksh each, I buy Daniel and me one each. I try to look beyond her dirty hands that have been turning the chapatti and head back around the corner to Ushirika where we enjoy our delicious chapattis outside in the Kibera air, listening to the songs of Michael Jackson being played at the World Music shop. I make a mental note to go there one day to pick up some music. The small shack has hundreds of probably illegally burned CDs for sale, ranging from reggae, to American hip hop to local African pop and gospel.

I catch a glimpse of Ruth and Anna watching Daniel and I eating our chapattis. It was such a small gesture but big enough to cause some jealousy within the team, as I realise how much of a luxury a simple chapatti is to my friends.

'Where did you get that from?' Ruth asks Daniel inquisitively.

'Belinda bought it for me!' Daniel beams proudly, thrilled at our small indulgence. I'm finding it hard not to tread on people's toes here. Offering one person a chapatti and not the others, or showing my photographs of a life more luxurious. But there is no hostility, we go back and have some chai with Ruth in the kitchen and tell her about our busy morning.

While taking a break with Daniel and Ruth outside the clinic, we are joined by Amos, the new nurse whose clinic I helped out with yesterday. Amos is very friendly and polite. He gives us an overview of his morning clinic, which he has managed well. He then suggests I join him for lunch at his place which is not far from the clinic. Amos says he often goes home for lunch. So, keen to have an insight into my colleague's life in Kibera, I accept the offer excitedly and we head off to Amos' house. As we walk comfortably together through Kibera, I learn *lesson number 7* in my Kenyan experience - *It's not far.*

This expression in Africa does not translate into 'just around the corner' as I expected. As was the case walking with Peter on my tour around Kibera, and with Ringo our driver on safari, and now with Amos, it turns out that this expression is, like that of African time, meaningless. Amos' house turns out to be at least a 30 minute walk from the clinic through the slums of Kibera. I remember this area from my tour with Peter and am surprised to see that Amos lives in one of these timber shacks, much like many of the patients he treats.

As we enter his place I notice that it is well furnished with colourfully crocheted covers on the couches and tables, and there are pictures of Jesus on the walls, something that is commonly seen around here. I remove my muddy boots at the front door and am led into the main room where I am met by what seems to be Amos' entire family! They are all so thrilled to have a mzungu visitor and welcome me so warmly into their home. Once again I feel like I'm being treated like a princess which, of course, I don't mind! Amos has two sisters, Phyllis and Margaret, and two brothers, George and Simon. His mother, Nayla, is also there but unlike the others she doesn't speak English. They already seem to know a surprising amount of information about me. Apparently Amos has admired me at work and his family continue to tell me how much they love Australia and how I must take them all back with me.

I am beginning to feel the awkwardness of this situation, realising it seems a little more set-up than I had expected. Amos' behaviour has also changed from his professional attitude at work to one of a man introducing his future wife to his family. I'm not quite sure what is going on and before I know it a table has been put out before me by Amos' sisters. They set the table with some cutlery then serve me lunch. It is a plate of *githeri*, a traditional Kikuyu meal which is mixed beans, corn and potato. I'm also served a mug of hot chai and a glass of water. They all sit around watching me as I eat. It's delicious, despite the uncomfortable surroundings of six pairs of eyes on me. Amos' family are friendly and kind as they encourage me to eat more before posing me more questions about my life and Australia.

Phyllis and Margaret pick up their magazines on the couch called 'True Love' and 'Parents', which prompts questions about how many children I want to have and questions about true love, to which his younger sisters giggle.

'Do you want children Belinda?' 'It's important to have a nice husband isn't it?' 'Have you found your true love?' I'm finding the situation very amusing by this stage, having been completely unprepared for this reception. Like they say, every day in Africa is another adventure. But where is this one headed?

Finally the time comes for Amos and me to return to work. It seems the African time concept also extends to lunch breaks, as I think of all of the patients waiting for him back at Ushirika. But he'll return when he's ready. Before we leave Amos' family insists on having our photo taken together. His sisters run off to get their camera.

'The future parents', they say, as they sit me down next to Amos and take a photo. I've got to get out of here! But not before several more photos, firstly with his sisters (now already calling themselves my sisters-in-law) then his brothers, his mother and then again with everybody. I thank Amos' family for their invitation to lunch and wave them goodbye.

Amos and I leave his house and start the long walk back to Ushirika. I am extremely grateful for the warm reception and the lovely lunch we shared. But it turns out that it's not over yet. As I turn around I find we've been joined by the whole entourage of his sisters and brothers who've decided to accompany us on our walk back to work! I have instantly inherited a family. I can't believe what has happened since finishing the immunisation clinic with

Daniel this morning and sharing our chapattis together. This experience is up there with other volunteers' stories of being offered cows as a dowry in exchange for marriage, or being asked by mothers to take their children back home with them. I'm learning that it is very difficult to read people here. Often when you think you're being friendly and kind, they interpret that differently or expect something more. It's my *lesson 8* in Kenya: *Sometimes you're in for more than you bargained for.*

I finally farewell Amos' family when we arrive back at Ushirika. Ruth looks over at me curiously. Eager to get back into work and to keep as far away as possible from Amos for the rest of the afternoon, I nominate myself to sort out the TB drugs into numerical order in the office ready for the next clinic. Anything to keep me busy and Daniel happy.

Chapter 12 – Sweet mangoes

At home in the evening I share the story about my surprise date with Amos' family with Alice and Molly. Alice finds it extremely entertaining as she laughs at my fear of being married off, while Molly insists I start wearing a wedding ring to send out the message that I'm married. We all get along like sisters in our Jamhuri apartment and this topic gets us talking about men in our lives. Molly has a close friend back in New York whom she refuses to label as a boyfriend, but Alice and I look at each other and decide otherwise. Since ending a relationship one year ago, I am single and not on the lookout for a man, preferring to enjoy my youth and independence, which is part of what brought me to Kenya.

Alice is 32 years old, not yet married but looking for a boyfriend and marriage. She is strong-minded, very driven in life and true to her Christian beliefs. Alice paints a negative picture of Kenyan men to Molly and me, describing them as dishonest, unfaithful and lazy. She's not surprised to hear of my experience with Amos, being the first to say that these men are after my money and a ticket out of Kenya. I'm surprised to hear Alice's views, and I can't tell where these strong opinions are coming from but trust that she has spent her whole life in Kenya, which is longer than my few weeks. She is set on looking for a boyfriend outside Kenya. Alice talks of having friends living in England, Ireland and Canada and says her dream is to go and live in one of these places one day and get married.

The next morning Alice, Molly and I share our breakfast of toast, fresh mangoes and chai masala tea. It's so tasty and a great start to another day. Molly and I head out together on our daily walk across the busy Kibera railway line where we greet our local friends. My chapatti lady from yesterday looks at me with eager eyes, keen to make another sale and some more money. It's hard to resist.

I'm met this morning by Peter at Ushirika; he's been helping me settle into my volunteer role and overseeing the HIV/AIDS project at the clinic. Despite participating in a range of different activities within Ushirika such as the outpatient clinics, TB and baby immunisations clinics as well as helping around the maternity ward and in the dispensary, I have not yet started the actual project in HIV/AIDS that I came to Kenya to do. The main reason this is not yet underway at the new facility in Ushirika comes back to the idea of African time; everything just happens on its own schedule. Unfortunately what I was told would be ready for me 'tomorrow' on my first day here, still does not look any closer to being ready. I am eager to invest all of my preparation, resources and ideas into the HIV project, even more so since witnessing just how desperate the situation is here in the slums of Kibera.

I express these concerns to Peter; that time is passing by and I am able to do more than weighing babies, as satisfying and enjoyable as this role has been. We spend a few hours this morning visiting different sites around Kibera and finally decide to head into the volunteer office to visit Irene, the program coordinator. This means taking a matatu into Nairobi city with Peter. He guides me through to the matatu depot in Kibera where we board a matatu painted in black, with big stickers of Puff Daddy glued over the side and back panels and a subwoofer pumping out Jay-Z louder than I've heard in most night clubs. Inside, a small disco ball hangs from the roof of the van. It really is a crazy experience.

We make our way into Nairobi which seems to be more hectic than usual. I have never seen so many people at once, and the traffic and matatu driving are unpredictable. I watch the matatus as they drive recklessly along the main roads. From the vehicle I observe the thousands of people within sight moving around this chaotic city. There is a mix of ages, races and religions. Some women are dressed in the Muslim burqa, others are in western clothes, and Catholic nuns wear their habits. Men dressed in business attire walk around with papers in hand. Homeless people covered in old dirty blankets sit outside offices and shops with their few belongings. And finally I can see beggars, young and old, weaving their way through pedestrian traffic and hovering around the windows of the matatus, pleading for money. I feel as though I have left the security I found in Kibera and its community and am back in this zone of unfamiliarity.

Peter and I walk into the volunteer office where we are warmly greeted by all the staff who are always so happy to have visitors. We speak to Irene who announces that, in view of the facilities needing completion at Ushirika, I will be starting work at a different clinic as of next week. It is an outpatient clinic that deals exclusively with HIV/AIDS cases and needs support for its projects and home visits in the community. I am excited to have a designated role in this new project. The past few weeks have been so enjoyable and rewarding at Ushirika, and I know I may return there when there is more work for me, but in the meantime there is work waiting for me in another of Nairobi's overburdened slums.

That afternoon I return to Ushirika with Peter. I visit Ruth in her kitchen, where she is washing and tidying up the dishes from lunch time. I sit and chat with Ruth, who I have really come to like. She is 34 years old, has 3 young children and works everyday of the week at Ushirika in her multi-disciplinary role of cook/cleaner/step-in-nurse/caretaker. Each day Ruth is there when we arrive in the morning and she stays until 9pm every night. She frequently tells Molly that she must take her back to the United States when she leaves. And of course, on alternate days, it's Australia, with me. Ruth has been sick for a few weeks with a cold and a bad cough, and I insist she sees a doctor. She tells me she can't afford it, despite working at the clinic. Life is so tough for her, for everybody here. I hate to think how much money Ruth is paid to work every day, but imagine it is only enough to provide food for her family.

It's warm outside and I feel like a refreshing drink and tell Ruth about the day I had a soda with Peter at the bar Sango. Ruth tells me that people in Kibera like herself cannot afford to buy sodas. Again, I feel pangs of guilt for bringing this up. I decide to walk down to Sangos myself and buy us each a cold drink to share. After all, it's Friday afternoon! When I return, with two cold Picana mango juices in glass bottles, I find Ruth more delighted than I have ever seen her. Each drink costs me 35kSH (about 80 cents). It is unbelievable how something so small to me can mean so much to her. We sneak the sodas into her small kitchen and, while everybody else is working, we drink them together, sitting on the little wooden stools. Anna, the caretaker, catches onto something happening and, feeling excluded, asks me where her soda is. Ruth offers to share her drink with Anna. So there we all sit, the three of us, beaming with delight as we drink our two bottles of mango juice together.

'So sweet, the mango!' 'Yes, it's very nice!' claim Ruth and Anna to each other. I realise it must be the first time they've ever had a mango juice.

Chapter 13 – Rain and Paranoia

Anyone who says sunshine brings happiness has never danced in the rain
– Unknown

The weekends are usually spent catching up with other volunteers or travelling outside of Nairobi. Today I am meeting with Susan and two of the other volunteers she's been working with at the orphanage, Jenny and Daina. We meet at The Junction shopping centre, which is a commercial shopping complex on Ngong Road and walking distance from Jamhuri. In contrast to the small street stands around Jamhuri and Kibera, The Junction consists of a big modern supermarket, Nakumatt (which resembles Walmart) and a selection of smaller shops including a book store, music shop, an expensive art gallery and some tourist shops selling over-priced jewellery and souvenirs.

It is a real insight to be around people who are wealthy enough to shop in these centres in Nairobi. Catering for the middle to upper class and expatriate population, there are more white people around me than I have seen since arriving in Nairobi. Each day at work in Kibera, the only white people I come across are other volunteers. It is that rare. Now I find myself back in an environment similar to home and the culture shock feels strange, considering where we are.

We stop to watch a coffee-making demonstration taking place in the centre of the mall, attracting everybody's attention with the demonstrators trying to sell their products. I'm suddenly aware of the big divide between the classes here in Nairobi. Families wheel big supermarket trolleys into the car park where their expensive cars are parked and guarded by armed security guards. I wonder where they live and who they are protecting themselves from. Their own people walking on the other side of the high steel fences? The people I am friends with and work alongside everyday in the Kibera slums? It's a contrasting image and another important lesson in my Kenyan experience. *Lesson 9 - The big social divide.* Looking around and experiencing these differences, I find myself torn between these two social classes that feel worlds apart. I'm confused about where I fit in.

I have lunch with Susan, Daina and Jenny at Java, one of the western-style cafes in this shopping complex. We're planning on taking a trip together to Mombasa, on the east coast of Kenya together, and have some organising to do. For lunch I order a tuna-melt sandwich which is served just as one would expect in an American diner, on a big plate with lots of fries and a salad. I pay about 450ksh, which is about $Au5. The same amount of money would have bought me enough chapattis to feed 50 hungry people in Kibera. I'm struggling a little with this transition from one life to the other.

Being the month of May, the wet season is approaching Nairobi. The morning has been filled with torrential rain and when it rains here, it really rains! After lunch, when the rain has temporarily eased, we all head down Ngong Road to Adams shops to visit the markets. But it proves to be almost impossible, for us mzungus anyway, to walk in this mud. All the dirt roads have turned into mud swamps with huge puddles of water. It's so slippery and each step is a risky one. In my big hiking boots, I pick up the mud on my shoes and they end up looking like mud-filled sleds as I carry more and more along with me with each step. We're a sight for all the Kenyans on the road: four mzungus walking one after the other in these conditions.

The locals we pass have no trouble walking in the mud and just stare at us. How do they do it? Must be genetically determined. We've become an attraction for all to see as we struggle down the busy Ngong road, attracting matatu toots and encouragement from nearby pedestrians! At one point Susan falls into the mud face-first landing on her hands and knees. Whereas we're used to saying 'Are you ok?' to such an incident, Kenyans always respond to a mishap like this with 'Sorry'. The passersby tell Susan 'Pole (*sorry*). Welcome to Kenya'.

After helping to clean Susan and realising we're not built like Kenyan women, we take a matatu the rest of the way down the road until we reach the markets. In the back seat of the matatu we find ourselves moving to Saturday Night Fever's 'Staying Alive' which is being played at high volume. Once at the markets, Susan, Jenny, Daina and I browse all the little shops set up on the roadside and listen to all the shop owners who call out to us to visit their stands. We sift through the mounds of second-hand clothing and laugh at the familiar brand names we see, wondering how these items have made their way to street markets in Nairobi. Big-W employee shirts, Target brands and Miss-Selfridge. I find a satchel bag that I've been looking to buy for walking to work and around the community. A newbie to the game of haggling, I'm sure I've been overcharged, but try to make myself feel better knowing that the money is helping someone who needs it.

I walk the rest of the way home to Alice's apartment in the afternoon. With the rain that has fallen during the day, a river has formed in the main street of Jamhuri, preventing cars from accessing a whole section of the road. One van has been abandoned, just left there in the middle of the flooded area, with the water level higher than the tyres. The wet season looks to be an interesting experience here! I manage to follow the tracks left by some of the locals to reach the entrance to Alice's apartment and finally make it back inside.

That evening, after dinner, Molly convinces me to go out with her and a group of other volunteers who have planned to meet at a club in Nairobi known as K1. I'd rather have stayed home happily with Alice in her apartment, but am persuaded to be sociable and discover Nairobi's night life. It is after all one of Molly's final weekends here in Nairobi before she goes home.

Molly and I share a taxi with a couple of volunteers living down the road from us. It doesn't take long for my paranoia to kick in as we leave the familiarity of Jamhuri behind us and start to take a series of dark back streets. Whether it be the side effects of my anti-malaria medications or being in an unfamiliar place I've become paranoid about situations I find myself in. Like being out at night in Nairobi. I know the direction to Nairobi city and that's not the direction we're heading in. I tell Molly and she laughs, aware of my tendency to be over-concerned. The taxi driver is taking streets left, then right. I'm sure we're going around in circles. I speak up, asking him where he is taking us.

'Are you taking us to K1? This doesn't look like the right direction', I state worryingly. 'I'm taking a shortcut' he responds. Hakuna matata, I remind myself.

The taxi eventually arrives at the club, much to my relief. Inside K1, the club is fancy and not unlike the bars I've been to back home. We're in one of the middle class suburbs of Nairobi, and it shows in the way everybody is dressed and behaving. The Kenyan men are wearing their stylish jeans, t-shirts and there's no shortage of bling. The women show off their curvy figures with short tight dresses. I am extremely underdressed, having only brought a supply of second-hand clothes to Kenya. I selected my pale blue three-quarter length shirt and my least daggy pair of jeans to wear with flip flops. I think it's the first time I've left the house without my hiking boots! I've worn some of my Masai jewellery bought from the markets when we were on safari, so that has thankfully dressed me up. We all share a few drinks at the club and play a few games of pool. Listening to the beats of the R&B and hip-hop music, I admire the way these women can move their bodies and know immediately that I will not be making an appearance on the dance floor this evening!

It feels surreal to be in a club on a Saturday night in Nairobi, doing the things I do back home. I never thought these types of experiences would be a part of my journey in Kenya. I'm continuing to see the divide in classes in this city, and I feel guilty enjoying these luxurious activities such as clubbing or going to the cafe for coffee when the other side of life is so near. I think of Ruth and Daniel at Ushirika, probably still working through their weekend just to pay their rent.

When we decide to leave, we call the same taxi driver to take us home. Still not convinced that it is safe to travel in taxis in Nairobi, I make everybody lock their doors once we're in, remembering the section on car hijacking from one of the many guide books I read. My friends think I'm ridiculous, but concede, desperate for me to relax. While travelling along the dark, isolated back streets, the driver suddenly pulls over and switches off the engine. Without saying a word, he gets out of the car. Paranoia has struck all of us by now, and we're wondering what on earth is going on. He lifts the bonnet of the car and checks the engine. Great, we've broken down, and at this time of the night there are no friendly Kenyans to give us a push along like last time. Not a soul insight. We convince Molly, the least anxious of us all, to ask the driver what's going on. I remind her that she is the one who talked me into coming out tonight so she owes this to me, to get us home safely. And alive. The driver stays outside for what seems like forever, before jumping back in the car. He tells Molly it should be ok, he was just checking something.

The taxi driver restarts the engine which seems to be working fine and we continue our long 'short-cut' route back to Jamhuri. We finally and thankfully pull up outside Alice's apartment to find a homeless man sleeping in front of the door.

We sneak past him and I hurry Molly along while she searches for the key in her bag. It feels eerie being outside in Nairobi at dark, and although I've had a nice evening I know I would have been just as happy at home with Alice, watching her television soapies and drinking chai. Still, this is all a part of the experience, I remind myself. Finally we're safely back behind her securely locked steel gates, and we find Alice still studying on the couch. I suspect she's been waiting up for us, making sure we return home safely. It really does feel like home.

Chapter 14 – The new girl in town

My exciting weekend continues having organised to meet Peter in Kibera. He's invited me to visit his small home town of Kamungi outside of Nairobi. I'm looking forward to exploring more of rural Kenya, and feel fortunate to have Peter to show me around.

I meet Peter outside Ushirika clinic in the early morning and can't believe he's on time. This is a first! We take a City Hopper bus into Nairobi city, before walking towards one of the matatu stations, searching for a matatu that is headed towards the town of Thika. Matatu stations in Nairobi can be hectic. There are dozens of different matatus parked chaotically, in no particular order or system, in this large open dirt space on the outer limits of the city centre. It is noisy with the constant sounds of matatu horns, music playing through the loud speakers, and the drivers yelling out their different destinations trying to attract passengers at a better rate than their competitors. It is rare to find upper class residents travelling in matatus. The drivers are considered reckless and the vans are frequently overfilled with passengers to an unsafe level. I stick by Peter's side as we meander our way through the congestion of matatus to find a van headed in the right direction.

Peter appears to be negotiating with a man who leads us into his van. He lets us take the front seat next to the driver, the one with the best view for the mzungu I suspect. We sit waiting for another ten minutes or so until the matatu is full before departing. This way the drivers make a maximum profit. Observing the culture of matatu travelling is fascinating. As a marketing tactic passengers are offered the best price and the more journeys made in one day the more money the matatu makes. As we take off, the driver's first priority is to turn up the volume on the vehicle's poor quality subwoofer. So we're all forced to listen to his choice of Snoop Dog and other American rap songs that make the van vibrate all the way down the road.

As we head out of Nairobi and onto the country roads, I take advantage of my front-row seat to observe the vast stretches of open fields and distant hills. About twenty minutes into our adventure I hear the driver shouting something in Swahili to all the passengers and he suddenly slows down and the music is switched off. I ask Peter what is going on. There's a police check on the road ahead, marked by giant spike grids that have been set up to ensure nobody speeds past them. We've all been told by the driver to put our seat belts on for the inspection. As we pull over, two heavily armed Kenyan policemen in uniform inspect inside the van, checking there are not more than the legal number of passengers and asking to see the driver's licence. Many matatus travelling around Kenya are overfilled. At times, over twenty people can be spotted crammed in like sardines into these fourteen seater vehicles. Peter informs me the police will stop any vehicle that's found to be travelling unsafely and the driver risks losing his operating licence. They give us the all clear and away we go. The driver keeps one hand on the wheel and reaches back to the passengers with the other, which is a sign we need to pay-up. We hand over our 40ksh. The music is turned up again and our adventure continues.

We arrive in Thika, which is a small town north east of Nairobi. Thika is a rural market town that is a popular stop-over point for people travelling to smaller rural villages. In Thika Peter directs me to a shoe cleaner working by the side of the road who's busily polishing a gentleman's black shoes. Peter wants me to have my boots cleaned. I'm not quite sure if it's for my experience, to help the hard-working man's business, or the fact that my boots really are filthy and I need to be made more presentable before meeting his family. Sitting on the stool I feel embarrassed paying somebody to clean my shoes on the street - almost humiliating. And yet it's something that everybody does here, not being bothered by the difference in class. The man does an incredible job, and it's the cleanest my shoes have been since I left Australia. If only I can keep them that way.

In Thika Peter and I take another matatu that is headed towards the village of Kamungi where his Mum lives. The matatu station is once again busy and this time there are dozens of young children carrying baskets of snack foods and water that they are trying to sell to passengers in the matatus. They are persistent and at times forceful. Even once we've boarded the vehicle they are pushing their arms through the windows of the matatu with water and food trying to make a sale. I seem to attract extra attention as mzungus are not often seen in these rural parts of Kenya. Even after closing the windows they bang on the doors to get our attention. Finally the matatu is full and we take off.

In true matatu style, Peter taps the roof of the vehicle twice as we approach an empty intersection to signal our stop and the driver pulls over and we jump off. Peter leads me down the road and starts to take me on a walk around this beautiful rural Kenyan village. The area is green and lush with a rich fertile brown soil and many plantations along the roads. The agriculture in this region is very important and productive. Peter points out the banana, coffee, avocado, mango, passion fruit, potato, sugar cane and pineapple plantations. I immediately notice the differences from Nairobi. The air is clean, fresh and unpolluted and it is peaceful, with no traffic or people about. There is one wide dirt road, which we walk down, surrounded by the fields of crops. Not a car, matatu, goat or even pedestrian in sight. We continue our tour and I am fascinated to learn about all the different crops and how they are grown. So much coffee is grown in Kenya and yet very little is consumed. Peter tells me tea is more affordable to the locals with coffee being one of the main exports to other countries.

The most fascinating part of my arrival in Kamungi is the reaction I receive from the locals. We pass a few people working in the fields and Peter greets them. I think he must know everybody here just like he does in Kibera. His friends all come out to greet me too, thrilled to have a visitor in these parts of the country. They stare at me, like they've never seen a white person before. Some of the local children start running out onto the street to see me. 'Habari?' 'Mzuri'. Then the chimes of 'How are you! How are you! How are you?' start, which sends more children running out to join them, recognising this as the call that a mzungu is in the vicinity. They compete to hold my hand as we walk along the road in what is simply a beautiful experience. When I crouch down to talk with the children a few of the young girls reach out and touch my hair, fascinated with how it is different to theirs. I watch another one touch my forearm and whisper to her friends that she has touched a mzungu. The children's mothers come out of their homes to see what is going on and smile welcomingly at me. Peter explains that it is likely that these children, and even the adults, have never seen a white person before. I feel elated and privileged to be one of so few people given the opportunity to explore such a beautiful and untouched part of this country. As we continue walking down the path, now and then I turn back to see all the children poking their heads out from their gardens, secretly catching a glimpse of me.

Peter and I meet his mother outside her Sunday morning church group. She's a very short and elderly lady, dressed beautifully in a blue cotton printed dress and small heals. Her hair is neatly tied back under a matching blue head scarf. She only speaks Kikuyu, her tribal language, so Peter must translate for us. We walk back to her house where Peter takes us on a tour outside. His mum grows bananas, potatoes, passion fruit, sugarcane, pineapple, tomatoes and has her own water bore as well as a goat out the back. Despite her age, she lives on her own and manages the property by herself.

The house is a largish timber shed with a few separate rooms and a central living area where we find a few small chairs and the gas cooker used to prepare the meals. All of the homes around here are without electricity and running water. Inside, Peter's mum prepares us some chai with fresh milk from her cows. She disappears into another room and returns with an apron over her lovely dress, in preparation for cooking lunch. Peter helps us to talk to one another; his mother is interested in my country and I am learning all about her culture. We all help to prepare lunch by cutting up some of the vegetables for the stew - cabbage, carrots, tomatoes and onions. When I start to slice the cabbage with my left hand, Peter's mum finds this so strange and watches me closely with intrigue.

'The right one is supposed to do all the work!' She says. We laugh a lot, the three of us together, over our different customs and cultures. For lunch she cooks the cabbage with onion over the kerosene cooker in the lounge room and it is served with rice. Then she offers me some yam soup to try, which is delicious. Peter's mum insists she would have prepared something more if she knew I was coming, and offers to send me home with a gift of some vegetables from her garden.

After lunch I take some photos of Peter and his mother then we all set out for a walk back towards the main street to wait for a matatu. We stop regularly in the street to greet the elders who know Peter and his mother and I am introduced to everybody. More children come out to see me and I have my photo taken with some of them, much to their delight and mine. Our numbers grow as we walk farther, collecting most of the children of the township on our way who seem to be following us in a small parade. Peter's mum insists on walking us all the way to the matatu stop to see us off. When we reach the town centre we say goodbye and I thank her sincerely for inviting me into her home. It's been a pleasure to meet her and the people in this town.

As Peter and I stand waiting near a tree in the town centre for our matatu, I notice the locals wandering up to stand near us. Some of them edge closer and closer staring at me with interest. I smile at them. I realise that they're not waiting for a matatu at all; they've just come by to see the mzungu who's in town. Word seems to have spread quickly! One man offers us each a banana in an extremely generous act of kindness. We're not able to converse in the same language but this offer of food says more than words possibly could. I feel welcomed into this small village and honoured to see the life these people lead.

From Kamungi, Peter and I take a matatu to Ruiru where his sister lives. Unaware that we have another stop before heading back to Nairobi, I follow my guide. Peter's sister, Maureen, works and lives at a prison in Ruiru where she trains the officers. We meet her and her children and share a soda together in their home. My paranoia starts to kick in again as I wonder if Peter has brought me to here to bail out his sister as their living situation seems quite strange. But I dismiss the idea, just as I dismissed the idea that Peter was going to introduce me to his mother as his second wife, which was a thought that occurred to me when we found ourselves alone in their home together. One never quite knows the cultural significance of meeting somebody's parents in their home, especially after my experience with Amos!

We don't stay long in Ruiru, since daylight is slowly coming to an end and I've told Peter I need to be home in Nairobi before dark. As it turns out we hit peak traffic heading back into the city. Our matatu suddenly pulls over onto the side of the road and everybody gets up and is rushed out of the vehicle. I have no idea what is happening but Peter urges me to follow the others who are being shown into another car. It's another example of spontaneous chaos in Nairobi. The new matatu we find ourselves in is larger than normal and decked out with flashing neon lights, loud music and fancy seat covers. It looks and feels more like a night club than public transport! There's even a television in the matatu showing video clips and we start to move along again to the sounds of the Backstreet Boys.

Finally we make it back into Nairobi where Peter and I squeeze our way onto an already full City Hopper bus that is headed back to Kibera. Using the public transport system can be exhausting and it's dark and late by the time we reach Kibera. I'm home later than expected but my concern fades instantly when I see the slums of Kibera lit up by candlelight for the first time. Most days I'm back at Alice's by sunset but here tonight I have the joy of seeing the slums at night. The sight is amazing. It's a sea of lanterns and candles bringing light to the small shops and businesses that are still open for business. The streets are still busy with pedestrians coming and going, and families making the most of the final hours before staying inside their small shacks for the night. By day or by night Kibera is alive and mesmerising. There is a feeling of security in an otherwise poverty-stricken area. This community really is something special.

From Kibera, Peter walks me back to Alice's apartment, as I have no flashlight on me and the back streets are covered in darkness. I've had an incredible day and am grateful to him for showing me around his hometown. He wishes me a good evening, *'jioni ngemi'*, as I enter the apartment. I have a nice Sunday night dinner with Alice, Molly and a new volunteer Young-Shil who has just arrived from Chicago today. I feel like the expert myself now, telling Young-Shil all the useful tips for living here, and yet it is only two weeks since I was the new volunteer in her shoes hanging onto every word Molly told me. You learn quickly around here!

Chapter 15 – Unexpected visitors

1st May 2006 – Nairobi, Kenya

Labour Day is a public holiday in Kenya. Despite its significance most people still go to work, especially in the slums. Public holiday or not they still need to provide a meal for their families to eat. I decide to go and help out at Ushirika for the day. Tomorrow I'll be starting my new role at the outpatient's clinic in Dagoretti Corner, so it is a good opportunity to finish some tasks and to see my friends again in Kibera.

I spend the morning helping out in the general outpatient's clinics. We see patients presenting with typhoid, malaria, urinary tract infections and a dog bite needing rabies injections. A young man presents with a sexually-transmitted infection for which I am called upon to deliver some sex education as well as some HIV counselling. I cannot force him to have a test for HIV but we strongly encourage it and provide him with all the information he needs. He takes this all in but insists on wanting to return for the test. We can only hope, as unfortunately many never return.

A surprise awaits me when I come out from seeing this patient in the clinic. It's Amos' family! His two sisters, two of their friends and his brother are all sitting in the waiting room amongst the patients. They tell me they've come to see me. *Ohhhhh god*! They want to know what I have been doing and when they can all come back to Australia with me! I take them on a tour around the clinic. I'm invited back to their house again for lunch sometime, which I thank them for, while wondering what excuse I'll be able to use to get myself out of this awkward situation.

But it doesn't end there! Back at Alice's house in the evening while reading my book, my phone rings. It's Amos. I take it into the bedroom to speak, where there is a little more privacy than sitting next to Alice, who I know will be listening in intently anyway.

'Hi Belinda. I hope you had a good day today', he says in his deep voice.

'Yes, yes, I did.' I respond, explaining how nice it was to return to Ushirika *for the last time*. And then he whispers softly, 'I just wanted to wish you a goodnight before going to sleep. I can't wait to see you again soon.' I manage to splutter out a 'thank you and goodnight', before quickly hanging up.

Aaaaarrrgh!!!!!! I return blushing and flustered to Alice in the living room who is finding the updates in my apparent recent engagement incredibly entertaining. I have got to end this and am relieved that as of tomorrow I'll be starting work in my new project, far from Amos and his family!

Chapter 16 – AMKA

HIV does not make people dangerous to know, so you can shake their hands and give them a hug: Heaven knows they need it - Princess Diana

Today's my first day in my new placement at AMKA clinic. Irene has arranged to collect me from Alice's apartment and drive me to the clinic which is in Dagoretti Corner. Dagoretti is another of Nairobi's big slums, located not far from our apartment in Jamhuri and in the opposite direction to Kibera where I have been working. When Irene arrives at Alice's, on African time of course, I hop into her car and closely follow the route she's taking so I can find my own way there tomorrow. We head out of Jamhuri and then onto the main Ngong road, passing the Junction shopping centre, before taking a left turn into the area known as Dagoretti Corner. The main road running through the middle of this slum is bitumen and is busy with cars, matatus, taxis, cyclists, pedestrians as well as wandering goats and the odd stray dog and chicken.

At first sight this slum is not as compacted as Kibera. There seems to be more space, but despite this the houses still resemble timber shacks and I can see overfilled dumps behind the many tiny wooden shops facing the road we're travelling along. There are signs of poverty all around; small toilet blocks in amongst the rubbish dumps, a few children sitting inside some old disused rubber tyres and women walking along the road carrying yellow jerry cans of water on their heads with their babies strapped to their backs. Along the main road, fruit and vegetable stands line the paths, with some women selling freshly cooked mandazis (a traditional fried bread, resembling a donut) next to others with big barrels of dried fish. I spot some men working in a small garden, bending over and cutting the grass by hand with a machete. People stare into Irene's car, spotting the mzungu, and curious as to where we're going. I'm new here, yet slightly less intimidated than my first days in Kibera. We turn onto a dirt track and pull into AMKA clinic, a small timber building hidden behind some maize crops in these slums.

AMKA health is the name of this project that was assigned to Sister Veronica by the Sisters of St. Joseph of Tarbes Catholic Church in Nairobi. AMKA is a Swahili word meaning *'wake up'* and was chosen to represent the message that HIV/AIDS patients can do a lot with their lives other than staying hidden in their homes. AMKA is a home-based care programme that provides medical, nursing and social support to members of the community affected by HIV and AIDS. The project's main centre is here in Dagoretti Corner. The clinic also looks after two additional catchment areas of Ngando and Gatina where a clinic is conducted by the team once a week to cater for patients who need outreach support in these large slums of Nairobi.

The clinic that I walk into this morning in Dagoretti appears new and well constructed compared to the timber-scrap shacks that surround it. Neat timber sheets and wooden panels frame the clinic building which has an enclosed outside verandah area and a blue painted roof. Several windows around the clinic provide light inside the building which contains a main common room and a door to a second private room with medical supplies that is used for patient consultations. Outside, the covered verandah at the front of the clinic serves as a waiting area for patients with wooden benches arranged in a manner inviting anybody to feel welcome to visit. I notice that there are no signs identifying the building as a health clinic. The issue of health, in particular HIV and AIDS, still remains a large taboo in these communities. Consequently the clinic is set back off the road and unidentified, encouraging patients to seek advice and support while remaining confidential.

The main room inside the clinic is a pleasant open space with a wooden table and some benches set up either side to provide a work space for some of the staff. There are a few wooden cupboards inside the room and a number of photos displayed that have been taken at a recent HIV seminar with patients and health care workers. I start to notice that the clinic has a role in building personal relationships with its patients in the community. Outside, there is a second entrance to another small consulting room, a kitchen, and a shed containing supplies for the program's patient food distribution. Inside the clinic I observe the posters attached to the timber-sheet walls of the clinic, campaigning for the prevention of HIV. One picture I'm drawn to is an image of a young man illustrating the dramatic transformation in his appearance before and after starting his anti-retroviral treatment. Another slogan reads *'If you're not infected, you're still affected'*. These pictures help me to understand where things are at in this community, with regards to HIV treatment and prevention.

I am introduced to Sister Veronica who is in charge of the AMKA health care project. Dressed in a white blouse, long navy blue skirt and wearing her black habit and gold cross around her neck, she is softly spoken and extremely sincere as she greets me with a warm hug. Her features are very soft and her nature very calming. Sister Veronica welcomes me to AMKA and tells me that she is delighted to have the help of a young volunteer like myself. They are very busy and under-staffed for the number of people in the community requiring their support.

Sister Veronica introduces me to Oloo, who is sitting down at the table with a large pile of paperwork. Oloo is an older Kenyan man, retired from his previous job in teaching and now works in the community as the social worker at AMKA. He is very tall, slim and dark, coming from the Luo tribe in western Kenya. Oloo helps to organise school sponsorship for some of the AIDS orphans who the project looks after, as well as some of the HIV-positive patients' children. Oloo stands up and shakes my hand gently with a very warm welcome. His lined forehead shows wrinkles from a hard life and his eyes connect with mine in a sincere and paternal bond.

Seated opposite Oloo is Solphine, the clinic counsellor. Solphine also stands to greet me, dressed immaculately in a traditional bright purple ensemble; the blouse tight and fitting with puffy shoulders and a matching long skirt hugging her curvaceous hips and flaring below the knees. This style is quintessentially African. It is feminine, smart and beautiful. And most of all it matches Solphine's bubbly and animated personality. She giggles at Sister Veronica and Oloo as they introduce 'the Australian volunteer' to the AMKA project. Solphine is delighted to meet me. I am greeted with the warmest and most sincere hug. Unlike the western world where handshakes and greetings can often become a formality, trivial and meaningless, every greeting I have experienced since arriving in Kenya has been heartfelt and meaningful. Solphine greets me today with the traditional hug as she leans in to embrace each shoulder in a way that is not rushed but is delivered with meaning and kindness. She continues to hold my hand as we stand next to one another, as new best friends do, and I feel so welcomed and special. Oloo comments on my height and says that if it wasn't for my skin colour I could be a real Kenyan woman from his Luo tribe, with my tall and slim figure, which makes us all laugh together inside the clinic.

Finally a young, tall and slender man wearing a stylish coloured shirt and fashionable jeans with polished black shoes enters the room where we are all gathered from the small consulting room at the back of the clinic. This is George, the clinic's nurse (whose role is the doctor). He comes across as reserved in nature and is a handsome young man. While I mingle with Oloo, Sister Veronica and Solphine, George stands back from the conversation somewhat mysteriously, carrying on with his own business and duties around the clinic. George, Solphine, Oloo and Sister Veronica together form the principal team at AMKA. There are many other people who help out invaluably with the project as volunteers.

Sister Veronica takes the time to sit down next to me and explain the set-up of the AMKA health project. I learn that the project has been running for a few years now, having branched off of the Riara Health project that was operating around Kibera and had been unable to cope with the growing demand for HIV/AIDS home-based care and support. AMKA was therefore established to cater for these principal catchment areas of Dagoretti Corner, Ngando and Gatina. The project is really the only one of its kind existing in these slums, catering for thousands of people living with or at risk of HIV in the community. While there are no facilities for patients to be admitted to the clinic, the medical program is equipped to treat opportunistic infections and other illnesses arising from the HIV virus. George is responsible for consulting patients who arrive at the clinic and distributes medications where appropriate. The clinic does not prescribe or supply ARVs but they are accessible to patients at a nearby designated clinic. Currently the project is taking care of over 250 patients living with HIV and 84 AIDS orphans.

In addition to the child sponsorship programs organised by Oloo the social worker, Solphine conducts individual as well as group counselling sessions at the clinic, which is an incredibly important aspect of working with HIV and AIDS patients. Amongst the most important work carried out at AMKA are the community home visits. Staff from the clinic visit new or existing patients in their homes in the slums, many of whom are too ill to walk into the clinic. Others are surrounded by the stigma associated with HIV and AIDS and do not want to be seen coming into a clinic. In these cases visiting patients in their homes is very practical. These visits are often conducted with the help of the clinic's incredible team of community health workers.

This morning I meet Evelyn and Immaculate, two of the volunteer community health workers at AMKA. Evelyn is a slim and stylish woman who has been helping at the clinic for some time now, knowing the AMKA team and patients very well. She wears a trendy grey hat on her short black bob and is bubbly and energetic to be around with a constant smile on her young face. Immaculate is an older lady who I learn comes from Burundi. Unlike everybody else I have met so far, Immaculate doesn't speak English, which is a part of the fun in conversing with her. A largely built African woman her hips swing from side to side as she walks and she's proud of it! She talks excitedly about me, grabbing my face with her two large hands and wanting to kiss me on the forehead. Evelyn translates for me, saying she has a daughter my age and that she thinks I am beautiful but would look much more elegant in a skirt like hers and not the denim jeans I'm wearing. A woman needs to show off her femininity, she explains to me, putting her hand on her hip and thrusting her backside out to the side, emphasising her point. This is not the first time I've been advised on my lack of personal style in Kenya and that I would be better off dressing like a woman in a skirt. I thank Immaculate for her advice. She smiles as she continues to talk away in Swahili and waving her hands at my attire.

I'm having a great morning at AMKA. My new colleagues are full of life and are fun to be around. So far there haven't been any patients come into the clinic and I ask Solphine about how the AMKA program works. The week is divided up into different clinics that the project runs around the nearby communities. Monday, today, is often spent doing paperwork or carrying out home visits with the community health workers if there are patients to be seen. Tuesday is a clinic day at Dagoretti Corner where patients come into the clinic throughout the day to be seen by one of the team depending on their need for medical, social or emotional support. On Wednesdays the clinic moves to Ngando, another slum not far from Dagoretti, to cater for patients in those areas. Similarly, on Thursdays, the clinic moves to Gatina, another catchment area. At each of these sites medical support is offered from George, social support with Oloo and counselling with Solphine. The community health visitors also conduct home visits in all of the surrounding slums to new and existing patients, taking the service into their homes, which in these parts seems to be the most effective method of outreach care. On Fridays the clinic moves back to its main centre in Dagoretti Corner where a food distribution program takes place in the morning for some of the patients, and in the afternoon there is a fortnightly group counselling session.

As I'm sitting down inside the clinic, two young schoolgirls come in to see Oloo. He warmly greets the two girls whose names are Eve and Lucinda. They are 9 and 13 years old and are AIDS orphans, having lost both of their parents to AIDS earlier this year. As their parents were patients of the clinic, AMKA continues to support the children through school sponsorship and the food distribution program. They are so young and shy around Oloo who asks them for their letters. The girls have to write a letter after each school term which is given to their sponsor who is paying their school fees. They also have to provide a copy of their results for Oloo to oversee.

Eve and Lucinda are introduced to me by Oloo and he tells them to shake my hand as a protective father would. I can see that he cares for these girls like they are his own. They politely greet me but are shy and withdrawn and don't say much. Soon after they have arrived the girls head home again, having to prepare lunch for their younger sibling. Oloo informs me that Eve and Lucinda and their younger brother live under the guardianship of their oldest brother who has just turned 18. As he's got a job and working most of the time, they have to look after themselves. Fortunately the school program provides them with a meal everyday at school. Being fed is often just as big an incentive for children to attend school in these communities as is the education itself.

Evelyn and Immaculate invite me into the kitchen which is a very small room, no more than $2m^2$, next door to the clinic's main room. Inside, there is a collection of pots that are used for preparing chai tea, a kerosene cooker and a few buckets for cleaning. The aromas of warm milky chai that Evelyn and Immaculate have been making fill the air. We're about to prepare for lunch. I watch as Evelyn and Immaculate work together to poor the chai into a couple of large thermos containers that we then carry into the main room of the clinic. The work table is transformed into a lunch room as the plastic cups and plates are taken out of the wooden cupboard as well as two loaves of sliced bread and a tub of margarine. This is the daily lunch at AMKA: bread and butter and chai. When everybody is seated at the table, Solphine leads the group in prayer, thanking the Lord for this lunch and she includes a special welcome to me and other new visitors to the clinic. I've quickly noticed the custom of prayer and the influences of the Catholic Church in the clinic. The thermoses circulate around the table as everybody eagerly fills their mugs to the top, and plates and knives are also passed around. As we take our bread I watch Immaculate as she leads the way making a triple-decker bread and butter sandwich. I start with two slices not sure how three would fit in my mouth.

The lunch we share is so very special, we all get along like we have known each other for a long time and I feel extremely comfortable. It's like I have always had a place in this team. When we finish our tea the second thermos goes around for seconds. Immaculate digs into the loaf of bread for another triple-decker sandwich as I watch in amazement. It occurs to me that this might be her only meal of the day, so as a volunteer with the clinic she's making the most of the lunch the clinic provides.

When we're finished, I help Evelyn and Immaculate to wash the dishes on the dirt path outside the clinic. Three large coloured buckets are filled with water; one is used to wash, the other to rinse and the third is for drying. I bend my knees, crouching down with a tea towel in hand, ready to dry the dishes that Evelyn passes to Immaculate who then passes on to me. We're a production line and an efficient one at that. Immaculate shows me the African style of washing - bending over the bucket, legs straight and backside pointed up in the air. Evelyn has the same position, which I've seen all of the Kenyan women around here do, when they're cleaning, washing clothes or buying vegetables at the markets. It might be awhile before my body learns to move and bend in these ways. In the meantime, I kneel down in my denim jeans on the dirt, thinking there may be is a reason why the western women stick to jeans after all!

After lunch Solphine explains that we're all going to visit one of the community health workers, Beatrice, who is at home with her ill son. He's in need of prayer to help his recovery. George, Oloo, Solphine, Evelyn, Immaculate and I all walk together through the slums of Dagoretti towards Beatrice's house. As we venture into the slums, there are many young children running about, some dressed in dirty tattered clothes and looking like they haven't bathed for days. We walk past a large dump that is filled with plastic bags and where goats are walking through the mounds of rubbish. I spot a single public toilet cubicle on its own, in the middle of nowhere, and a young well-dressed man walks in to use it. These slums are dirty and yet there is plenty of life all around us. The slums of Nairobi, after all, are home to over half of the city's population. Kids kick a ball of rubber bands back and forth across the dusty ground and women are outside chatting around the local corner shops. There is a strong sense of community where the locals all know each other well.

We arrive at Beatrice's small timber shack. We remove our shoes which is customary before entering someone's home especially for me with my mzungu boots. I place my mud-covered boots next to Solphine's spotless black flats and George and Oloo's polished black lace-ups. How is it that I cannot manage to stay as clean as them? Beatrice invites us into her home. Inside there is a small couch and table and a curtain separates the main room from the bed that is behind. Beatrice's son Peter, who is 17 years old, has been battling lymphoma for several months and has been in and out of hospital. The team at AMKA have organised a collection for Beatrice, knowing that she is struggling to care for her family and her sick child, and Solphine presents her with the envelope. Beatrice calls to Peter to come out and see his visitors, which he does. He is shy and withdrawn and has a lump the size of a tennis ball protruding from his neck, disfiguring his face. Beatrice explains that he cannot leave the house because of how he looks. Again, there is a stigma and lack of education associated with illness, not just HIV. He's since become isolated from the community and spends all his time at home.

We come together and Immaculate initiates a prayer. Everybody in the room joins in singing this uplifting and spiritual Swahili song. It is very touching. A procession of individual prayers follows as one-by-one everybody prays for Peter and Beatrice's family; wishing them strength, power and recovery. I'm not quite sure how to follow as everybody closes their eyes and I look around the room. I'm amongst people who have little possessions and money and yet they have put all that they have into this small envelope for their friend. They also have their faith which no amount of money or material possessions can replace. This time spent in Beatrice and Peter's home is inspiring and for them it is precious. They know that they are not alone in their battles, as I see for myself how strong the ties are in these slum communities. I feel privileged to be present for this ritual and blessed to join the wonderful people who are part of the AMKA team. My first day here has shown me that they are truly very special people.

Chapter 17 – Ngando
Do what you can and pray for what you cannot yet do
– Saint Augustine

Today I'm preparing to go to Ngando, one of the other slums where AMKA holds a clinic on Wednesdays. It is also the site of the convent where Sister Veronica resides. Our temporary clinic room is set up inside this building. The region of Ngando is not far from Dagoretti, to the west of central Nairobi. To get there I've arranged to meet Solphine, the counsellor at AMKA, outside The Junction shopping centre on Ngong Road.

But first of all I'm collecting Emilie, a new volunteer who has just arrived and will be working with me at AMKA. Emilie is from Vancouver and is living with a host family in Jamhuri not far from Alice's place. I'm excited to have another volunteer join me in the project. As I approach her apartment I spot the obvious mzungu standing there with her new backpack and short curly blond hair, eagerly looking out for me. I remember that first day feeling as well as the day my shoes were as white and spotless as hers are right now. Emilie is chatty and energetic and she tells me how she has volunteered for a couple of years in a clinic for HIV-positive people back in Canada. She wants to be a doctor one day and sees this experience as a great stepping stone in her dream to help underprivileged countries around the world. With plenty to talk about we walk up the main road of Jamhuri in the direction of our meeting point with Solphine.

We stand waiting at the busy corner intersection as Emilie asks me if I know where we're going today.

'I have no idea.' I respond. 'It's a place called Ngando where the clinic is held once a week. Being my first week with this project I have no idea how to get there'.

I wonder what our chances are of finding Solphine amongst all these busy commuters this morning, standing on this main road heading out of Nairobi. Emilie checks the time in western fashion and points out that Solphine's already 10 minutes late. Having just arrived in Kenya a few days ago Emilie will have her own lessons to learn in adapting to the different culture and way of living here.

Another quarter of an hour passes before we can see somebody waving their hand out of the window of a crowded matatu on the other side of the road, yelling 'Belinda, Belinda!' In true Kenyan style, it's Solphine, and we dash across the road as she tells the matatu driver to wait for us so that we can join her. Everybody stares as we duck our heads to board the van which has no remaining seats so we're forced to squat in the aisle, illegally, as the bus driver tells us to keep our heads down low so as to avoid being pulled over by the police. Just another Kenyan adventure as we make our way into work.

After a short ride Solphine taps the roof of the matatu and the matatu driver swerves immediately off the road to let us off. Emilie and I look at each other in relief that we've made it here in one piece. Solphine, who is today dressed radiantly in a matching green ensemble, is delighted to meet Emilie. She takes one of our hands in each of hers and walks us proudly and caringly along the narrow paths of the Ngando slum towards the clinic. Around us are the usual small shop stands set up on wooden tables selling small electronics, cotton kangas, shoes, fruits and vegetables and second hand clothes. Women are carrying their empty jerry cans as they walk towards the water tanks to fill them up. I can see people's shabby timber shacks constructed all around. Like Dagoretti Corner, this slum is more spread out than Kibera and although there is not the stench or visible sewage I saw in Kibera, the area is still extremely poor and the people face many hardships.

As we pass the large Catholic Church at the entrance to Sister Veronica's convent, Solphine pauses and makes a small prayer with her hands in front of the church's doors. The convent is modern and built solidly of bricks which is a rarity in these slums. We pass a number of young nuns as we walk through the corridors, each one stopping to greet us welcomingly and pleased to meet Emilie and me for the first time. Solphine shows us into a main room at the end of the hallway which is the space AMKA uses for the Wednesday clinics. We find Oloo and George already waiting for us and Emilie is introduced to them. We recount our morning experience on the matatus which makes everybody laugh, knowing what an adventure this normal daily routine for them is to us mzungus. Kenyans always seem so proud to have visitors trying to be a part of their culture, whether it is tasting their food and tea, travelling in matatus, walking through the muddy streets or attempting some phrases in Swahili. They are a very proud race.

The room we'll be using for the clinic is large and there are curtains which we have drawn to create a small private consulting area for George. Emilie and I are given the task of assembling the chairs and tables. We set up a small table with two chairs for George's room and the same in another corner of the room for Solphine to carry out her counselling, as well as for Oloo. We're shortly introduced to Joanne, one of the community health workers for the Ngando area. We'll be carrying out some community home visits with her this morning to check on some of the patients in the Ngando slum. Joanne is extremely welcoming and kind. She's wearing a colourful long skirt, sandals and a blouse. When I comment on her beautifully beaded bracelet and matching earrings, Joanne tells me she made them herself and is trying to set up her own small business for all the jewellery she makes. Joanne sits down with Emilie and me and talks to us about her role as a community health worker, helping to identify people in need of support in the slums as well as educating the community about HIV.

Joanne explains that many misconceptions and myths still exist about HIV in the slums that they are working hard to dispel. Amongst these myths include the belief that HIV only infects homosexuals and drugs users, that HIV is transmitted through touching or sharing the same cutlery with an infected person, that HIV and AIDS is a poor person's disease and that being infected implies immediate death. The myth of the 'virgin cure' is perhaps the most widely entrenched belief amongst the uneducated, whereby it is believed that having sex with a virgin or a young child will cure a person of AIDS. This has sadly lead to a significant increase in the number of rapes of women, young children and babies throughout Africa, particularly in South Africa. These are just some of the challenges that face HIV educators.

A few regular patients have already arrived and sit patiently outside the clinic room on some long benches that have been placed along the wall in the corridor. Before the morning clinic starts, Solphine, Oloo, George, Joanne, Emilie and I join the patients outside in this waiting area to open the clinic with prayer. Solphine leads the Morning Prayer, thanking the Lord for this facility to use and to bring strength and good health to all of our patients today. We all join in with 'Amen' before returning to the clinic room. George starts off the clinic by calling for his first patient, a lady who has been waiting patiently and is a regular at this clinic. He closes over the curtain next to his desk as he conducts his consultation. Everybody does their best to respect patient privacy despite the challenges of all being in the one clinic room.

Sister Veronica arrives during the morning clinic and takes the time to speak with Emilie and me to help define what our role will be in the AMKA project. We will be involved in the community home visits within the slums, reaching out to people living or affected by HIV and requiring support. Due to the stigma associated with HIV, bringing the support to people in their homes is often the most effective and sometimes the only method of providing help. There are many patients that are not ambulant and require assistance in their homes, in the form of massages and simple stretches, to help with their rehabilitation. We will be assisting Solphine in arranging the group counselling sessions where patients talk about their concerns and experiences living with HIV. Oloo is often overwhelmed with requests for arranging child sponsorship programs, and the community health workers require help with the food distributions that are conducted weekly to families in need. There is much work to be done to support this project with patient numbers growing bigger every day. Sister Veronica encourages Emilie and me to work together and welcomes all our ideas and suggestions for improving the service. We will be working on seminars that are being organised for patients and health care workers, and campaigns to increase the awareness of HIV and AIDS.

I'm excited to start my position in this clinic. In addition to the medical, nursing, social, emotional and nutritional support, AMKA also looks out for its patients' financial situation which obviously plays a big role in their overall wellbeing. The clinic encourages its patients who are physically well enough to work to support themselves. A common misconception is that HIV positive people are unable to work and are bedridden at home. While this is the case for some, many people who are taking ARVs are still very fit and capable of working, which is strongly encouraged so that they can remain active in their community. A positive and healthy mind helps to maintain a healthy body. All the HIV patients I meet are desperate to work, to be given that chance at doing something positive and having a sense of accomplishment in their day, not to mention the financial security in provides. A part of Oloo's job is to visit patients in the slums to observe how they are supporting themselves. Sister Veronica emphasises the importance of not giving hand-outs to patients. The project assists in providing food, medicines and counselling, but not money. One new project the clinic does help out with is starting up patients' small business activities that in the long term provide them with a sustainable income.

We meet Mary this morning in the clinic. She is 31 years old and has just seen George for some medications. Mary is HIV positive and taking ARVs. She has a healthy looking appearance and smiles when she meets us. Emilie and I are going to Mary's home with Oloo this morning to look at her idea for a small business plan to see if she is eligible for the program's support. We head out of the clinic and Mary leads the way through the slums towards her home. The main dirt road outside the convent that is lined with muddy puddles from recent rain is filled with pedestrians, the odd car and bicycles loaded with fruits, vegetables and jerry cans. Dogs and goats also come and go amongst the traffic. We cross the road and head into the smaller narrow tracks leading away from the roadside shops and towards the small timber home. A private gate leads us into a group of shacks where Mary lives.

Mary has two small children but they are not home today. She invites us into her home and inside it is a typical slum residence with one main room and a sheet dividing the bed from the cooking and sitting area. It is very small and the dirt floor is covered with cooking utensils, pots and plates. Off to the side of the room Mary shows us a collection of supplies she has set aside for her business. She has started to sell charcoal and soaps, which she shows us. The charcoal pieces have been grouped into small plastic containers, each one containing one dozen pieces of charcoal for the price of 20ksh. Mary explains how she bought the charcoal in bulk at the markets for about half the price. In selling them this way she will make a small profit with each sale. To the side are some soaps that Mary is selling too, which she has made herself. She has the basic ingredients needed to make the soap and is trying to sell them alongside the charcoal. Mary explains that at the moment the soap is not as popular but that the charcoal is selling well.

Oloo enquires about Mary's children and how they are doing. She tells us that they have been staying with her mother recently, who lives in the country, but they will be returning to live with her soon. I ask Mary how long she has been living here in

Ngando and she says she moved here not long after she was diagnosed with HIV. She is doing well with the support of the clinic and has friends who live nearby. Oloo is impressed by what Mary has been able to show us of her business. She is just managing to cover the price of her rent at this stage and, unlike many people in the slums, she has shown an understanding of how to budget her small amount of money. Mary tells us that she feels better about herself when she's working as it's the only time she stops worrying about her health. AMKA helps support small business plans such as Mary's through providing them with a small amount of money to start up or develop their business idea, which the patients must repay from their revenue. Oloo explains that Mary will be a suitable candidate as she's demonstrated initiative and stability in her situation. This small financial assistance will enable her to buy extra supplies from the markets and ingredients for her soap making which will hopefully further develop her business. We leave Mary's house advising her to come and visit us at the clinic next week. She is happy to have had visitors and some hope to hold onto for her business.

Next we visit Martin, a young man who lives in the slums. Earlier, I had been talking with Martin's brother at the clinic, who comes in regularly to collect Martin's medications and reports to George and Oloo on his brother's progress. Joanne accompanies Emilie and me on this home visit and leads us down the muddy paths of Ngando and around the back route behind a few shacks before arriving at Martin's place. We open the wooden door, which is secured by a small latch, and step into the darkness that typically characterises these tiny homes. Lacking electricity, the only light is natural light, and we find Martin lying on the couch inside his sombre timber shack. He is home alone, his brother having gone to work to support them both. Martin appears immobile and weak. His long skinny legs are stretched out on the couch. And yet he greets us with a large smile as Joanne asks him how he is going. He reports he is feeling better. Martin, who is no older than 30 years old, has just recently started taking ARVs. The effects these have had on his health, both physically and mentally, have been extremely positive.

Joanne describes the positive transition that these patients undergo in accepting they are HIV positive and starting ARV treatment. Patients who are bedridden can soon regain their strength to go outside and even work again. This of course carries many positive psychological benefits, allowing them to reintegrate into the community and have some purpose to live. Despite this, there is still a lot of stigma that exists, especially in these slums. Many patients will not come into the clinic for fear of being seen and labelled as HIV positive, which carries the risk of being thrown out of their family and abandoned on the streets. An article in the Kenya Daily Nation highlighted the stigma, discrimination and misunderstandings that still widely exists about HIV. A young boy, whose parents both died of AIDS, was being kept by his grandmother in a cage in their backyard with the animals. Despite not being HIV positive himself, he was treated like an animal and considered to be harbouring evil spirits passed on from his parents. His grandmother refused to allow him in the house or to use the same eating utensils as him. Fortunately neighbours found out about the young ostracised boy and the situation was reported to the authorities.

There are countless examples of discrimination, stigma and myths surrounding HIV, many of which have been developed from a poor understanding of the illness as well as conflicting religious beliefs and tribal customs. It is for this very reason that visiting people in their homes within the community is such an effective and needed form of help. Walking back to the clinic after our home visits this morning a young woman, no older than 20 years of age and holding a young baby in her arms approaches me.

'Take my baby' she says, smiling.

Stunned and not sure I'd heard her correctly, I respond:

'Why do you want me to take your baby?'

'For money', she pleads.

She's serious. I glance over to Joanne who gives me a look suggesting it's not the first time she's seen this happen. I'm shocked and not quite sure what to do. I reassure her she has a beautiful child who belongs to her and insist I cannot take her baby. As we continue our walk back to the clinic this image of the young mum wanting to sell me her baby on the street stays with me. This is poverty.

Chapter 18 – Mombasa

May 2006 – Mombassa, Kenya

This weekend I'm heading to the coast for some sunshine and to enjoy the beautiful beaches of Mombasa with Susan, Daina, Kate and Jenny. Mombasa is the second largest city in Kenya on the coast of the Indian Ocean. The ten hour bus journey between Nairobi and Mombasa is busy and frequently travelled by many Kenyans.

After packing my bags at Alice's and then trying to cross the huge pool of water that has formed outside our house following the heavy rains, I head off to meet the girls. Every step here is not without an obstacle! We take a matatu into Nairobi city where the night buses leave for Mombasa. The departure location is on River Road. Locals tell me that this is the side of town to stay away from in Nairobi, especially at night. I can see why. It's about 10pm and Susan, Daina, Kate, Jenny and I are waiting in a dark isolated street with our big packs on our backs and all our supplies for the next few days. There are strange people lurking about. I can't wait to be on the bus and moving. Finally the driver lets us get on and before we know it we're on our way.

We've come prepared with some entertainment for the journey. It is just as well because it's a long and bumpy ride and these buses aren't equipped with movies or air conditioning like other long-distance journeys we may be used to. Susan has lashed out on an imported issue of The Sun from London. It was last weekend's issue but she's thrilled to have found a copy here in Nairobi and intends to read it all from front to back. A little piece of luxury from home. I've brought my mp3 player along with extra batteries on hand to get me through the journey. It's customary for theses night buses to have a security person on board alongside the driver. It's no secret that the Nairobi to Mombasa route is at risk of hijackers, especially in recent times. Just last week I saw on the news a bus that was pulled over by a group of armed bandits who robbed all the passengers of their money and belongings. I watched, sitting concerned on the couch next to Alice, who reassured me we'll be fine since we're travelling at the start of the month. The hijackings are apparently more frequent at the end of the month when people are travelling with more money. So I sit up the front next to Susan and the overnight security guard. I'm not sure if his presence makes me feel safer or more worried about the journey.

Halfway through the night our bus pulls over onto the road. Those who were sleeping wake up to see what is happening. Others like Susan and I, who have stayed awake watching the driver's frightening night driving, wonder what is going on. On the opposite side of the road we see another bus that has been travelling back along the same route towards Nairobi. It has reared off the side of the road and nose-dived into a deep ditch. Nearby is a semi-trailer parked diagonally across the road. These roads are dark and dangerous and more often than not the drivers speed. Everyone on our bus starts to peer out the windows at all of the passengers standing by the roadside next to their bus, some visibly injured. I see one man with blood running down his face. I start to feel very uneasy; firstly to have come across an accident during the night, secondly I'm not sure if we should get off the bus and help these people, and thirdly I'm not feeling that great about being stationary on this isolated road in the middle of the night. We wait for over an hour while our driver helps out with the situation. We're told somebody is still trapped at the front of the bus. I experience a feeling of guilt, knowing that I'm a health care professional and trained in first aid, but unsure about offering my help in this scary situation. I stay on the bus with the others. Eventually our driver returns and we head off again, leaving behind a bus full of passengers on the dark roadside, not knowing if anyone will come for them.

My batteries hold out the journey and we arrive in sunny Mombasa early the next morning. It's beautiful and worth every hour of the previous night's long and perilous journey. We get off the bus at the Mombasa bus station, and it's bustling with people everywhere. I can taste the salty sea breeze and soak in the warmth of the early morning sun. We're finally on the coast! Mombasa has a very mixed ethnic population with a strong Muslim presence, and all around us I observe Muslim women dressed in their traditional burqas covering everything but their eyes. This is the first encounter I've had with this custom and I'm fascinated. I'm fascinated by the culture, the tradition and more than anything the mystery of what is underneath their veils. These women are beautiful and I feel the presence of centuries of history and tradition in this city.

Susan, Daina, Kate, Jenny and I find ourselves a taxi that drives us to Diani Beach where our accommodation is located. For the weekend we've rented a big beach-front villa with three large bedrooms, a kitchen, a lounge room and a verandah terrace looking onto the beach. It's incredible. Outside in the gardens that overlook the beach, baboons jump about in the tall palm trees. Over the next few days we're going to swim, eat, relax and enjoy a break from our work. Going away for the weekend is encouraged by our volunteer organisation. It gives volunteers a break from their work which can become very intense and emotionally challenging at times. It's considered important in refuelling volunteers' minds to continue their projects. We're of course constantly aware of our good fortune in being able to remove ourselves from these hardships by travelling to the beach or anywhere for that matter. For many people the slums are their lives and there is no escape.

Chapter 19 – Beach boys

To myself I am only a child playing on the beach, while vast oceans of truth lie undiscovered before me – Isaac Newton

There is a local fruit man that passes our villa every day with a basket full of fresh tropical fruits for sale: mangoes, papayas, paw paws, pineapples and bananas. We make big fruit salads for breakfast which we share out on our patio, overlooking the beautiful beaches with their crystal blue waters and deep white sand. The rest of our time is spent reading books on the deck chairs, playing cards, taking walks on the beach and swimming. In the evenings I enjoy listening to the calming sounds of the waves breaking on the beach and watching the incredible sunsets.

The beaches here are frequented by local boys who are very talkative and always trying to sell their small souvenirs and crafts to anyone on the beach. We call them 'the beach boys' of Mombasa. It is impossible to take a peaceful walk or spend an afternoon sunbathing without them approaching us to buy their items or to talk with them. Although they're friendly, they also hassle a lot and wait on the beach for us to go down every morning.

I find myself lying on the beach reading my book when a young man approaches me with a handful of beaded bracelets and jewellery.

'What is your name? Where are you from?' He persists with his questions, determined to start a conversation with me. It feels rude to turn them away, but the questions and constant following around on the beach becomes irritating and intrusive and forces us to enjoy the beauty of the beach from the villa's garden instead.

Susan, Daina, Kate, Jenny and I decide to head into the local shops and hail one of the local matatus driving down the main road. In addition to buying some supplies for dinner, we visit some of the tourist curio shops selling paintings, wooden ornaments, jewellery and all things Kenyan. Despite being keen to buy a few souvenirs, the shop owners hassle us to come in and buy everything we look at, which eventually turns us away and we take the matatu back to the peacefulness of the villa. Inside the kitchen we discover one of the big baboons has found its way in through the window and is holding one of our bananas in its hand. We scream in surprise and amusement as we try to shoo him back outside, wondering what else has been taken by our little friends.

The four days of sun and relaxation pass quickly and before we know it our Mombasa weekend comes to an end. We pack our bags and prepare to take the taxi back to the Mombasa bus station. However, in typical Kenyan style the taxi does not arrive and we start to cut it pretty fine for the bus' departure time. With only one night bus leaving for Nairobi we don't fancy being stranded in Mombasa overnight with nowhere to go. At the very last minute the driver arrives and once at the bus station we run into the office with all our bags to confirm our tickets and are relieved to see the bus hasn't left yet. We climb onboard and are met with a number of unhappy passengers. Clearly we're the mzungus who have held up the bus. We push our way through the full bus to find the only remaining seats left, right up the back. It's an old coach and the air inside smells stale, a combination of perspiration and a lack of ventilation. It's going to be a long ten hours back to Nairobi.

To make matters worse, just before leaving the villa at Diani Beach I started to feel unwell with that familiar unpleasant feeling in my stomach that sent me running for the toilet right before the taxi arrived. I took a few of my loperamide tablets and take another one now. It's not going to be an easy journey back and all I can do is to hope for the best. There's nothing like bad timing!

The bus ride is long and the driver makes only one stop at the five hour mark. I plug in my headphones and meditate to my music, trying anything to pass the time and not to think about the obvious as I become more and more desperate for that toilet stop. As I see the driver approach the roadside stop, I tie up the laces of my boots and run faster than I can remember doing for a long time. I am the first one off the bus into the most disgusting roadside pit toilets. But I've made it! Back on the bus I reassure the girls that I'm holding in there. I prepare myself for the next five hours, pop a few more pills and put my headphones back on.

We eventually arrive back in Nairobi earlier than expected. It's about 5:30am and because we're ahead of schedule and it's still dark outside, everyone just stays seated on the bus. So Susan,

Daina, Kate, Jenny and I decide to go along with it and sit waiting on the bus too. I'm not sure what is worse, these shady streets of Nairobi at 10pm at night or at this early and equally dark hour of the morning. We're probably better off on the bus. A little while later people start to get off the bus as the sun slowly starts to rise and Nairobi city starts to come to life. So we decide to follow. I say goodbye to the girls who are taking a matatu back to their orphanage, and then I look for a bus headed for Kibera. I climb on board a City Hopper bus which is packed with passengers and struggle to squeeze my way through towards the back seat, knocking everyone I pass with my big blue backpack. It is so tight that I cannot even turn around, so I spend the whole ride wedged in backwards apologising to the poor old lady I keep pushing into.

'Pole sana' I say, *I'm very sorry*. I'm now getting used to the many stares I get in and around Kenya. I can only guess what the locals must be thinking of the young white girl with the oversized backpack wedged in backwards on the bus!

I arrive back in the familiar surroundings of Kibera, and I walk back over the railway line and into Jamhuri. I'm greeted by our watchman who lets me through the big steel gates into Alice's place, where I find her in the kitchen drinking her morning chai and getting ready for work. It's so nice to be home! I sit down with Alice and we have some breakfast and more chai, as I share my stories about Mombasa, the long bus journeys, the baboons invading our villa and the beach boys. She's particularly amused to hear about my desperate runs to the toilet on the bus ride home, laughing openly about my unfortunate experience. At least now, back in the security of Alice's apartment, I manage to see the funny side to it too.

While I was away over the weekend, Alice bid farewell to Molly whose time in Kenya came to an end and she flew back home to New York. I'm saddened to return to an empty room, having shared so many exciting experiences with Molly. She made my transition into Kenya easier and more fun than I could have expected and was my first friend here.

Chapter 20 – The women of Jamhuri

Standing on a street corner waiting for no one is power - Gregory Corso

I'm eager to return back to my work at the clinic today following my time away in Mombasa. It's Wednesday, which is the day we hold the clinic in Ngando. I leave Alice's place and head up the road where I meet Emilie. She is staying in a street not far from me with a single mother, Beatrice, and her young daughter, Natasha. Together we walk up the main street of Jamhuri, past the few local shops and towards the busy Ngong Road. There is always plenty of activity in Jamhuri. Even early in the morning, many of the locals have been up for hours. Young men who have been fortunate to secure work are busy constructing new houses, children walk unaccompanied to school with their little bags on their backs, and there are women walking with large packages of food or jerry cans of water on their heads. Cars also come and go through the main street. There is an air of optimism about what this new day might bring.

Every morning walking to work I pass a small group of women who are dressed brightly in a range of colourful kangas and sitting patiently on a couple of large boulders that form the corner of one of the main crossroads in Jamhuri. Each morning as I pass them on my daily walk to work we greet each other, and exchange smiles as I pass by. As Emilie heads into one of the shops this morning I stop to talk to these women. I meet Janice, Pamela, Meredith, Esther, Faith and Dorothy. Some of them are regulars to this corner spot, while others come less frequently. It is early in the morning and they inform me they've already been waiting here for a couple of hours. When I ask them what they are doing they tell me they're waiting for work. They will quite possibly sit on these boulders all day waiting for somebody to offer them a job, whether it is washing clothes, cleaning a house or cooking. Janice explains that a load of washing might earn her 40ksh (less than $Au1). That will be enough to feed her family of five.

I am grateful to have made myself some new friends today. Meeting the people in this extraordinary community reveals their individual stories and daily challenges. These women of Jamhuri are courageous, never letting go of their hope and pride.

Emilie and I hail the matatu number 111 that we take to go into Ngando. Just making it into the clinic from where the bus drops us off is an obstacle course today. The long rains have been continuing and the dirt paths that form the backstreets to the clinic have turned into thick mud, filled with deep puddles of water. Emilie and I follow the busy flow of pedestrians making their way up the street. We hold onto the fence and pull ourselves along, just as I remember doing as a child when I tried ice-skating for the first time and was too terrified to let go of the edge. The locals watch us with big smiles on their faces, aware of how much of a problem the mud and water is for us. For them it's the smallest barrier they'll encounter in their day.

We finally make it through to the clinic, carrying an extra few kilograms of mud each on either shoe. Once again I stare in awe at the women wearing their clean sandals and the men in suits and their shiny black leather shoes, which are still shiny and black after their trek through the mud. Unbelievable! Emilie and I stop outside the clinic door where we try and clean up and make ourselves look a little more respectable and less muddy before going inside.

We're greeted by some of the other Sisters who work in the convent, as well as a few patients who are already waiting patiently to be seen. Inside the clinic room we find Oloo, Solphine and George, who has already started consulting his patients. Josephine and Rosalie, two of the community health workers for this area, have also joined us for the morning's clinic.

Today's clinic is fairly quiet. The mud can pose a problem for some of the locals in the slums. Some of the timber shacks can even become completely inaccessible with streams of water and mud blocking residents in. Emilie and I head out with Rosalie and Solphine to pay a few home visits. Solphine's young giggly laugh and commentary keeps us entertained as she sees how Emilie and I struggle to walk around. Our colleagues enjoy the role of guides through the slums particularly in these conditions, and show off their experience and skills as real Kenyan women.

We reach an area on the outskirts of the slums where a group of people have all come to a stop, unable to go any farther. Without stepping into knee high mud and water, it is impossible to get past to access the homes on the other side. Solphine and Rosalie decide we should head back to the clinic. Although they wanted to visit a young woman who is unwell in her home, we simply cannot get there today, and will have to go another day. We can only do our best.

Back at the clinic Emilie and I interview two young children who come in to see Oloo regarding sponsorship for their schooling. Brian and Peter are a few of the many AIDS orphans that AMKA continues to sponsor. Brian and Peter's father died last year of AIDS and left behind their mother with her four children. They have been out of school for a few months and Oloo is finalising their documentation for funding so they will be enrolled in school next term. We help out Oloo with his paperwork, as it seems he has been overwhelmed with applications. Each child filled out a page with all their personal details, and attached a photo that will be sent to their sponsor. I try and talk with the boys but they are shy. Many of the children we meet have a lot of respect for their elders, even Emilie and I, and often talk very softly with their heads turned away. Their personal circumstances and experiences are also likely to have affected their behaviour and lack of confidence.

On the way home from work Emilie and I stop at The Junction, the upmarket shopping centre on Ngong Road. It's always a strange feeling to enter into the elaborateness of this shopping mall, especially after spending the day working in and around some of Nairobi's worst slums. Dressed in our muddy shoes, jeans, long sleeved shirts and backpacks, we brace ourselves and head on in past the big security gates and armed guards. I feel rather out of place in an environment that a few months earlier I would have felt right at home in. As it is, the colour of our skin suggests that of all the customers here we're probably the least likely to be considered out of place. We stop at the supermarket to buy a few supplies before heading straight out again. I feel overwhelmed by the commercialism and enormity of this shopping centre and its exclusion of the surrounding communities. I'm relieved to walk back down the street towards my home in Jamhuri, its small roadside stalls and the welcoming community that I've become a part of.

Chapter 21 – Gatina

The base for our Thursday clinic is Gatina. Spreading outwards from Dagoretti into the area of Kawangware, Gatina is another of Nairobi's large slums. After I finish lacing up my boots, I head out of Alice's apartment and walk towards my meeting spot with Emilie. Each morning we always have stories to share about our evenings at home with our host families. We often compare what we've eaten for dinner the previous night which, unfortunately for Emilie, does not seem to change much at all.

'Ugali and beans again?' I ask her when I arrive.

'Hmm' she nods. 'Yep'.

I pass my new friends sitting and waiting as always on the corner of the road. Janice sees me and waves, and the other women call out my name. We stop to say hello, wishing them a good day, *siku njema*, before continuing on to take the matatu on Ngong Road to Gatina. It's such an uplifting start to the day to know we share a friendship with these women in the community.

Once in the matatu with the music blaring and the driver recklessly swerving around the big pot holes in the road, we notice a routine police check point up ahead. The matatu pulls over to where the officers are standing in their blue uniforms and guns slung over their shoulders, which is something I always find intimidating. They inspect the driver's papers and then inside the vehicle. We all sit still inside the van, seatbelts fastened, and wait for the officers to give the driver the okay. Fortunately today the matatu is carrying a legal number of passengers. The driver pulls back out onto the road, cranks up the music again to its unbearable volume and we're back en route to Gatina.

Emilie and I signal our stop by tapping the roof of the matatu and it immediately swerves off the road to let us jump off - literally - while it's still slowly moving forward, before pulling out again. Phew! We exchange looks of relief after another hairy matatu ride.

Emilie and I walk up the long stretch of dirt road that heads into the central area of Gatina. As always, people are smiling and friendly as we walk up the street past the chickens, goats and dogs, and around the small children who have squatted down to play with the dirt on the ground. On either side of the road, there is an endless collection of shops, made up of wooden logs and benches, and displaying anything from snacks, to clothing fabrics, to hair products and electrical devices.

There are many clothing stands lining the road, with piles of assorted second hand clothes from 10ksh a piece. One of our patients at the clinic has his own shop selling clothes. Each week he travels into the big markets where he buys his items of clothing, which he then carries into Gatina in large canvas sacks and puts all the clothes out on display for sale. It's a successful small business which the clinic has supported to get him started and now he has become self sufficient.

I'm amazed at the range of clothing brands we find when sifting through these stands. The international brands we see represent the variety of countries these clothes have come from. Today I see an AFL Hawthorn polo t-shirt and a pretty New Look blouse. My friends have been proud to sight their university hoodies worn by middle aged men. My favourite has been the business man I saw dressed smartly in the purple, green and yellow striped Subway employee polo-shirt. This mix of clothing that has come from all corners of the world and converged in the slums of Gatina is incredible.

We finally enter the large white gates that lead into the facilities of our Gatina clinic. Inside the large compound is a Catholic Church and to the right is a primary school. It is through Sister Veronica's contacts at the convent that the clinic is allowed to use a small room at this site for our Thursday morning clinic. The children are running around playing in the yard, dressed smartly in their tiny royal blue uniforms. It's a small private school here in the slums. A group of young girls are playing elastics with dozens of large rubber bands they have knotted together. It works impeccably. Nearby the boys are kicking around a soccer ball made from dozens of plastic bags scrunched up together. In these parts of the slums a real soccer ball is a rare sight. In fact I'm yet to see one. Instead, everybody plays with these plastic-bag balls.

As some of the children spot Emilie and me they charge over to us and, before we know it, we're surrounded by about fifty small adorable children all wanting to get closer to us and touch our hands. 'Howwareyouuu' they all chant excitedly as their mzungu call. 'Howwareyouuu howwareyouu howareyouu'. This is our Thursday morning greeting at the Gatina clinic. It's very special.

As the school bell rings and the children run off towards their classrooms, Emilie and I can finally make it up the stairs and onto the balcony where George, Solphine, Oloo and the local community health worker, David, have been standing and laughing at all of the attention we've generated among the school children. We greet each other and then Solphine opens the morning's clinic with a prayer.

We head inside where there is a large open room that the school permits us to use. George, Oloo and Solphine each set up a table in opposite corners of the room to try and have a small amount of privacy from one another while consulting their patients. George always carries a backpack full of his essential medications which he starts to unload next to his desk. Oloo is carrying, as usual, a mountain of paperwork consisting mainly of numerous sponsorship papers for the children. Oloo is incredibly good-natured and hardworking and yet, as Emilie and I continually remind him, completely hopeless with the concept of filing or organising his papers which we always find scattered everywhere. It's no wonder he keeps misplacing his papers and having to redo some of the sponsorship forms! We promise to buy him a small portable plastic wallet to help him store and organise all of his papers.

We start the morning's work with a home visit to see Nancy, one of the clinic's local community health workers. Nancy is also a patient of the clinic. She is HIV positive and has recently been sponsored by the clinic to start up her business plan, and generate income for her and her family. Emilie and I have been sent off to visit Nancy's home in the slums and to assess her situation and progress.

The clinic's support for patients' income-generating activities is one of the most successful programs they offer. Nancy presented Sister Veronica with her business plan a few months ago. Her idea was to set up a small fruit and vegetable stand here in Gatina where she lives. Lacking the money to start this project, AMKA lent Nancy enough money to buy all the fruits and vegetables she needed to start (600ksh), with the agreement that she would pay back this money in monthly instalments from the small profit she makes while also keeping some money for herself to pay her rent. If the patient is unable to pay back the money after the first few months in business, then the program's sponsorship does not continue.

We arrive at Nancy's home. Nancy is a single mother of three children who are all at school. We walk in through the wooden door to the single room shack. It's dark, as she has no electricity, and there is a row of yellow jerry cans lined up against the wall which is her water supply. A sheet hanging from the roof separates one side of the room as a bedroom. Nancy informs us that her three children share the bed at night and she sleeps on the floor. Her place is tidy and organised. Nancy invites us to sit down on a few small cushions on the dirt floor, as she brings out her small notebook which contains a record of her business expenses and revenue. Nancy's records show that her business is viable and she has already paid back half the loan that AMKA gave her. Nancy explains how happy she is at the moment to have a job each day, working at her small stall, and how much of a positive influence it has also had on her health. Before, when she was struggling to pay her rent, she was constantly stressed and depressed and her health subsequently declined. She explains how grateful she is to AMKA for their support, and that this is why she volunteers as a community health work to help out other women in her situation.

We head back to the clinic and report positively on Nancy's situation to Oloo and Solphine. They're delighted to hear about the progress in her business and her health. Although many patients are given the opportunity to start up an income-generating activity, unfortunately some fail. Sometimes this small amount of money is the largest some patients have ever dealt with and they are just unable to save or spend it wisely, having only ever had enough money to meet basic needs. For most, bank accounts do not exist. Nor do savings. If they have money they spend it because tomorrow it might be gone again. One lady bought a television for her child out of the grant and then had nothing to eat for a week. These income-generating activities are all about teaching the patients about how to manage their money.

We finish the morning clinic by helping Oloo with the food distribution program. AMKA's food program entitles many of the patients who are in difficult situations to a weekly handout of food to help them and their families. Since arriving in Kenya I've observed that one of the biggest challenges remains that of nutrition. While medications and ARVs seem to be widely available, basics such as food and water remain a daily struggle for many.

There is a large container located around the back of the school where Sister Veronica stores large bags of flour, rice, beans and Nutrimix (a nutritional flour mix to which water is added to make porridge). Patients who are eligible for food support have a small coupon which they present to us in exchange for one portion of the rice, beans, flour and Nutrimix. In many cases this can be enough food for a week. I climb into the large storage container where Oloo is working to help him out. I dig into the big sacks of beans and pour the two cups into a plastic bag, tie it up, then do the same for the rice and the flour as Oloo ticks off each patient's name who comes by on his list. The patients are extremely happy to head home with their food. As I continue pouring the flour and getting it all over me, I stop to think how it really feels like we're doing a lot of good work for the community here. We're just a small team, but a few hands can go a long way to put smiles on people's faces.

As the clinic finishes, George, Solphine, Oloo, Sister Veronica, Emilie and I have lunch together at the nearby cafe. 'Cafe' in this setting does not mean alfresco seating with toasted focaccias. The cafe is called 'Fair Deal Cafe' and is where the staff are invited to eat by Sister Veronica each Thursday when the clinic comes to Gatina. It's located on the main street in Gatina, next to the church and school where our clinic room is situated. The owner is Moses, a friendly and always smiling man, dressed in his infamous red polo t-shirt, track suit pants and flip-flops. He comes out to meet us and shakes our hands. We're invited to clean up out the front, using the plastic bucket with water and soap. The front of the shop is painted pale blue with some creative illustrations decorating the timber exterior. An old wooden advertising sign with the cafe's name and specialities, no longer readable as it has now faded so much, is perched against the wooden picket fence to the side. We walk in and sit down at one of the wooden benches Moses directs us to. It is small inside with only enough space for a few groups to eat.

The menu is simple Kenyan food: rice, beans, chapatti, ugali or chips. I've seen how most of these small cafes cook all of their food in re-used oil to save on costs. I try to work out what would be best to order and listen to what the others are getting. Solphine orders *matumbo* and thinking she's playing it safe, Emilie says she'll have the same. I decide to take the chapatti, my favourite Kenyan speciality, with beans. Our dishes arrive, served on old enamel plates. Emilie sees what Solphine is served and asks her what it is.

'Matumbo! It's very delicious' Solphine says smiling. George helps Emilie out by saying its sheep's intestines. We can see the small villi of the intestines curled around in a soup. Emilie's jaw drops and her eyes widen. The expression is priceless. I think she's learnt her lesson not to order what the next person is having! She ends up having the same as me, chapatti and beans, which is delicious. Moses serves the chapatti chopped up into little squares, and as I look around our table I notice that Emilie and I are the only ones to be given a knife and fork. I ask George if it's another tradition to eat the chapatti in these small pieces with a knife and fork to which he responds: 'No, it's just the mzungu way'. From this day onwards Moses will always serve us our chapatti chopped up and with cutlery.

Later as we walk home, I stop by the fruit and vegetable stand in Jamhuri to see my young friend Stanley. He is there smiling as always, and delighted to have a customer in an otherwise long lonely day standing on the street. We talk for a little while and I ask him about his family and school. He says he finished school but he has to work in this shop for his Dad every day. I buy some bananas to take back to Alice's. Stanley says he has the perfect pineapple for me, knowing what I usually come for. 'Okay!' I agree, thinking it will be nice to share with the others after dinner. I pay for the fruit and then wish Stanley a good evening, *jioni njema*, and *tutuonana*, that I'll see him soon.

Chapter 22 – Natalya

It's Friday and the clinic is back at its base today in Dagoretti Corner. Friday is food distribution day for this area and when Emilie and I walk past the tall maize plants outside the clinic and up the gravel path, there are already a dozen patients waiting patiently out the front. They're here for their food handouts, coupons in hand. I love the job of getting into the small food shelter which is amusingly the most secured part of the whole building (double padlocked every night to protect the food from thieves). As was the case in Gatina, there are large sacks of rice, beans and flour and today there is maize too. All the food is donated by sponsors. During the week Emilie and I spent an afternoon with Patricia, one of the community health workers, measuring and pouring the flour, rice and beans into the small plastic bags, tying them in knots, and putting them aside ready for today's distribution. Patricia enjoyed pointing out my clothes to everybody at the clinic once we'd finished. My tracksuit pants were covered in flour, while her black trousers were impeccably clean.

'It's good,' she reassured me. 'Now you look like a real working African woman!' I accepted the compliment proudly, as Solphine ushered me over to the water tank to clean me up.

Evelyn pays the clinic a visit during the morning. One of the roles of the community health workers is to report back to the clinic on how patients within the community are doing, whether there are any significant changes or requirements, as well as identifying new patients and bringing them the support they need. Emilie and I now know Evelyn well, having accompanied her on a number of home visits in the Dagoretti area, and today she informs us that she knows of a young woman who is very sick in the slums. We organise to go and visit her together and to assess her situation.

Evelyn, Emilie and I head out of the clinic and through the slums of Dagoretti. Evelyn shows us the way through the small dirt paths that lead off the main road, greeting many of her friends as we go. This is her neighbourhood, having lived here with her family for some time. I pass some young children sitting and playing inside a large rubber tyre. Another young boy is squatting low and defecating outside his house. A bit further away I see a large rubbish dump next to a single-standing toilet cabin and two goats are sorting their way through the rubbish. These slums are always a sight to see. Evelyn points out the entrance to the young woman's shack. It has been constructed from a combination of different materials, with wooden planks forming one side and dozens of scraps of metal having been put together to form another wall, along with some netted wire. The door is half-complete, made of various wooden planks and has *Hotel 46* hand-painted on the top corner. Next to this some of the scrap timber sheets have been painted white with an Arsenal logo (a popular team amongst Kenyans) drawn onto them. From the outside this shack is a mess, one of the worst living quarters I've seen yet. We brace ourselves as we always do before heading inside.

Through the squeaky wooden door, Evelyn, Emilie and I enter into the darkness of the home. The air is stagnant and it smells terrible. In the darkness I can see some posters that have been attached to the walls, some empty jerry cans lying on the dirt floor and an old sheet divides the small room. We follow Evelyn who makes her way towards a mattress on the floor and lying curled up like a skeleton under a sheet is an extremely ill girl. She is young, no older than 20 years old, and does not speak other than nodding or answering Evelyn's questions. We introduce ourselves and explain why we're here. She doesn't move. I see the shadow of a rat scamper by in the corner of the room.

The girl's name is Natalya. She's extremely fragile, both physically and emotionally. Learning that she hasn't eaten anything for a few days, we decide straight away that Natalya needs to be fed and hydrated. Does she live here alone? How did she get so unwell? Does she have HIV? All these questions can wait. For now, it's survival mode. We form a plan to buy some vegetables and fruits and to cook her a much needed nutritional meal. Given the state of her place we can't do it here, and Evelyn volunteers the use of her house which is not far away. We reassure Natalya that we'll be back shortly and head outside into some fresher air and daylight. I take in a big breath as I absorb what we've just seen. We're shocked and concerned about the state of her health. It is obvious that she has been through some trauma that has caused her body to shut down, mentally and physically.

We stop by the local market and buy some food (potatoes, tomatoes, onions as well as a few bananas) and head to Evelyn's house to cook. Despite living just a few minutes away from Natalya's corner, Evelyn's place is well built and spacious. It's a brick house and she has the good fortune of having running water and electricity. We walk through the solid security gates, past her living room which is fitted with a big television and into the kitchen. Evelyn starts preparing the vegetables. She's going to make a popular dish *matoke* which is mashed potatoes and plantains with tomatoes and beans. It's very nutritional and is what I ate with Peter on our tour of Kibera.

We get talking with one another, and as she starts cooking, Evelyn reveals to Emilie and me that she is HIV positive. She describes her own battles with stigma and discrimination since being diagnosed, and how just 12 months earlier she was critically ill herself and thought she would die. Since then she has accepted her illness, started ARV treatment and turned her life around. Evelyn talks openly to us about what it is like living in the slums in Kenya and the burden of being HIV positive. She is no longer ashamed of her status, as she once was, and uses her role with AMKA and at the clinic to help other men and women in her situation. She's truly inspirational.

We return to Natalya's house with the meal that we've prepared. We find her lying as we left her in the bed, under the covers. Evelyn explains that we'll help her sit up so that she can eat something. Natalya's extremely weak and as she moves her fragile bony limbs I become even more concerned about her state. Every rib is visible through her thin t-shirt. She has not showered for some time and the mattress looks to be soiled. Evelyn spends some time talking to Natalya in Swahili as Emilie and I stand back, unsure of what to think or do. She doesn't want to eat in front of us, so Evelyn leaves the food next to her mattress with some water. We can't push her, so we leave her to eat alone and reassure her we'll come back again tomorrow.

Walking away from Natalya's house is more difficult than it was entering a few hours earlier. How can we leave her like that on her own? Shouldn't she be taken into a hospital? To me she looked to be close to death. Here in the slums, the doctors, nurses, social workers and carers are the people like Evelyn; the people who live in the community and look after each other. I'm starting to realise how effective the clinic's system of home visiting is. It's the people like Evelyn who live in these slums, who come to know of people in trouble like Natalya, and they are the best people to offer support and take action. How would an outsider like Emilie or I know that there was a young woman dying in her bed there today? There is also a confidence that Evelyn provided Natalya with, in being a neighbour and a friend, which we are not always able to offer.

We report back the details of our home visit to George at the clinic who assures us we've done all we can for today. My western mentality is running through all the possible options that could be done to help Natalya: send an ambulance, blood tests, medications, saline hydration, and psychologist - get to the bottom of it as soon as we can. That's not how it works here. This is my first serious case but for my colleagues it's one of thousands they encounter in their work. Listening to stories from Solphine, George and the other community health workers, there are periods where every week they'll carry out a home visit and find a patient passed away in their home.

Solphine recounts a story where just a month ago a poor man's body had been left and became infected with maggots by the time she visited him. His family had abandoned him and the community ostracised him once they found out he was HIV positive. Finally the reality of my work is hitting me today. It's not all about laughing about walking through the mud, holding hands with the cute children and hearing the good stories of patients making a better life for themselves. The reality is that these are some of the poorest areas in Africa where every day there is a case like Natalya's. This is the biggest challenge I've faced in this journey. Seeing Natalya lying lifeless inside a shack made of timber and wooden scraps was shocking and saddening and it has touched me in more ways that I'd expected.

Chapter 23 – Kevin and Helen
'Life here is so hard' – Kevin

The weekend passes quickly and Monday morning soon arrives. Emilie and I are both keen to return to AMKA and to visit Natalya to see how she is going. She's been on my mind all weekend. I told Alice about Natalya and she also found it very distressing. Being able to go home at the end of the day and share our stories with our host families and fellow volunteers is an important part of the debriefing process. The weekend break lets us catch up with our friends and step outside the intensity of work we're involved in. We're lucky to have that 'option out'. For our friends like Natalya, her life *is* here in her timber-scrap shack in the slums. There's no stepping in and out of reality for her.

Evelyn comes into the clinic in the morning and I head off with her and Emilie to see Natalya. We arrive at the Hotel 46 timber shack and let ourselves in. Inside it is exactly as we left it on Friday - dark, filthy and glum. Natalya is under the covers on the bed and I'm relieved to see her tiny chest is rising and falling under the sheet. But she doesn't look good. Today she is having difficulty breathing as she sporadically gasps for air. We offer to give her a bath, which will make her feel a lot better, and she agrees. We warm some water over the gas cooker and gently sponge her dry scaly legs that look like bones. She lifts her t-shirt off allowing us to wash her upper body, and we gently rub her back for her.

To help Natalya regain her strength, Emilie and I prepare to visit her most days to help her stretch her legs and to give her massages. I unpack my small container of lavender oil from my bag, a precious gift from a colleague back home. I was told a few drops onto my pillow would help relieve any worries from my work and help me sleep. I've found a better use for it. A few drops onto my glove and I start to gently massage Natalya's legs. I'm careful not to hurt her, asking if she's in pain, *'Unasakia uchungu?'* I also massage her feet which are slightly swollen. The lavender oil is soothing and the physical contact through bathing and the massage is important in our care for Natalya. She remains quiet but I continue to talk to her as I rub her back and her legs. When we're finished we reassure Natalya we'll return again tomorrow for another massage. She has some food left next to her bed to eat and water to drink. It's a beginning in what looks to be a tough road ahead for this young woman.

The same afternoon there is a shy young man waiting inside the clinic with Sister Veronica and Oloo. His name is Kevin and Emilie and I introduce ourselves to him. Kevin has been a regular visitor at AMKA for some time now. He is the son and sole caretaker of his mother, Helen, who is HIV positive. They live in the slums of Gatina. Kevin is 18 years old and dropped out of school to take care of his mother last year. The clinic was sponsoring his studies but his need to earn money for his mother became more important. Helen has been bedridden for a long time now, unable to weight-bear because of weakness in her legs. Kevin has come to report to the clinic about his mother's condition. Emilie and I are sent out on a project with him to visit Helen in their home in Gatina.

Young Kevin is softly-spoken and shy. He avoids direct eye contact when talking to us, responding to our questions with his head bowed. His forehead is very lined for such a young face and his big brown eyes are heavy with worry. He's dressed in jeans, flip-flops and a bright blue and yellow Nelly the rapper t-shirt. I ask him if he likes Nelly and he smiles. It's a rare smile I suspect for a young man who seems to have taken on a big number of adult responsibilities.

Kevin leads Emilie and me towards his house through a secret short-cut route through some maize fields, over some stepping stones in a creek, we slide over a concrete ramp, and walk hesitantly over a wooden plank that forms a bridge over a river of sewage.

'We're trusting you here Kevin' says Emilie. We seem to have a friendly bond with him, much like that of a younger brother. He holds our hands to help us over the creek and then waits patiently for our slow but sure performance over the wooden ramp. It's obvious we've never done this before and he can tell! We finally come out at the main road leading into Gatina.

Heading up the familiar path to our Gatina clinic site, we take a left and pass the biggest rubbish dump I've seen yet, right in the middle of the slums. Ironically a large hand-painted 'no dumping' sign oversees the piles of rubbish that have been mounting up over the years in this dump sprawling over an enormous area. Next to the dump there's a shop selling dozens of full-sized coffins and I watch a few young men who walk past us carrying one on their shoulders. The streets are filled with activity and when we approach Helen and Kevin's place, several young happy children come running out to see us. Their mothers all gather around too, wondering what is going on. Two mzungus are in the neighbourhood. We ignore the attention and follow Kevin into their shack.

Kevin and Helen's place is made of wooden boards and inside the layout is typical of most homes in the slums, a curtain separating the bed from the small kitchen space, no electricity or running water. It is no bigger than 15m^2, and inside Kevin has arranged everything very tidily. A small window lets some light in and outside the shack there is a small open space offering them some privacy from other homes in the slum. Kevin invites Emilie and me to take a seat opposite Helen, who sits up to greet us from her bed. Helen is in her forties, she has very short dark hair and a soft and graceful face. She takes our hands, one after the other, to greet and welcome us into her home. Like Kevin, Helen speaks good English. Helen is interested to hear about our lives, where we come from and our families back home. She never has visitors. Her husband, Kevin's father, died 2 years ago from AIDS and now Helen's health is also failing her. She has an older son who lives and works in a village in western Kenya, leaving Kevin to care for his mother on his own.

As I watch Kevin take care of his mother, I realise what a difficult life this courageous boy leads in these slums. He opens a thermos of tea that he has prepared for Helen and pours her some to drink, offering Emilie and me some as well. He stands by Helen as she talks to us, wiping her forehead in a gentle and paternal manner. I am overwhelmed by the gentle and caring nature of this young man, as I think of all the 18 year old boys I know and how none of them are like Kevin. Kevin is desperate for us to help his mother regain her strength, knowing that she is all he has left. I can see how close they are. Emilie and I plan to visit Helen on our regular home visits to help her regain some movement and strength in her legs with some rehabilitation exercises. It's been about 18 months since she last walked. I take out the lavender oil and gloves and give Helen a massage around her feet and her legs which are limp from muscle wastage. She enjoys the feeling of being nursed which gives her new hope for getting better.

Helen and Kevin are incredibly grateful for our visit and uplifted to know we will be visiting them on a regular basis. Emilie and I pack our bags and say goodbye to Helen as we step outside. Our new little friends are waiting in the yard to see us. Their young and big wide eyes stare up at us inquisitively, wondering who we are and what we are doing. I'm often aware of the attention we attract as mzungus in the slums on our community visits. Although our visits are carried out in confidence we can't help but generate some interest amongst the locals who spend their days outside their homes, wondering why we are visiting a particular person in their community. It's a natural concern knowing some of the stigma and discrimination that surrounds HIV as well as other illnesses in these areas. However, despite this concern for our patients' anonymity, I've realised that our visits to otherwise forgotten corners of the slums are appreciated by those in the community. They are grateful to have somebody take an interest in them and that they are not forgotten. As we head off, the young children's mothers smile at Emilie and me, making us feel welcome and appreciated.

Kevin kindly offers to walk Emilie and me back to the clinic in Dagoretti Corner, aware that it would be a miracle for the two of us to retrace the perilous short-cut he led us on earlier. Although we walk mostly in silence, we feel a special connection with Kevin. Once back at the clinic he doesn't bother to come inside, he just makes sure we're back safely. Kevin looks at us both with sincerity, hope and gratitude.

'Thank you and God bless you both' he says softly, offering to come and pick us up from the clinic in a couple of day's time to visit his mother again. He has been touched by our visit, as we have by his strength, maturity and gentleness. We hug him goodbye, knowing we'll see this special person again very soon.

Chapter 24 – New Hope

Those who educate children well are more to be honoured than they who produce them; for these only gave them life, those the art of living well
- *Aristotle*

I've been invited by Susan, Daina, Kate and Jenny to spend the weekend at the orphanage where they have been volunteering. I'm excited to travel somewhere different and to see inside another volunteer project. Above all, I can't wait to meet the beautiful children whom I've heard so much about.

I meet the girls in central Nairobi on Saturday morning and we spend some time looking around the City Hall and Masai markets. One word can describe this experience - exhausting. The many little shops and stands display a typical selection of African souvenirs ranging from beaded jewellery, wooden bowls and utensils, to dyed prints and colourful scarves. From the moment we step inside City Hall markets, we're hassled by every market-owner to enter into their shop and to see what they have.

'No pressure, look only!' they reassure us with their big smiles, but their eyes tell us they're after more. I cling onto my bags and have a look around. The salesmen and women are friendly and kind, but never cease to pressure every potential customer into buying something. This is, after all, their job.

When the hassling becomes too much after awhile, we head around the block to the outdoor Masai markets. Set up outside in an open square, there are dozens of different stalls to look at, many selling the same things as the previous City Hall markets and similarly competing for our attention and business. From the moment we step foot into the market place the hasslers arrive, their hands full of leather belts and beaded necklaces they insist on showing us. There is no appropriate place to look as no matter where I glance, there is a stall and the owner seems to catch my glance which he interprets as a strong interest in his stock. I walk around the markets with Susan, where we are constantly followed by friendly young men wanting to take us to their shops, their friends' shops and their uncles' shops - there is no escape!

Susan barters with a man from his original offer of 1000ksh for a scarf down to 100ksh and walks away with a bargain for her friends back home. Daina spots some jewellery she likes but when the man refuses to drop his price she walks away. Timed to perfection, a minute later he reappears behind us agreeing to meet her price. Sold. That's how it's done here. Their mark up is incredible, and having been here for some time now we know what a reasonable price to pay is. Still, as discussed over lunch in the city, there is that feeling of being torn between paying a good price and knowing that for us it still only converts to a few dollars for something somebody has probably spent hours making by hand. There's a pride in not wanting to be overrun by the system of bartering, but also a moral responsibility towards respecting these people, their trade and their only source of income. There's not always a simple answer to these difficult questions that keep appearing during this experience.

Once we're all shopped out, which does not take long, I follow the girls to the big matatu station in the city centre. The area is bustling with dozens of matatu vans parked everywhere, drivers calling out to passengers to choose their vehicle and passengers searching for the matatu heading in the direction they want. The matatu station is always chaotic, but not as intimidating to us as it once was, having become more experienced at negotiating and navigating our way around Nairobi and its outskirts. Daina and Kate spot the matatu we're after, and instantly object to the mzungu price of 60ksh they quote us, knowing for certain that it's always a constant 40skh for this route. They agree, realising we're more local than they expected.

We sit waiting inside the van in the matatu park until there are enough passengers for it to take off. I'm all the way in the back seat with Susan, not able to hear a word because Shakira's 'Hips don't Lie' is blaring through the speakers right next to my ears. Even once we've started moving, the driver stops to take on more passengers through the streets of Nairobi, squeezing them up the aisle of the Nissan minivan. I now have a lady sitting on my lap and cannot see or hear a thing. We eventually make it onto the main route, and take off towards the area of Uplands where the orphanage is located. It's about a 25 minute journey and our matatu is over-filled with passengers. I just hope there's not a police check on this route today.

Daina taps the roof signalling the approach to our stop, and we push our way through from the back seat to the sliding door and jump out of the matatu with relief. We're on the outskirts of Nairobi. Having left the busyness, chaos and pollution of the city behind us, there are now large open fields, some filled with crops and others completely bare, which line the road we walk along. I have the feeling of being in the countryside. It feels great! I follow the girls as we set off on our walk towards the orphanage. There's a dusty path cutting through a large grassy field that leads us around to a church, which Susan points out is where the children go for their Sunday mass. We're very isolated out here; there are no houses or shops. As we continue walking I can see the nice and brightly painted building that is New Hope Children's Orphanage.

Standing on its own and painted in a light blue, this modern looking brick building is a change from the timber-sheet shacks of Kibera. Space is abundant out here in the Uplands and as we approach, I can see the large outdoor areas to the side of the orphanage where the children are playing, and rows of clothing are hanging out to dry. We've arrived, and we enter through the gates to greet all the children who have gathered at the fence to see their visitors.

As we walk through, all the children come running out to greet their friends Susan, Daina, Kate and Jenny, crying out their names in excitement and grabbing their hands. Despite not knowing me, it makes absolutely no difference and the children fight to hold my hands too, not concerned by an unfamiliar face but rather excited to be around a new visitor. I'm given a short tour of this outdoor area where the children are playing in the dirt.

The children at New Hope Orphanage range from babies of just a few months old to older teenagers. At the moment there are over sixty children housed here, some having just arrived in the last week or so, others including some of the older teenagers, having lived here for most of their lives. The one thing they all have in common is they are orphans. Some of the children have one living parent whom they have contact with, but who chooses to send them to an orphanage where they can sleep, eat and be taken care of during the week while they work. These children sometimes return to their parents on the weekends. There are many others who have no family at all. Their family is here at New Hope. The children's stories for arriving here at the orphanage vary widely. Many are very sad. Some children were found as young babies, dumped in public spaces and brought into the orphanage. Others were abused, physically and emotionally, in their previous home environments. But stories are not revealed or talked about at the orphanage. The centre is a fresh start for many of the children. It is a warm, caring and safe home where everyone is family.

Anne is the courageous lady who established and runs New Hope. Addressed by everybody as 'Mama' for her maternal love for the children, she treats them as though they are her own. This remarkable lady set up New Hope in 2000. She previously worked at Barkley's Bank and with her business skills and help from the missionaries she succeeded in raising enough funds to start up the orphanage and construct these excellent facilities. She continues to receive sponsorship from many of her contacts to fund the centre. Mama is an incredible woman. With a large African build, short black hair, and her constant warm and welcoming smile, Mama is the one person who has brought together all these children and who continues to make them feel safe, happy and healthy. She has help from other people working at the centre, including Susan, Daina, Kate and Jenny, as well as local volunteers. Daina and Kate live at the orphanage where they are with the children all the time, while Susan and Jenny stay with a host family not far away.

I'm introduced to Mama and she welcomes me warmly to the orphanage and thanks me repeatedly for coming to visit. We sit down in an open lounge room where there are a few couches and chairs. While Mama talks a little about the centre and its organisation, children keep running in and out of the room to see her, desperate to touch her arm or fight to have a spot in her lap. They want to be close to her and it's clear these children see Mama as their mother. Even Daina and Jenny have managed to each gain a few followers, with some of the children they've become so close to during their stay here following them around everywhere they go.

As dinner time approaches I wander outside to join the children. Some of the older teenagers have the responsibility of preparing and cooking the chapattis for dinner. They are sitting huddled around the gas cooker and hot plate, dressed in their warm coats and beanies. Out here in the countryside it gets cooler at night. I can see what a big job they have here, working in a team with one of them rolling out the chapatti, another spinning them around on the hot plate and, once it's cooked, somebody else ready to open up the plastic container and adding the chapatti to the growing pile. Cooking enough for the whole orphanage and breakfast tomorrow means at least a good hundred or so chapatti. But the children are happy with their job, sitting singing songs together as one does around a campfire. They giggle about boys and make silly jokes, just like any group of teenage girls. They're all best friends, family even, and are happy together in the comfort and security of this home.

Unlike the slums I've spent my days working in, this centre is a home tucked away from the visible signs of poverty and disease. Standing on its own with empty and peaceful surroundings, the children's home consists of a nice new brick building with designated bedrooms, a long corridor and family rooms inside, all of which are secured with proper doors and windows. There is routine here. While food is not abundant, there is always something to eat at every meal. There is not a daily struggle for something to eat, or the concerns of violence happening outside on the streets. Here the children have their own space, where it is quiet and secluded from the stretches of poverty in central Nairobi. At New Hope all the children have a mother, in Mama, who is caring, compassionate and somebody who everybody counts and depends on. And perhaps even more importantly they have each other. Everybody here is family and tonight I feel I'm a part of that.

Outside I'm led by my new little friends towards the back of the building where the few animals they care for are kept. A new calf was born just a week ago and all the children are excited to show me the new addition. As we approach I can see it sleeping in the corner near its mother. Around me, some of the smaller children are playing a game of tag and chase. A young boy called Brian, who is no older than 4 and dressed in a blue pair of overalls, is playing with a set of plastic racquets with 3 year old Alicia, who is wearing a tiny pink knitted cardigan and small colourful beads hanging from her braided fringe. I join in their game, having fun running around with this racquet, despite having no ball to play with. The children are energetic and delightful, young enough not to be worried by their past or concerned about their future. Alicia, I'm told, has no parents or family. She has already been at the centre for some time and will likely finish her schooling here. And then what? I wonder. What happens when they are old enough to get a job? How do they integrate back into the outside world where life can be difficult and challenging? I know I'm getting ahead of myself as for now they are children and that's all that matters.

Before we eat dinner, Mama introduces a new visitor at the centre to the children who they are asked to perform a song inside for. Various visitors come by from time to time, from the church, the local community and overseas organisations, each one an important prospect for supporting the centre. Some of the older children gather around a brightly painted mural lining the corridors inside the orphanage. They arrange themselves into a choir and proceed to sing some prayer songs in front of Mama, her special visitor and the other children. Their voices are beautifully tuned and in harmony. Listening to them sing I can tell that singing brings them joy, as much as the words they are singing do. They feel special performing for their visitor who is extremely impressed by the performance. He's invited to join us for dinner, which is announced to be ready.

I follow as the children, excited and proud to lead the way, know exactly what to do at dinner time. We're served our plate before all the others, being guests at the orphanage, and I gratefully take my plate of chapatti, beans and potato over to the couches with Susan, Daina, Kate and Jenny. Then, one by one, the older orphans serve up the other children's plastic plates, half a chapatti, beans and potatoes, and a plastic cup of water. They happily take their plates with them and find a place to sit and eat with their fingers, most sitting on the floor along the main corridor in a neat little row. This routine is familiar and extremely well regimented at the centre. The children are well disciplined and very respectful of their elders, whether it is Mama or the older children they also look up to.

The meal is delicious and I find it even more enjoyable given the company that I have the privilege to be amongst this evening. What a difference it makes sharing a meal with others, compared to being on your own. I've really come to appreciate this throughout my stay in Kenya. Even though we just eat bread and butter everyday for lunch at the clinic, sharing this amongst friends with laughter and stories is so special. Tonight I feel the warmth and love of this tightly knit family and their openness and willingness to welcome any new face into their home.

Once the children have finished their dinner, one by one they start to collect their plates together, even coming over to us inside Mama's family room, to collect our empty plates. We're being treated like royalty. The children collect all the plates and put them into the big plastic containers where they will later be washed, ready for breakfast tomorrow.

The fortnightly ritual known as Fellowship at the orphanage begins after dinner has been cleared away. All the children move into the small family room, competing for a place on the couches, the tables, or sitting on the floor as close as possible to Mama where they'll be close to the action that is about to take place. Fellowship is another reason that my friends have invited me out to the orphanage this weekend, and also the reason why all the children are in a state of excitement. It is an evening of singing, dancing, prayer and welcoming of new children into the orphanage. It's an evening where they all express their faith which bonds the family together.

Some of the older children start the proceedings by initiating the first song, to which everybody joins in; Susan, Daina, Kate and Jenny included. They've learnt many of the songs in the short time they've been here. I gaze around and listen in amazement to the wonderful music being made together. Some of the children start dancing as they sing, many hold their hands up firmly to the sky, reaching up towards their Lord. Everybody is united together. Mama then welcomes three of the new children who arrived during the week. For these children it is their first experience of a Fellowship, and like me, they are quite overwhelmed by everything that is happening around them. I think about what they must be feeling and thinking, where they have come from and this new home and family they have found. Not all the children are ecstatic and singing and dancing. There are some who watch passively, their faces blank and withdrawn. It's a reminder that many of them are still healing.

The songs become louder and louder, and now even the small children are up on their feet dancing about. I join them, feeling inspired by the energy and the faith around me. Then some of the children have the opportunity to perform individually. One girl sings and then a boy performs a break dance on the floor. Everybody is laughing, encouraging him to continue and he receives an enormous applause from everybody. It's now my turn to introduce myself, as a new visitor, frantically thinking what I could possibly do that would entertain the children. I introduce my name to which they all chant: 'Praise God!' and then I thank them all for inviting me to join them in their Fellowship, which is followed by 'Praise God Again!' and that I wish everybody a lovely evening. 'Praise God Again, Amen!' they cry. The unison of the voices is moving.

Mama then clears one of the tables and starts a special presentation for the volunteers, marking their contribution to the orphanage. Daina and Kate, having already been in Kenya for 6 months, will be leaving in the coming weeks. A large cake is brought out onto the table, along with some small bowls of chips, to which the children applaud with excitement. This really is a special occasion for them. Everybody is served a small piece of cake which is a real treat. Mama delivers a speech thanking the girls for all their love, support and assistance with the children at New Hope. Then Susan, Daina, Kate and Jenny are each presented with a small knitted bag that one of the children, Minnah, has made. They're extremely emotional, knowing how attached they have become to the children and how difficult it will be to say goodbye.

But for tonight, it is not yet goodbye and the songs continue on until later than the normal bedtime. Some of the younger children start falling asleep, and I watch as their older brothers and sisters take care of them and put them to bed. Finally Fellowship comes to an end and we all head back to our rooms for the night. I'm sharing a room with Susan, Daina, Kate and Jenny which is well set up with a few single beds and some space for our bags. Next door, the older children are busy tucking in the smaller ones, who are often two or three to a bed. Each room has a few bunk beds and the children are happy to share with the others for the company. We clean our teeth outside just before the generators are switched off for the evening which leaves the centre in darkness. It's lights out for everyone.

I wake up early in the morning to the sounds of children's voices and tiny footsteps running down the corridors. I slept really well after such an exciting evening. Before breakfast I sit on one of the couches in the family room and suddenly I am joined by four of my new small friends. It's incredible how quickly I've bonded with them. Around the room there are a few pictures on the walls and a book case containing a collection of books for the children.

One of the young boys brings me a book that he wants me to read to them all. I open it and I start reading, noticing that they all know the story by heart. They snuggle into me trying to get as close as possible. We then have breakfast together, which is a mug of chai tea and a chapatti that has been heated up from last night. Once again, it's delicious. The children then get ready for their Sunday morning church service.

A young girl, Minnah, who had made all the girls each a small bag last night at Fellowship, approaches me. We have not yet met, but Minnah presents me with a small knitted bag of my own. She has been busy making it since last night, seeing I didn't have one. It's knitted with royal blue, green and white wool. Inside are a few small handwritten notes on paper written by the children to me. One of them reads: *'Belinda, I am happy you come see us. Please stay, I love you. Monica'*. I'm overwhelmed by their kindness and open hearts. I give Minnah a big hug, unable to express just how much this means to me. As I pack my bags this morning, I'm sad to leave the orphanage. In less than a day I've made so many friends here and am touched to know that all these children have a safe home, away from the troubles of their past.

As all the children set out on their walk to the Church, dressed in their smart school uniforms and black shoes, I follow them on the path towards the main road where I'll take the matatu back to Nairobi city. I thank Mama for a wonderful stay and reassure her that I will come back and visit again. I say goodbye to Susan, Daina, Kate and Jenny and take my matatu back to Nairobi. On the journey home I think about my fabulous weekend and how refreshed it makes me to return to my patients at AMKA: Natalya, Helen and Kevin and maybe others who are awaiting our help. The children at New Hope are inspiring and have left a lasting impression on me.

Once back in Nairobi, I change from my matatu onto another bus that takes me towards Jamhuri. I walk through the markets at Adams where I run into Debra from Ushirika. I'm so excited to see her, as she is me, having not seen my friends at Ushirika for awhile. She informs me that they are all well and waiting for me to come back. On a sadder note she informs me that her younger brother passed away this weekend at her family's home, which is upcountry in western Kenya. She'll be travelling up to join them for the funeral. It seems like tragedies never seem to stop affecting people here. It's sadly common to hear of babies and young children dying in this unexpected way. I console Debra for her loss and promise to come by and see her at the clinic soon.

Finally I walk up the entrance to Alice's place and I'm back home. I don't remember at what point Alice's house became home, but it has certainly felt like that for some time now. It's the place where I feel safe, where I have family here in Kenya and where I have my few possessions. Like at New Hope, it's here that I have my meals morning and night, where I talk with my housemates about my day, where we laugh and where we are safe from the troubles going on outside. I hug Alice as I put my bags down. She wants to hear all about my weekend and I bring out my camera as well as the few gifts I was given by the children to show her.

Our household is now growing with another intake of volunteers having just arrived. Christine's a middle-aged nurse from Australia who has come to participate in the HIV program and will be staying with us at Alice's. Set in her ways and independent, she has been an interesting addition to the otherwise smooth dynamics in our household. Alice quietly informs me that over the weekend Christine complained about not being given enough food to eat, being woken up early in the mornings and that we eat dinner too late. I have a laugh with Alice in the kitchen as we catch up on household gossip like reunited sisters.

I always enjoy this time with Alice in the kitchen, talking together and helping with dinner preparations. She shows me how to sort through the rice, taking out the tiny stones, and tells me off for throwing out the ends of the vegetables insisting nothing goes to waste here. Tonight as we're preparing dinner we have a power outage in the apartment. Electricity cuts are a common occurrence here, happening at any time of the day and lasting for any length of time. Alice is quick to light a few candles that she places on the living room table. Young-Shil, Christine, Alice and I sit around the table together and share our dinner and conversation in what is a peaceful and pleasant candlelight evening.

Chapter 25 – Annie

As I step outside Alice's apartment on Monday morning I meet our new neighbour who is moving in to the apartment that is in front of ours. His name is Leon and he's just arrived in Nairobi from Congo to study architecture and English. I introduce myself. Leon is my age and is very kind but also quite shy. I realise that, even for him, the culture and language here in Kenya are different to where he's from and he's also adjusting to life in a foreign country. I explain that I live with Alice and some other volunteers from different countries and that we are all working here around the slums in Nairobi. Leon seems impressed and intrigued by our lives as volunteers.

When Emilie and I arrive at the clinic there is a staff meeting that has been organised with the principal team of Sister Veronica, George, Oloo, Solphine, Emilie and me. We feel privileged to be recognised amongst the keys members of staff and to be included in the meeting. Sister Veronica discusses what's currently happening with many of the clinic's different projects and how AMKA is providing support to all the surrounding slums. We learn of plans to rebuild a new centre in the Ngando area, where the current Catholic convent is located. This project will be funded by Sister Veronica's convent.

George, Oloo and Solphine present an update of their work in each of their disciplines. Then it's Emilie and my turn to provide our report. We describe our two most recent patients, Natalya and Helen, and the regular visits we will be making to their homes and the support we will be providing in terms of massages, stretching as well as reporting back their condition to the others. Sister Veronica is pleased with our organisation and instructs Emilie and me to take responsibility in looking after these patients. We're now capable of finding our way around the slums to visit these regular patients on our own.

During the meeting Sister Veronica assigns Emilie and me the task of developing the program's income generating activity (IGA) project. Our role in this project, which we have already shown a keen interest in developing, is to set up some documentation and planning for the clinic's support of patients' business plans. We will be responsible for researching these business ideas, by visiting patients' homes and assessing their input and output expenses and evaluating whether these patients are eligible for financial support from the clinic.

Emilie and I set to work straight away on our project. We construct some rules and requirements for patients to be eligible to participate in the program and design a table containing all the relevant information we will be required to collect. We brainstorm some ideas for supporting the patients, which includes a method for teaching them simple business record-keeping skills, as many of the patients we have visited simply remember their figures off the top of their heads. They have never been taught the concept of keeping a budget and recording their expenses and profits. We decide to invest in some exercise books and pens so that we can provide each new IGA patient with a pen and a book where we will draw up a table of expenses and income. We will teach them how to manage their business and keep track of their loan repayment to the clinic. This will also be the record that we will check to monitor the viability of their business during the evaluation stage.

On the way home from the clinic I stop at Nakumatt Junction to meet up with Kelly, Suen and Galvia. It's really nice to catch up with some of the other volunteers who started out with me and to hear how they are going in their placements. Like me, they're busy with their projects teaching and looking after the children at the orphanage, and have also been doing some travelling on the weekends. I continue on the road back home to Alice's, passing Stanley along the way where I give him a wave, and receive a huge smile in return.

Later that night at Alice's, I wait for the arrival of my dear friend Annie. Annie, a close friend and colleague from the hospital I work at in Adelaide, is joining the volunteer program for 6 weeks and will be staying with us at Alice's. I can hear the van approach and I step outside to give her a huge welcome hug and help her inside with her all her bags. I'm so excited to see Annie and she's had a long journey from Australia. We pass our new neighbour Leon who is coming home from school and says hello. Inside Alice's, Annie is introduced to our household and we all sit down to talk before having dinner together. One of the first things Annie says to me is that I look so happy and at home here. Her words stay with me and make me realise that she's right. I love my job here, my routine and the friends I continue to make. This is exactly where I want to be right now and I cannot wait to show her everything.

Chapter 26 – Hunger

If you can't feed a hundred people, then just feed one – Mother Teresa

This morning Annie, Emilie and I head off to our Ngando clinic. It will be Annie's first day at AMKA and I soon realise it's impossible to explain everything about Kenya and our work here to her. She will just have to see it all through her own eyes. It all starts as we walk through Jamhuri towards Ngong road where we take the matatu. I show Annie how much of a local I've become when I tap the roof to alert the driver of our stop, and we stumble out of the van one after the other. Much of the mud from the previous week has hardened up so the walk up the long road to the clinic is a lot easier today. I point out the goats, the small road-side shops, the open sewage and timber shacks to Annie, sights that have become every day for me now, yet never cease to attract my attention.

On arriving at the clinic, we greet some of the regular patients who are already waiting patiently on the wooden benches to see George. Annie stays at the clinic to meet Sister Veronica, Oloo, Solphine and George as Emilie and I are sent off on a home visit to assess a patient's small business plan.

Beth is a patient who we have met before at the clinic, but we have never seen or learnt about her income-generating activity. Beth leads us to her home which is not too far a walk from the clinic. It is a typical slum home, built of wooden planks and inside there is the single room with a bed and some kitchen utensils and pots. It is clean and Beth stays here on her own. She has three children but they all live with her sister out of Nairobi. I write down some of the details about her living situation into our record book, including the rent she has to pay and expenses for her children. Beth then takes us to her shop where she sells fruits, vegetables and plants. It is located in a good position next to a larger road where there are many passers-by. She informs us that she has been earning more money lately and that the business is allowing her to support herself as well as her family. Emilie and I take note of everything we've seen at Beth's and will report back positively to the AMKA team on her IGA.

After the morning clinic we set up the room for lunch. Some of the community health workers have been preparing the chai and Sister Veronica asks Emilie and me to buy some bread. The table is then set: chai, bread and butter. Everybody takes a seat as we all pray at the table and Annie is given a special welcome to the team. Then lunch begins. It's always a pleasure and an excitement to have a new visitor and everybody has many questions for Annie. What do you do in Australia? Are you married? Do you have children? Do you like Africa . . .? Annie loves the closeness of the AMKA team and the specialness of our lunch together, just as I always have since my first day at the project. She's excited to be joining us on our mission.

After lunch I help to pack up the clinic, wash the dishes, clean the floors and put everything away before Oloo, Solphine, George, Annie, Emilie and I walk back to the clinic in Dagoretti Corner. It's a nice 30 minute walk from Ngando through the fields, around the mud, across a railway line and then back through the slums. Sitting outside the Dagoretti clinic we see Kevin, who's been waiting patiently for Emilie and me. He's come to collect us so we can go and visit his mother Helen.

This time accompanied by Annie, the four of us set off, heading towards Gatina. Kevin leads us through the short-cut route, where we slide across the cement embankments, balance on the branch to cross the stream and walk over the unstable wooden bridge. When we arrive at Helen's house, she appears to be in good spirits and is so happy to see us again. I think she looks better which is extremely encouraging. The swelling in her feet has gone down slightly. I introduce Annie to Helen whom she is also delighted to meet. When I ask Helen how she is doing today, she tells me that she is hungry. She has not eaten anything all day since her cup of chai for breakfast. This is always so difficult to hear. Eating is one of the most fundamental ingredients for a recovery plan and yet is still often unreachable for so many. Helen has her free ARVs and other medications to take, but no food. The ARVs are especially strong drugs and it is important to maintain good nutrition and energy levels. So while Emilie carries out the stretching and massaging of Helen's feet and legs, Annie and I head out to buy something from the street stands for Helen to eat.

We find a small shop not far from her home where I buy some ugali mix that Kevin will be able to prepare for them both and some bananas. As volunteers we're always aware that our role is not to give handouts, or to make people dependant on our aid. The aim is to encourage people in the community to be self-sufficient so that in the longer term, when we're no longer able to visit every few days, they can manage to look after themselves. There are, however, times when we just have to help out. Like today. We take the food back to Helen's house, where Kevin is extremely grateful. I help Emilie finish the massage and together we help Helen to sit up and, supporting her under both arms, we help her walk a few steps outside to where Kevin has put a chair in the sun next to the avocado tree.

Sitting outside on a chair under the sun makes Helen's day. I don't know when she last left her bed as she's unable to walk on her own. I feel that she is already making progress and know that we will be able to improve this with our regular visits. We insist on the importance of drinking water, *maji*, and remind Kevin that he can come to the Gatina clinic on Thursday for the weekly food distribution. We can check with Oloo if they are entitled to some extra bags of food. We reassure Helen that we'll be back to visit in the next few days and we can see the difference that this makes by the smile on her face and the hope in her eyes.

At the end of a busy day, I walk back home where I meet our new live-in housemaid Lucy. With a growing number of volunteers in the house and Alice's night school starting again, she has hired a young Kenyan woman to do the cooking and cleaning in the house. I introduce myself to Lucy. She's young and has a timid smile. I offer to help Lucy with the cabbage or tomatoes, as has been my job with Alice in the kitchen, but she doesn't want to let me help, insistent that it's her job and worried what Alice might think if she sees me helping out. Lucy makes a great dinner that we all share. As I'm sitting in the living room eating I can see Lucy sitting on a chair in the kitchen having her dinner on her own. I encourage her to come out and join us, unaware of the usual customs for a housemaid in a Kenyan house, but she's committed to making a good impression on her first night and doesn't leave her kitchen.

Chapter 27 – Harvest

Never doubt that a small group of thoughtful, committed citizens can change the world; indeed, it's the only thing that ever has
— Margaret Mead

It's Thursday morning and our clinic is in Gatina today. Emilie, Annie and I head off on the journey into work. At the top of the main street in Jamhuri, we pass the women sitting and waiting on the corner. There are many today, dressed brightly and looking about optimistically at the chance of finding work. I wave at Janice and her friends and we continue on our way.

The walk into Gatina from where the matatu drops us off is, as usual, fascinating. The gospel music is already blaring. Emilie, Annie and I walk past the goats on the road, avoiding the open sewage and looking over at the enormous rubbish dumps. Children run over to say hello to us, as do many polite and friendly adults. They stop to shake our hands on their way to their own jobs or simply wandering about in the slums. Once at the clinic, Emilie, Annie and I sit amongst the patients for awhile in the morning and talk with them. I meet Patrick who is a charming 18 year old boy who comes in regularly to collect medications for his HIV positive mother. We talk about football and music together. We also talk with Mary, Bonfar and Ivy. It's such a pleasure to meet with all these people and to listen to their stories.

During the morning I conduct two more interviews for the IGA project that Emilie and I have been organising and which is coming along well. One of the patients we're assessing is Darlene. After talking to her at the clinic, Emilie and I set off on a walk with Darlene to visit her home. In true African style, the walk which we're told is 'not far' proves to be several kilometres away from the clinic, and we continue walking on and on, following Darlene's unrushed footsteps. Nobody is ever in any hurry here. We eventually arrive at her home where she lives with her two young sons. Like many, Darlene is a single mother. Her partner left her when he learnt he was HIV positive. Not long after she too was diagnosed positive. Darlene has a small business selling charcoal in a shop. She buys the coal cheaply at the markets then marks up the price. Still, she is struggling with her rent, telling us that she is already late with her payments and the landlord is starting to threaten to throw her out if she doesn't pay. We record all the details we need before leaving Darlene's place and make the long trip back to the clinic.

When we arrive, the clinic is closing and Oloo is busy organising the food distribution. Most of the patients have already been and gone. For lunch we all head to our regular lunch spot, Fair Deal cafe, where Moses is waiting for us excitedly. Emilie, Annie and I order our chapatti, beans and cabbage while the others take their matumbo and ugali. George makes a joke by asking Annie if she's sure she doesn't want the same as them, saying how delicious it is. We all laugh, remembering Emilie's mistake on her first day in Gatina. George informs us he'd visited Helen this morning while we were out with Darlene. He is pleased with her progress, noting her brighter appearance and the improvement in her legs. He checked her medications and told Helen and Kevin that we'd be around again for a home visit tomorrow.

After lunch the whole team heads back to Dagoretti Corner through what is becoming known as the famous shortcut thanks to Emilie and me. We struggle through the obstacle course, poor Solphine tripping at one point and grazing her leg. But that's not enough to take away her smile as we laugh about it, and eventually make our way back to the clinic in Dagoretti.

Emilie, Annie and I arrange to visit Natalya this afternoon. I'm keen to see how she is doing but at the same time I'm also slightly worried about what we might see. We set off on the road out of the clinic and through central Dagoretti. We stop via Evelyn's house to see if she wants to join us in visiting Natalya. As a local, she communicates better with Natalya than we can and has gained Natalya's trust. Evelyn answers the door and is delighted to see us, warmly inviting us into her home explaining she has some guests. As Evelyn ushers us through to the living room, we can hear the voices of a small gathering inside and finally see the faces of many familiar as well as some unfamiliar faces in Evelyn's lounge room. We're greeted excitedly by everybody. They are delighted to have some unannounced visitors.

Today is their meeting day for a women's group that they have created amongst themselves in the slums. There are about thirty women inside Evelyn's spacious living room. All of these women are HIV positive. They have come together today in the first of many planned future meetings to help themselves in their constant battle to support themselves. They have established a name for their group today, *Harvest*. One woman informs us they'd just finished praying together for help and support when we knocked on their door. 'God has sent you to help us', they tell us.

I'm invited with Emilie and Annie to sit down and listen to Evelyn's guests speak. These women want to work. They want to help other women who are HIV positive and living in the slums. Because help has not been offered from anywhere else they have come together today to help themselves. Women are twice as likely as men to become infected with HIV through unprotected sex. This is one of the leading reasons behind the higher population of women living with HIV in Africa than men. Another disturbing fact is that almost half of Kenyan women and girls experience some form of violence (physical, sexual, verbal or emotional) in their lifetime.

These women I am sitting and talking with are inspiring, each and every one of them. Some talk openly about their situation, their children, their health, while others remain quiet but offer their support. Annie shares our story of how, similar to their women's group today, we organised a big cake stall in the hospital where we were both working in Adelaide before coming to Kenya to raise some funds. She explains how all the staff members took the time to contribute cakes and biscuits for the stand in an effort to help us raise funds. We finally raised several hundred dollars to bring to Kenya with us. With this, the women all start to applaud our efforts, feeling the inspiration from working together to help a needy cause.

I see Joanne, one of AMKA's community health workers, who is today wearing a bright yellow t-shirt displaying the words: *'HIV and Positive'*. I didn't know that she is HIV positive and a patient herself at AMKA. Her own battles, experiences and decision to accept and live positively with her diagnosis make Joanne an invaluable role model for other women in the slums, whether they are HIV positive or not. As she is taking ARVs, Joanne manages to lead a positive lifestyle through working and interacting in the community. Today, her t-shirt tells everybody that there is no shame in being HIV positive. And that it is possible to live a positive life with this virus. It's a powerful and affirmative message that I am touched to see.

I also talk with Grace, who I have previously met at AMKA's group counselling sessions. She tells me how she would do anything to be given a chance to work, to be given a small shop and some materials so that she could start her sewing business. She points to her friends who, she explains, would work with her. These women are pleading to be given a chance. As visitors today, Emilie, Annie and I are the ray of hope for these women. They're counting on us to make a difference in their lives.

Unable to make a promise to give them jobs, I do promise to remember them. One lady, Joan, touches me with her words when she says 'Belinda, please don't forget us. So many people come through here, and promise us the world. And then they leave, returning to their country, and they forget us'. I'm so struck by what Joan tells me.

'I won't forget you' I promise all of these women at Evelyn's today. I may not be able to promise them money or jobs or security or good health, but I know that I will not forget any of the stories they have shared with me.

Following the meeting at Evelyn's, we're even more inspired to visit Natalya and to help her out of her bad state. We head back through the interior of the slum, around the towering rubbish dump that is still occupied by the resident goats, around the single standing toilet block and out towards the easily identified timber scrap box that is Natalya's home. Hotel 46, as I've come to call it now. I push the timber door in and go through into the darkness of the shack. I call out to Natalya but as usual there is no response. I wander through to her bed where she is lying curled up in the foetal position, frail and distant.

Natalya doesn't respond much to our questions about how she's going and whether she's in pain. We're desperate to help this young woman but we feel like there's a big barrier we can't break down. The state of her home seems to be worsening, if that is possible. There are small fleas in the air that I try to brush away from my face with my hand, desperate not to inhale them when I speak. Emilie holds her t-shirt up to her face to keep her mouth covered. It smells terrible inside. Outside, Natalya has two brothers who are just hanging outside the house, one older and one younger, with nothing to do. They too look malnourished and withdrawn. Neglected. We decide the best we can do today for Natalya, as she is not communicating or cooperating with us, is to buy some food that her brothers can cook for her, and at least ensure she is eating something. We will return tomorrow having reported back to George at the clinic.

I'm convinced after today's visit to Natalya's that we can no longer help her without knowing the source of the problems that have brought her to this state. She clearly has many emotional and psychological issues that are discouraging her from any form or attempt of recovery. She needs to help herself in order for us to help her. All of the possibilities for her health run through my head. Is she HIV positive? We don't even know that, and it is such a sensitive topic to broach, particularly in these communities. She is not improving and her state is critical. It worries and saddens me to think I'm not doing anything more. My biggest fear is that when I open the door to Hotel 46 that I may find Natalya not responding at all.

These are the challenges we face on a daily basis carrying out this type of work in the slums. The reality is that people do die in the slums every day. In Kenya alone, an estimated 400 people die every day from a HIV related illness. On my walk home from the clinic this afternoon I decide to visit my friends at Ushirika to say hello. I always enjoy the walk into Kibera, crossing the busy train line and then walking past the women sitting at their stands stringing beans and cooking chapattis. Despite not coming into Kibera every day, these women still remember me and their smiles are welcoming, which gives me the lift I need after a tough afternoon at the clinic. I greet my friends, these women of Kibera, and head on through to the big white gates of Ushirika. At the gate I am greeted excitedly by Anna and Ruth who are delighted to see me. We hug each other and I tell them about what I've been up to. I then head on through to the clinic which is fairly quiet this afternoon and I see Debra, David, Judson and David. I'm so happy to see my friends whom I no longer see every day since starting my work at AMKA. I tell them all about my work, the projects we are developing and the community home visits in the slums.

'You're very busy' Judson tells me, followed by 'When are coming back to work with us?' I feel happy and at ease to be back amongst these friends. It makes me realise just how many people I've bonded with since arriving, whether it be the smile I share with the women stringing the beans who only speak Swahili but whom I manage to communicate with nonetheless, my friends here at Ushirika, my new colleagues at AMKA, the women who sit on the rocks in Jamhuri, Stanley who sells me fruit from his little stand or the many locals I pass every day in my walks around the slums. I am blessed to be welcomed here in so many ways.

    I stay at Ushirika for a little while catching up on the news at the clinic. They're still in the development stages for their HIV clinic, which is no surprise, knowing how long some things can take in Kenya. But they're not concerned, there is no hurry, it will all happen in its own time, *African time*. *Hakuna Matata*. Then another familiar face comes out from the consulting room to see me, it's Amos! He's especially excited to see me, a big smile spreading over his face. I glance over at Daniel who knows about my stories with Amos and he flashes me an even bigger cheekier smile at my awkward meeting. I stay a little longer talking with everybody at the clinic before heading home to Alice's. I promise to return and see them all soon. As I walk back across the train line and into Jamhuri, I feel such a warm feeling about my visit to Ushirika where I first started my adventure in Kenya.

    Back at Alice's, Lucy has been busy preparing matoke and rice for our dinner which is shared amongst the six of us: Annie, Young-Shil, Christine, Alice, Lucy and me. Alice now sleeps on the couch, next to Lucy in the living room, having kindly given up her bed for Christine. As we share dinner, Lucy finally adjusts to being invited to eat in the same room as us and she's even developing some confidence in laughing at our jokes and Kenyan experiences. We share our work stories from the day. Christine talks about the clinic where she's working as well as a local orphanage where she's been helping out. Annie and I describe the Harvest women's group we visited and our home visits in the slums. Young-Shil works at Ushirika in the medical program and treated somebody with a machete wound to the head today. Not an evening goes by at Alice's without a new adventure or story from just another day's work volunteering in Kenya.

Chapter 28 – Challenges

Do what you can, with what you have, where you are
– Theodore Roosevelt

It's Friday, the weekly food-distribution day at the AMKA Dagoretti clinic. That means a busy and active morning handing out the bags of rice, beans and Ugali mix that Annie, Emilie and I have been busy sorting out during the week. I love Fridays at the clinic. When we arrive we're greeted by a few patients who have arrived early with their small food token cards in hand. We help Solphine and George bring out the wooden benches that are stored inside the room overnight, dragging them onto the gravel path under the clinic's verandah. When Oloo arrives we all stand together with the patients who are waiting, and open the morning clinic with a prayer. Solphine thanks the Lord for this day and for the strength and means to support the people in the community. 'Amen', we all say in unison.

I wander around to the food shed and start to organise the process for its distribution. Pen and paper in hand, we record the names of the patients who come to collect their food. It's always a positive feeling to work in the food shelter, handing out the rice, beans and flour and seeing how happy our patients are to walk away with something in hand. A guaranteed meal for their families. We carry on throughout the morning and I do my best to finish without too much flour all over me. I still haven't quite mastered how to do it like an African woman!

Once finished with the food distribution we lock up the shed and our next duty is to start preparing the chai for our lunch. Annie and I warm the milk with the tea powder in the big pots inside the small kitchen space. We pour the tea into the three thermos flasks and take them inside the clinic where Emilie and Solphine have prepared the table with the plastic plates and mugs, the loaf of bread and the tub of Blue Band margarine. Lunch is ready. As usual a prayer is said before sharing our meal together.

We talk about our plans for the weekend. Emilie, Annie and I are going on a weekend trip to Mount Kenya with some other volunteers. Solphine is travelling upcountry to visit her daughter who is in boarding school and whom she only sees every few months. Understandably, she's very excited to be reunited with her daughter even if it's for just the weekend. George will be studying all weekend for his diploma in advanced nursing practice. Oloo has his set routine of visiting friends and going to church on Sunday. After lunch, the men carry on with their work and Emilie, Solphine, Annie and I take care of the washing and drying up outside the clinic using the big plastic buckets and jerry cans of water. One bucket for washing, the next for rinsing, the third for drying. We've got the system down pat and work perfectly as a team.

Emilie, Annie and I decide to pay Natalya a visit after lunch. George calls Evelyn to see if she is available to come on the visit with us. Just as we finish washing the lunch plates, Evelyn walks into the clinic to join us. We head out towards the now very familiar Hotel 46, passing a young man riding an old bicycle with four large 20 litre jerry cans of water strategically hung onto the frame of his bike. A single one of these jerry cans, which is typically filled with water and carried by a woman on her head, weighs 20kg. Children are out playing in the black rubber tires again and small groups of women are standing around outside their homes and talking.

We open the door and walk in to see Natalya. The fleas are still about, and the stale air and smell are suffocating. It's almost unbearable. Evelyn greets Natalya in Swahili. She's still lying in the bed, her legs stretched out before her and she turns her head to see Evelyn. They speak for some time. Suddenly I feel like there are too many of us in her small room; Evelyn plus Annie, Emilie and I, all peering over this poor vulnerable girl. I decide to go and wait outside, leaving Annie and Emilie at Natalya's side.

They stay inside for some time. Emilie has carried the gloves and oil to give Natalya a massage if she's feeling like it. As I wait outside the timber sheets that form Hotel 46, I find myself still thinking about the women I met at Evelyn's house the day before. Their stories and words still resonate in my ears. I feel a strong desire to help these women. I keep thinking about how we can raise some funds to help give them the start they need for their business plans, in the same way that AMKA is supporting its patients' income-generating activities. I make a note to talk to Sister Veronica about the idea of establishing some sort of project to help these women.

A short while later Evelyn, Emilie and Annie step outside of Natalya's shack, squinting as they readjust to the bright daylight and relieved to breath in some cleaner air. They report that Natalya is keen for a massage, having helped her to stretch her legs and to even walk around the room, which they have encouraged her to continue doing every day. As we head back along the main road of Dagoretti towards the AMKA centre, Evelyn starts to share with Emilie, Annie and me some of the details Natalya has opened up to her about today. Evelyn has also learnt some information about Natalya from some of the other women living in the community. Sometimes a little gossip can be helpful!

Evelyn tells us that Natalya, who is just 20 years old, has a daughter and recently fell pregnant again. She, like many women in the slums, resorted to an abortion to terminate the pregnancy by seeing somebody who works locally and cheaply and conducted the abortion using unsterile and unorthodox equipment and methods. He's apparently a local medicine man. As Natalya did not have the money to consult a qualified doctor, who may not have agreed to terminate the pregnancy, she paid this man to do it. Now she is clearly suffering from a severe infection and possible internal damage. The reasons behind her pregnancy and social relations are unknown to us, but have clearly caused her severe depression together with the trauma of the abortion.

Natalya's decision to share this information with Evelyn is a big step in her recovery. Evelyn reassured her she does not need to be ashamed, and that nobody judges her and that she can trust us. She also informed her that George will come around later with some medications for her that will be important for her to take in her recovery. Natalya's younger brothers, who are dependent on her for money and food, are living with her in the shack. They also seem to be neglected and malnourished. Natalya's parents live outside of Nairobi with her young daughter.

To hear a story like this is distressing, even to Evelyn who knows that situations like this are not unheard of in these slums. We return to AMKA feeling better about the progress we've made, but equally saddened about Natalya's circumstances which are complex and not easily resolved. And that is one of the biggest challenges we face as volunteers in a country like Kenya. We sometimes arrive with the attitude of having the power to solve every probleso. Natalya's case is one of many that show how money cannot solve her problems, nor can food, nor can medications alone. The problems go much deeper, touching on social, psychological and physical issues that are all woven into her cultural and social environment.

Even now I'm convinced she should see a doctor, but George and Evelyn say that it is just not possible to take every single patient like this into Nairobi Hospital. With some medications to counteract her infection, relieve the pain, and some food and water to have over the weekend she will be all right until we visit her again on Monday.

At the end of the day I take the bus into Nairobi city with Emilie to visit our coordinator, Irene, at the volunteer office. On the bus I prepare myself for the hustle and dodginess of *Nairobberie* city. It is a contrast to the poverty-stricken slums which despite being poor, unsanitary and riddled with disease and malnutrition, feel so much more secure to me than the mix of people and activity in the city. The slums have become my working environment, my base, and this is where most of my friends, colleagues and patients live; the people I trust and care for.

We jump off the moving bus on the busy Kenyatta Avenue and walk towards the office. Having emailed Irene about our project at AMKA to kick start patients' income-generating activities, she has agreed to use some of the funds to buy the materials we have requested, namely exercise books and pens which we will rule up and give to the patients we'll be following. Irene, as always, greets us with a beaming smile and laughs as we describe our journey on the bus into the city and how it's always a relief to step off the streets and into the office! We sit down for awhile and talk about the work we've been doing, enthusiastically describing all the current projects and the patients we're trying to help. We take the money for our materials and arrange to return soon to catch up again. Once successfully boarded on a City Hopper bus headed back towards Jamhuri, I can relax again, knowing our mission in and out of the city has been accomplished.

I walk home through the markets at Adams shopping centre, and spot Stanley standing on his own at his small fruit stand near Alice's. As he spots me, he smiles excitedly, which I hope is as much about seeing me as it is about the prospect of getting some business. I tell him I haven't seen him for some time, worried he'd moved his stand from Jamhuri elsewhere, and he tells me he's been unwell but has now recovered. I'm glad he's back. Stanley asks me what I've been up to during the day and I explain about our clinic in Dagoretti, visiting some patients' homes in the slums and then our trip into the city centre. He tells me I've done a lot for one day and instructs me to go home and rest. I agree and buy a few bananas and a mango to share at Alice's. I say *kwaheri* to my young friend Stanley and head home.

Chapter 29 – Karibu Kenya

There are many paths to the top of the mountain, but the view is always the same – Chinese Proverb

The next morning Annie and I head off early on the City Hopper bus from Kibera into Nairobi city ready for our weekend trip to Mount Kenya. We meet Emilie and several other volunteers in the city and from here we all board a matatu that is headed for the rural town of Nanyuki, at the base of Mount Kenya. The ride is typically bumpy and at times hairy on these roads and we're all pleased when we arrive at our first stop - the crossing of the equator. We jump off to have a photo taken with the sign where we are also predictably hassled by a number of men trying to sell us certificates stating we've officially visited the equator. Another man is conducting an experiment to show that there is a change in the direction that water moves on either side of the equator; anti-clockwise on the southern side of the equator; clockwise on the northern side and directly down directly over the equator. We're left feeling no further convinced about the phenomenon than before. After reboarding the matatu we head towards Nanyuki, our destination for the evening.

Nanyuki is a bustling rural town at the foot of Mount Kenya. Because of passing tourists like ourselves, the town has many curio shops selling the usual souvenirs accompanied by friendly salesmen. I walk through the town with Annie where we are persistently followed by locals trying to sell us jewellery, clothing and small snacks. A young lady approaches me and tries to hand me her baby. I'm shocked to have had this experience for a second time. One particular souvenir shop that attracts my attention has a big sign out the front with its name: 'Hassle-free Curio Shop'. Contrary to its name, the owner calls out to us as we walk past inviting us in to see what he has inside. 'Good price, negotiable, no hassling,' he reassures us. 'No hassle, free to look,' he continues on as Annie and I laugh together.

We spend some more time walking about the town. Hearing a lot of voices and seeing people crowded around the corner, we approach to see what is going on. We find a man standing on a wooden block preaching loudly in Swahili. His technique is loud and aggressive. He has attracted quite a crowd, the people following each of his statements with a supportive cheer, their hands held proudly in the air. The majority of Kenyans are Christian with about 45% of Kenyans being Christian-Protestant and another 33% Roman Catholic. Smaller percentages support Islam and indigenous tribal religions. For the dominant Christian population their faith is extremely important to them. I find it encouraging seeing these people holding on strongly to their beliefs in situations where they have little else from which to take strength.

We spend the night in Nanyuki at our hotel, Simba lodge. I eat at the hotel's small restaurant for dinner with the other volunteers. Afterwards we sit outside together sharing stories from our volunteer experiences and making plans to climb a part of Mount Kenya the next day. We are a mix of old and new volunteers, some still adjusting to the life and routine here in Kenya, others well adapted and settled in their programs.

I share a room with Emilie at the hotel for the night. On entering the room we discover a toilet and shower in one contraption - a new concept to the both of us. Under the beds we find complimentary pairs of flip flops. Used, of course. And odd sizes. Since Emilie's arrival in Kenya we have shared a joke about experiences like these that are new and unlike anything we've encountered before. Emilie calls these moments 'Karibu Kenya', the Swahili for *Welcome to Kenya*. We laugh about our hotel room. It's a Karibu Kenya moment.

The next morning we get up early to watch the sunrise over Mount Kenya, which is spectacular. Mount Kenya is the highest mountain in Kenya and the second highest peak in Africa after Tanzania's Mount Kilimanjaro. The country was named after this mountain when it became the Republic of Kenya in 1964. At sunrise, the mountain appears as a blue shadow, which shines like a silhouette against the pink swirls of the morning sunlight. We have an early breakfast at the hotel before setting off in our group to start our trek up Mount Kenya.

Arriving at Mount Kenya National Park there are open green fields which lead into an area of denser vegetation and forest reserve at the base of the mountain. It is very green and the soil is very fertile making it a great area for agriculture. The bus drops us off at the main gates where we prepare for our walk. But the start of our journey is not without another Karibu Kenya moment. Emilie goes to use one of the toilet cubicles and finds herself locked inside and unable to reopen the door. We ask one of the men who works at the park entrance to help. He arrives and has a look at the door then walks off again to get something. When he returns, he has a giant machete in hand! If only Emilie could see the situation from our side of the cubicle, she would be laughing right now at the sight of this man using the multi-purpose Kenyan machete to open the toilet door. It takes some time but eventually he succeeds, and Emilie is liberated from the confined pit toilet. 'Now that was a Karibu Kenya moment,' she says.

The incline up Mount Kenya starts off fairly gradually as we appreciate the foliage and trees around us. The vegetation is diverse and thick. Along the dusty path Emilie points out some large animal tracks. We're not able to work out what animal made the tracks and are worried about what we might come across on this hike. They are huge - could they be an elephant's? Are there elephants in these parts of Kenya? We carry on, enjoying the clean fresh air up here in the mountains. Suddenly we hear some loud rustling in the bushes and we all scamper for safety, which there is none of at this point in the park. It is probably a wild boar we're told by our guide Wilson, and so we carry on.

Emilie and I talk about our plans for the future. She tells me it is her dream to become a doctor one day and to come back and work in Africa. She wants to apply for pre-medical school next year and her experiences so far have confirmed her plans to follow this path. After about an hour and a half of walking we decide to head back down again with all the other volunteers knowing our bus will be leaving later today. To get to the top of Mount Kenya is a minimum four day trek and well worth it according to other volunteers who've accomplished the feat. The descent is long and tiring and we eventually reach our bus at the bottom, relieved and satisfied with our efforts.

Our group stops for lunch at a small restaurant in a nearby town which is en route to Nairobi. We all choose something from the typically Kenyan menu. As the wait for our meal stretches out to over an hour and a half it becomes obvious that the staff must have gone out to buy the chickens that they will then kill for our meal, along with buying all the vegetables required. Through the kitchen I can see one of the cooks walk through with a feathered chicken tucked under his arm. Talk about made to order!

Eventually our meals are brought out and they are very tasty. I ordered the *mukimo* which is a Kenyan specialty of mashed potato with spinach, corn and beans. Green in colour, soft and mashed in consistency, its appearance is quite intriguing. It is good and much appreciated after our long walk up the mountain this morning.

Following lunch we board the matatu to head back into Nairobi. The ride back is bumpy and noisy. We pass some interesting rural towns. Through the scratchy windows of the matatu I see some large outdoor markets where dozens of locals have gathered around the many small market stands selling foods, clothes, jewellery, buckets and shoes. The colours are bright and vibrant and many of the women working at the stands are sitting on the dirt ground under colourful umbrellas, blocking out the warm sun. It looks like most of the town's residents have come together in the central market place which is the hub of the community.

Finally we arrive back in Nairobi where Emilie, Annie and I farewell the other volunteers we've spent the weekend with, and we find a City Hopper bus to take us back into Kibera. It's peak hour for the locals heading out of the city, so it's a fight with the locals to jump on one of the buses. Like real Kenyans we follow the bus as it pulls into the stop and are forced to grab hold of the silver bar and pull ourselves up onto the moving bus, pushing our way through the crowd. Once on I check over my shoulder to see if the others have managed to make their way on too. They have. Meanwhile the bus is already on its way down the road.

We finally make it back to Kibera from where it's just a short walk over the railway line to Alice's apartment. We arrive, exhausted, but having had a nice weekend outside of the city. Already I find myself thinking about going back to work tomorrow and what will await us there. The work at the clinic is what I've come here for, and as much as I enjoy travelling on the weekends, the clinic is where my heart is.

Chapter 30 – Mandazi Day

Out of difficulties grow miracles – Jean de la Bruyere

Every day on our walk from Jamhuri into Dagoretti Corner, Emilie and I pass the small road-side shops made from scraps of wood and timber selling everything ranging from clothes and food to second hand mobile phones and hair pieces. Amongst these stands are the *mandazi* stalls. These are the sweet, deep fried triangular pastries that are handmade then cooked in big pots of oil and lined up one by one for sale. They cost 10ksh each. Every morning on our walk into Dagoretti, the smell of the mandazis is sweet and appealing and it's so tempting to stop and buy some to take with us. Emilie and I have decided today is Mandazi day. On our walk into the clinic we stop at one of the stands and buy 20 mandazis, enough for all the staff at AMKA, which we will share for lunch with Emilie's bottle of maple syrup from Canada. Once at the clinic we put them safely into the cupboard with the bread and butter until lunch time arrives.

The morning clinic is busy and many of the regular community health workers have come to help and report back to the clinic. Margaret is there with Immaculate and they are laughing and dancing about as usual. The atmosphere is positive and refreshing. I have the feeling it is going to be a good day.

Emilie, Annie and I decide to head off to visit Natalya, having not seen her since Friday. We head out of the clinic and back down the usual path towards her Hotel 46 shack. But before we arrive, heading up the road towards us, just 50 metres from Natalya's house, I see the most remarkable sight up ahead. Walking together on the street are Evelyn, Joanne and Natalya. All wearing big smiles at the sight of our delight. I cannot believe my eyes. Having been prepared for the worst inside Natalya's shack, here she is walking proudly yet still fragilely on her own two feet. And above all she is smiling! She is a different person from the frail, withdrawn and despondent girl we visited just days earlier. Emilie and I have tears in our eyes as we take in this very special moment together. It's a huge turnaround and we all couldn't be happier. I hug Natalya warmly as we greet each other in the middle of the road, oblivious to the activity around us with cars and goats moving about. I tell Natalya how delighted I am to see her outside, walking and smiling. I hold her hand as we continue slowly walking towards the clinic, savouring every minute of this elating story.

Back at the clinic we are greeted by a large gathering of women, patients and community health workers, who have come to visit AMKA today. Natalya sits outside on the benches that have been put outside under the sun with Joanne and two other patients, and the women talk amongst themselves about Kenya, the weather and their community. There is laughter and support without broaching the topic of health. It is the perfect reception for Natalya, to feel needed and engaged in a community of such kind-spirited women. Looking at these women sitting next to each other on the wooden benches outside the clinic is an empowering image, knowing that each and every one of them have stories of hardship and joy to share. But today it's all about being positive and having hope.

Margaret continues to play the clown with her jokes and movements, keeping us entertained as she wiggles her big bottom around from side to side. George and Solphine join us outside to see what all the excitement is about. Oloo walks over and stands next to Emilie and me, telling us it is like we have put the life back into Natalya. I still can't believe it. I don't want to take my eyes off her, dressed in her skirt and t-shirt and an old pair of blue thongs. Her hair is untidy and dirty. But inside she is alive again, and that is already huge progress.

Natalya spends an hour or so at the clinic and George gives her some more medications to take home. Today, it is important for her to be among friends, and to put aside the troubles from her recent past. The patients all head home as it approaches midday. It seems even more fitting that today is the day we've organised a small party with our team to share our mandazis. After the events of the morning it feels fitting that we have something to celebrate. It's been a great morning. The chai is prepared and the table is set. George, Oloo, Solphine, Margaret, Immaculate, Joanne and Evelyn are excited about eating the mandazis we've bought. It is such a treat to have something other than our usual bread and butter. Evelyn says grace for us all, thanking the Lord for a miraculous morning at the clinic and this opportunity to share a special meal amongst friends. We serve the chai and Emilie passes around the bottle of maple syrup, another first for our Kenyan colleagues, to eat with the mandazis. It all goes down very well with the team!

After we've enjoyed our small celebratory lunch marking the inaugural Mandazi Day, we tidy up the kitchen and Joanne tells us about a new patient, Stella, whom she has been to see in the slums of Ngando. I organise to go and visit this lady with Annie and Joanne. I realise that our work here is never done. As one patient is helped there are still many others who are unwell. The cycle is ongoing. We've enjoyed our morning which has been enlightening and rewarding. In struggling times it is important to enjoy the highs when they come before the next low arrives.

Joanne leads the long walk out of Dagoretti and into Ngando, the bordering slum. On the way she describes Stella's situation to us. Stella is 30 years old, HIV positive and now battling the onset of AIDS. She's in a very poor state, refusing to eat, drink, or go into hospital which is what she needs. She's refusing to live. When we arrive Joanne leads the way up and behind an old wooden shack to where Stella's place is located. As she opens the door I feel like I inhale a mouthful of the tiny black fleas that are floating around this closed confined space. Stella's body is so emaciated and skeletal that I hardly see her lying under the covers on the old mattress. This picture before me is disturbing and saddening. We walk in sensitively, aware that Stella is very vulnerable and not in a state to want visitors.

Joanne has already visited Stella and so introduces Annie and me today. Stella doesn't move as Joanne sits on the small stool next to the bed. I listen to Joanne as she talks sternly in Swahili, explaining to Stella the importance of eating and drinking, and giving her reasons to fight for her life. Stella has two small children who are not living with her. Joanne has known Stella for a few years, from the time she was well and taking her ARVs, working and living positively. I can only imagine what a turn around this must be for her to see now. Somebody who is younger than her and HIV positive too.

Stella has given up. She is dying and stubbornly refuses any help. I look around the lifeless room and at Stella's body on the mattress. She can't weigh any more than 30kg. I look over at Annie's face and can see her desperation and frustration, wanting Stella to accept our help and knowing she can still live healthily in her life. Joanne eventually sits up and says it is time for us to go. We will come back again tomorrow.

We head to the clinic to report back to George on Stella's state. What a day it has been! The highs of Natalya and her miraculous turnaround and the lows of Stella facing the end of her life. The emotions I'm experiencing are challenging and unlike any I've had to deal with before. The challenge is to know how to process these emotions and how to deal with these situations we encounter in our everyday work here.

I walk back home from the clinic on my own this afternoon, feeling like I need time to myself. Annie is also feeling the same strains and takes time for herself too. Does the work we do make any difference when just around the corner there is another tragedy? Today I'm faced with the enormity of the poverty and the problems it creates here in the slums. How can one or even one hundred people make everything better? Is that our goal, to make everything better, as international volunteers? The people at AMKA: George, Solphine, Oloo and Sister Veronica don't strive for perfection as we do, they don't strive to solve every problem. It's *lesson number 10* in my growing list of lessons here in Kenya: *To deal with each situation as it arises* and not to look too far into the future. It's the here and now. It's about managing and about surviving from one day to the next. We can't achieve the unachievable and we can only do as much as our hands will allow.

On my way back to Alice's I stop by to see Stanley, knowing he will help to pick up my mood with our regular chat about our day. There he stands, a big smile on his face, holding out a pineapple for me to see. I smile, grateful to have this friend in our neighbourhood.

'I have a fresh pineapple for you today,' he beams. It's just what I feel like. Stanley also says he has something else for me. Out of his pocket he pulls out a small book called 'Christ's Journey'. We've often talked about faith and religion and he says I should read his small book. I smile again, touched that he's offered me one of the few objects he probably owns and something that is so precious and important to him. This act of kindness couldn't have come at a better time as I search for the answers to deal with so many of my questions.

Chapter 31 – Show bags and seminars

Always walk through life as if you have something new to learn and you will – Vernon Howard

Sister Veronica and AMKA clinic have been organising a seminar for our patients to attend on HIV and many of the issues associated with the illness. Today is the day of the seminar. Annie and I leave Alice's house early as we have been given a meeting time of 7am at one of the local bus stops in Dagoretti. Unfortunately Emilie has become unwell with what she thinks may be malaria, so she'll be staying at home and resting.

Annie and I walk to the designated meeting spot in Dagoretti. As we head down the main street, we pass many young children dressed up in their school uniforms, white socks, black shoes and backpacks, heading off early to school. We can't help but think it is so early for these young girls and boys to be walking on their own to school at 6:30 in the morning. It is such a long day for them before returning about the same hour in the evening. For many parents their children are sent to school early where they eat breakfast before starting, which in many cases is more than they would get at home.

Annie and I spot a group of our patients and community health workers waiting anxiously on the corner in Dagoretti. There is Joanne, Grace, Darlene, Mary, Margaret and James. They are all dressed up and so excited about this big day. It's an outing for them and everything has been put together for them by the clinic. Sister Veronica tries to organise regular seminars as a part of patient and staff education on different topics concerning HIV and AIDS. The aim of these seminars is to bring everybody together to listen and to learn. Our patients have been talking about the seminar for weeks now.

We all stand by the roadside waiting patiently for our bus and driver to turn up. Solphine arrives and joins us, as do several other patients. There are a few men who have come to join in, and some women have brought along their children for the outing. It is not every day they get to take the bus out of the city. As I wait with Joanne, she informs me that Stella was taken back into hospital yesterday due to her worsening condition. Hopefully there she will regain the strength to fight her illness. It is yet another reason to be a part of this seminar today to empower and educate people in the community about HIV and to reduce the number of cases like Stella's. Finally the bus arrives to pick us up one hour later, just as we're starting to worry about missing the beginning of the seminar. *Hakuna matata*. We all board the bus excitedly.

The venue for the seminar is a Catholic Youth Centre. A large outdoor tent has been set up next to the centre with chairs and tables for everybody as they arrive. The seminar is opened by the centre's director with some prayer and music. We're all invited to stand and sing the gospel songs together. I look around the room at the fifty odd people, mostly women but also some men, who are smiling and raising their hands with joy to the music. There is a feeling of union today in this space.

One by one we're all invited to introduce ourselves in front of the group. Some people choose to reveal more about their lives and their battle with HIV than others. One lady shares her struggle with her family to be accepted despite her illness, another admits having been in denial for months until just recently accepting her status and starting on ARVs. Everyone applauds her encouragingly. It's now my turn to introduce myself. I stand up and put together my principal Swahili phrases: '*Jina langu ni Belinda* (my name is Belinda), *Natoka Australia* (I come from Australia), *Ninakaa Jamhuri* (I am living in Jamhuri), *Asanti sana* (thank you very much)'. I'm welcomed by everybody before sitting down. Annie and Solphine take their turn to introduce themselves too.

During the morning session a speaker talks about the HIV virus and presents the myths and facts to the seminar group. Many of our patients are often well informed about their illness; it is more often their family members and other people in the community who are not. We are then divided into smaller focus groups and given a pen and a large sheet of paper and a topic to discuss together. I find myself in a group of seven and don't know any of the other people in my group. The topic we've been assigned is to look at the social consequences of being HIV positive and how these affect us. The women in my group start to interact and share their ideas, writing them down one by one on the large sheet of butcher's paper.

The list starts with words such as *discrimination, stigma, isolation* and *outcast*. These are many of the typical reactions that these women encounter in their community. To my amazement these words are just scratching the surface of a much more complex and sensitive issue. The words keep coming and as our list goes on I see that the members of my group are opening up more and more about the reality of their situations. *Loss of jobs, loss of house, husband runs away, children taken away*...right up until the final words that are written across in black capital letters: *threats of killing*. The young woman said it honestly and openly adding her personal experience of being told by her grandmother that she did not deserve to live with this illness. It is one thing to have read the many guide books on HIV and the types of challenges that patients are faced with in third world countries. However, being a part of a seminar is showing me that these problems go far deeper than I ever knew or could have been prepared for. Victims fearing for their lives, not from the virus, but because of social reactions towards HIV and AIDS.

Following the exercise, each focus group stands up and presents their topic in front of the big group. All of the topics have been chosen to promote a discussion and to make people feel comfortable about sharing their experiences and to show them they are not alone. The atmosphere is open, non-judgmental and supportive. There is even laughter in the tent at times, when the women talk about their husbands that walk out and leave them, as another yells out spontaneously 'Let him go, we don't need them!'

We all take a break for lunch and are served some ugali, chicken, greens and bananas. It is a good nourishing meal for everybody. We sit around the long tables that are inside the youth centre, near the kitchen where the food has been prepared, talking openly with each other and enjoying the meal. I continue to meet many inspiring new people; everyone is so friendly and welcoming.

The afternoon session opens again with some more prayer and singing. We then listen to some presentations about good nutrition when living with HIV which is followed by dealing with the stages of grief. A nutritionist has been invited who draws some diagrams on the board of the food groups these patients should be concentrating on to remain healthy, especially while taking their ARVs. The stages of grief are also very important and interesting. Some of the patients share their experiences of denial, anger, bargaining, loneliness, depression and their final acceptance of their illness. I think of many of the patients I have met in my work at the clinic, those who have bargained with their religion to be cured, and others who choose to accept and fight the illness.

The afternoon passes by very quickly. We finish the seminar with more songs and this time everybody gets up and dances too. The participants in the seminar have been enlightened and inspired by the day's events. They know they are not alone in this fight, and what's more they have a voice to try and make changes for the future. The day is topped off when everybody is told they will go home with a bag of food: rice, beans and ugali mix. They are delighted and turn around and hug each other saying thank you with such sincerity and excitement. It is the equivalent of a party bag filled with lollies and chocolates or the complimentary pens and notepads given out at work conferences back home. Today, each person who has attended is handed a reused plastic shopping bag containing enough food to make a proper meal for their families at home which may even last a few nights. It is the perfect end to an inspiring day.

Chapter 32 – A special gift
Poverty often brings out the true generosity in others – Nelson Mandela

Today is Thursday, our clinic day in Gatina. Annie and I leave Alice's place and head towards the meeting spot with Emilie. It is her first day back at the clinic after having taken some time off to recover from the malaria she contracted. She's lost a few kilos and is still taking her medications but is feeling a lot better and has her bright smile and bubbly personality back. I tell her all about the successful HIV seminar.

We take the matatu into Gatina clinic where we meet Solphine, George, Oloo and Nancy. Our first visit for the day is to go and see Helen and Kevin. Their place feels like our second home now we've become so accustomed to walking around there, and greeting all the small children that are always playing outside and helping Helen. Emilie and I go inside where we find Helen sitting upright in her bed looking happy and relaxed. Her condition has continued to improve since we started visiting and encouraging her to move and to walk around. With our assistance Helen can now walk, and we support her under each shoulder to walk outside and sit in the fresh air. We spend some time talking with Helen who is always interested to know about our lives back home as well as what we've been doing and discovering in Kenya. She has heard from Kevin that Emilie has been unwell and enquires about her health like a concerned mother.

As we talk with Helen I watch Kevin outside playing with the young children. He takes care of them as if they are his own, showing paternal skills that are uncommon in such a young man. One of the young girls is called Brenda, she has long braids and a podgy stomach that sticks out of her pretty dress. Kevin helps to comb her hair back, which has become tangled while playing with the other children, and invites her inside where he gives her some of his bread to eat.

Today Emilie has some important news for Kevin. She has decided that she would like to sponsor his education, to enable him to return to school and graduate with a qualification. Emilie shares her personal story with Kevin and Helen of her own mother's death when she was young, due to cancer, and how she is reminded of what it is like to grow up with one parent. She sees Kevin as a brother and is inspired to help him in whatever small way she can. Kevin and Helen are overwhelmed and extremely grateful. Helen takes Emilie's hand in her own, saying we are like daughters to her. For Emilie and me it is a pleasure to meet and visit such kind and caring people, and sponsoring Kevin's studies feels like the least we can offer him.

As we finish the stretching and massage and head back towards the clinic from Helen's place, Kevin comes running after us, telling us he has something he wants to give us. He holds out his hands and gives both Emilie and me a small plastic bag each containing a silver necklace. We pull out the chains which both have a single charm hanging from them. They are a gift from Kevin. I can't help but think how this young man has probably just spent his week's food allowance on these extremely precious gifts for us.

'Nelly!' I exclaim, my customary nickname for Kevin. 'What's this?'

Kevin tells us it's to say thank you for all the kindness we've shown him and his mother, in helping her to get better. I am so overwhelmed by how generous people can be when they really have nothing to give. My eyes are welling with tears as I give Kevin, my African brother, a big hug of gratitude. Emilie is already crying, knowing she is leaving Kenya soon and will dearly miss the special bond we have formed with this family. We head back to the Gatina clinic together proudly wearing our new necklaces. I haven't worn any jewellery since arriving in Africa and this feels more precious than anything I've been given before.

Kibera slum, Nairobi

The daily crossing of the railway line from Jamhuri into Kibera

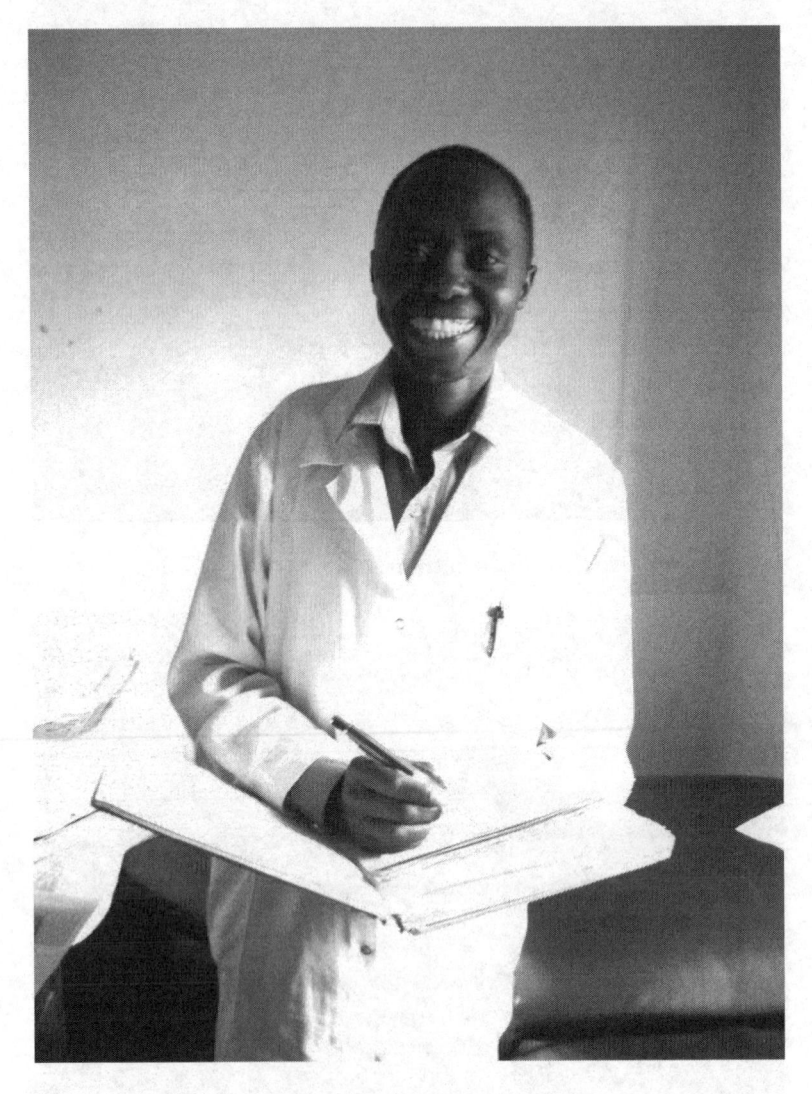

Nutritionist Daniel at Ushirika Medical Clinic, Kibera

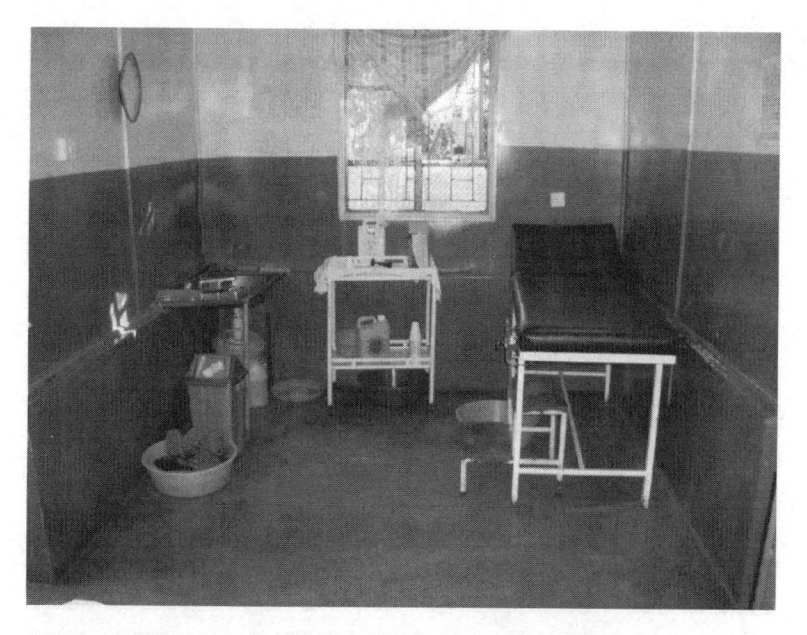

Delivery room at Ushirika Medical Clinic, Kibera

Rose sitting in the kitchen at Ushirika Medical Clinic, Kibera

Peter and his mother outside her home in Kamungi

AMKA team: Sister Veronica, Belinda, Solphine, Oloo and George

The women of Jamhuri sitting on the corner

Home visits: Solphine helping a volunteer cross a bridge over a stream of open sewage in Gatina

Thursday lunches at Moses' Fair Deal Cafe in Gatina

Belinda with Helen and Kevin outside their home in Gatina

'Mandazi Day', sitting outside AMKA clinic

Chapter 33 – Carnivore

Annie, Emile and I have organised to take the afternoon off work at the clinic today. George can see that we're looking quite tired and worn out, having had a couple of busy weeks full of home visits, project planning and travelling. We're going to make the most of a quiet period. Emilie heads home to rest, while Annie and I go shopping for a kanga to wear to our volunteer dinner later tonight at Nairobi's famous Carnivore restaurant.

I'm keen to buy a brightly coloured kanga in Gatina. Every day on our walks through the slums my eyes are drawn to the small stands selling dozens of different patterns and designs. If it's not the stands, it's the women walking along the streets dressed colourfully in their beautiful kangas who catch my eye. I love this image of the African woman and tonight I will be making my own debut. I've decided to hang up the jeans and the boots for the night and go African style. Annie helps me look through the display of kangas until I find one that I like. It's orange, yellow, red, black and white which to me represents the colours of Africa with some Swahili words written around the border. I hand over my money to the lady who seems delighted to sell me one of her kangas and as we leave she reminds me to bring all my friends to her stall.

Back at Alice's, I call on Lucy to help me get ready and to properly tie the kanga around my waist. I show her the one I've chosen before putting it on which she admires immensely. She giggles as she wraps the kanga around my waist telling me it doesn't usually go this many times around an African woman's waist, but says it is okay. I feel slightly uneasy about it falling down, knowing it's just been tied on the side, but Lucy reassures me it will be fine. When Alice gets home from work she finds Annie, Christine, Young-Shil, our new volunteer Katie who's just arrived from Canada and me all sitting down in the living room ready to head out. Katie is a psychology student who will be volunteering at an orphanage in Kibera. I've immediately warmed to her openness and sarcastic sense of humour which always makes me laugh.

Tonight Alice is coming with us to the restaurant and she has invited Lucy to come along too, which of course we're delighted about. We all love Lucy, her fun personality that has started to shine through, and we especially like her cooking. Lucy has put her best outfit on for the evening. I ask her where she got it from and she says it's her suit she wears to church on Sundays. She looks beautiful and slightly intimidated to be going out with all of us. Alice, too, puts on some makeup, a lovely necklace and her high heels. It's like a group of girlfriends ready for a night out in Nairobi!

Our vehicle comes to pick us up and we arrive shortly after at the stylish restaurant Carnivore which is popular with tourists. From the outside it is already a lot classier than anywhere I've been in a long time, definitely different from what has become my regular eatery with Moses in the Gatina slums. Carnivore is built for the tourist market and on entering the restaurant I see more foreigners than I have seen in a long time. We have reserved a big table for all the volunteers and we take our seats. The waiters, dressed smartly in small safari hats and vests, bring us some drinks. Alice takes a beer, as Annie, Young-Shil and I tease her and warn her not to have too many. The dinner consists of a constant serve of meats that the waiters bring out: beef, chicken wings, lamb, crocodile, ostrich and camel. It is protein over-load for all of us who have adapted to a diet without meat since arriving in Nairobi.

I'm sitting next to Lucy and am aware of how awkward this situation is for her - the upper-class restaurant, the service and the food. She has never been to a restaurant like this nor been waited upon in this manner. She hesitates when the waiter asks what drink she would like and she watches my technique for laying my serviette on my lap and using the knife and fork. The environment is unreal compared to our daily lives in Nairobi, and I am unsure how to take it all in, given how I've adapted to living here. We've suddenly stepped back into a lifestyle that was the norm for us volunteers up until arriving here, or has never been within reach in the case of Lucy, and now it feels out of place. Even the prices, although affordable for us, are ten times the price of a bowl of rice and beans in Jamhuri. I watch Lucy look around at the people at other tables, indulging in their food and wine and listening to the live music. I feel like I am seeing the situation through her eyes. Again there's the guilt of having a luxurious meal that for most people in this city is completely out of reach.

Overall our evening is thoroughly enjoyable. It's nice to go out as a family and to see Alice and Lucy enjoying themselves. There are many laughs among the volunteers and stories shared around the table. There is a competition among the boys about who can eat the most meat and win the flag on the plate marking the 'champion' of Carnivore. It's another contradiction between western culture and the average Kenyan household in this ongoing lesson in the big social divide.

Chapter 34 – Support group

Coming together is a beginning. Keeping together is progress. Working together is success – Henry Ford

It's another Friday morning at AMKA clinic and we all help out with the regular food distribution in the morning. Emilie, Annie and I are used to the routine now so we take complete responsibility for coordinating the program. I go and visit Evelyn's house with Emilie once we've finished, and then we go around to see Natalya who is continually improving. She is walking around outside her shack when we arrive, smiling, full of confidence and talkative. Just being in Natalya's presence these days is such an uplifting experience, given how far she has come. We walk down the main street together, hand in hand. We stop halfway down the street to greet some familiar patients, and Natalya rests her head on my shoulder, as a sister does to her sibling. I feel extremely close to her, a special bond has formed after all we've been through together. There is a trust and compassion between us. Natalya tells me she has something to show me. Out of her pocket she pulls out a $1 Australian coin, which she says her father has given to her. I'm so surprised and proud of the connection she feels with my country. I make a proposition to her. Seeing as the current exchange for $1 is 50ksh, I offer to trade her Kenyan shillings for the coin. I feel like it is a good deal, a way of giving her a few shillings but in exchange for something. She's delighted and we make the deal.

Emilie and I return to the clinic in time for lunch together with the team. In the afternoon we help Solphine prepare for her fortnightly support group counselling session. In these sessions patients come and have the opportunity to talk about whatever problems they are going through in their lives, whether it is related to their HIV status or not. Solphine, as the clinic's counsellor, can offer support and guidance for these patients. Most of their support comes from each other. Emilie and I help set up the two long wooden benches outside the clinic which is where the session will take place. On schedule, some patients start to arrive and take a seat outside, talking amongst themselves. Along with the the fifteen or so patients, Joanne and Evelyn have also come to participate today. Their experiences and attitudes will be fundamental to other less confident patients in the community. Solphine opens the session with a group prayer and then starts the discussion by asking how everyone's week has been. I listen in as one by one they share their challenges and worries.

Some patients explain their financial difficulties and describe situations where they are unable to pay their rent and subsequently forced from their homes. Another patient talks of the stigma and isolation that she still encounters in her community for being HIV positive. Her local shop no longer welcomes her to buy her fruits there so she has to go elsewhere. She is offered support from other patients who have been through the same experiences, giving her advice and offering sympathy. Other patients discuss the problems that exist within certain communities concerning HIV positive people; the negative attitudes, the stigma and discrimination, and the groups that falsely claim to be able to cure AIDS through religious or money-making schemes. The group counselling session is exactly what these patients need; somebody to talk to and somebody in the same situation as themselves. They have the opportunity to share their concerns, to be encouraged to continue on and reassured that things will get better.

Amongst the serious stories and concerns, there is also laughter and more positive news in the support group session. One man Rob has finally found himself a job, and other patients report on their children's good results in school. We close the session by sharing some afternoon tea together - a thermos of chai and a plastic bucket filled with slices of bread is passed around the group. We drink our tea and eat our bread together, feeling united and supportive of one another which is as much as one has to offer here. Sometimes that is the most effective form of help.

Chapter 35 – Family

Treat your family like friends and your friends like family
– Proverb

This weekend I've decided to stay home, to catch up on some of my jobs and to just relax. It's been a busy time at the clinic recently. I have a nice breakfast with Alice in the morning of chai, fruit and pancakes which Lucy has kindly prepared for us. I always feel that we're so well looked after at home. Alice and I enjoy these moments of having breakfast together in the mornings. I then get to the dreaded task of doing my hand washing which takes me most of the morning to get through, given how dirty our clothes get walking out in the dusty slums all day long, and the tedious process of scrubbing them all clean.

I've organised to meet George for lunch at The Junction. I wander down and we find a nice table outside on the terrace to eat together. This environment is such a contrast to where we work every day. It is nice to share lunch together and to have the time to talk, away from our work. I'm glad he has decided to come, as George has been so busy with his work and studies that he never takes time out and I've seen him getting more and more run-down by his responsibilities at the clinic. We talk about our plans, our lives, and our families and of course we can't help but talk about work. Sadly, George informs me that Stella passed away in hospital last night. Despite all the help that was given, she just couldn't fight her battle any longer. It's news like this that unfortunately dominates our work here.

We finish our lunch and head our separate ways. I walk down Ngong road towards the Adams clothes markets. I'm in need of some more clothes and decide to sift through the many stands of second-hand clothes to find myself a bargain. I find a second-hand blouse with a flower print and some jeans. I'm excited to have a bit more selection to my wardrobe and all for the price of 30ksh!

Later, I help Lucy prepare dinner in the kitchen. She's finally come around to the idea of letting me help her in her job and what's more, tonight she's making chapatti. My favourite! I'm excited to help roll out the chapattis ready to be cooked on the hot plate. It's Young-Shil's last night with us before she heads back to

Chicago. It's always sad to see volunteers go home as we form such a tight friendship together. We're family here.

We share another entertaining moment when Alice decides to pick something up from the shops and realises we've been somehow locked inside her apartment. After laughing at the situation, Alice tells me I should call Leon to come out and unlock our door, knowing I've met our neighbour on several occasions. With Alice and Lucy laughing, I reluctantly pick up my phone to call Leon and explain the situation. A few minutes later he's out the front of our apartment and is met by a row of smiling faces up against our front window waiting to be released. Leon kindly sets us free and Alice invites him in to meet everybody.

We eat our wonderful dinner while watching what has become a popular weekend ritual, a Venezuelan TV soap opera called *Secreto de amor*. With its scandalous storylines and poorly dubbed English, *Secret de amor* is Alice's favourite show. Now I'm becoming just as addicted. Tonight Maria Clara has arrived in the hotel room of her boyfriend Carlos, only to find his new fiancée Barbara with him. Alice and I giggle throughout the show at the poor acting, the long dramatic pauses and the strange English translations. After dinner and another entertaining episode of *Secreto de amor*, the taxi arrives to take Young-Shil to the airport. We all say a big goodbye, sad to see one of our family members leave. I'm pleased to know that it's not me yet, knowing how settled I feel here and how much more I have to do before it's my turn to say goodbye. Alice and I wish each other a good night and sweet dreams, *lala salama*, before going to bed.

Chapter 36 – Goodbye Emilie

Don't cry because it's over. Smile because it happened – Dr. Seuss

It feels like a time of goodbyes in Nairobi as Emilie's last day arrives. Annie, Emilie and I walk into the clinic together. Emilie takes in every last sight including the matatu ride and waves to her friends in the streets. We have a lot planned for the clinic today, including home visits to many of the patients she'd like to see before leaving. We start the morning with a visit to Evelyn's house, where she is hosting another meeting for her women's support group, Harvest. We're warmly welcomed by all the guests who are saddened to hear it is Emilie's last day. They are all so interested to hear about our plans for the future when we return to our countries and what we want to do with the rest of our lives. Hearing about our plans to study at university, to work wherever we choose and to live wherever we want, fills them with optimism and excitement for us. I know they are thinking if only they had the same possibilities. Evelyn organises a small presentation for Emilie. They have become very close since working together to help Natalya. Evelyn presents Emilie with a special kanga and a head scarf, which they dress her in. All the women applaud and the room is filled with laughter and smiles. After staying awhile and talking with our friends, the time comes to say goodbye. Annie and I promise we'll return to see them soon.

Back at AMKA we share lunch with the team - Oloo, George, Solphine, Emilie, Annie and me. Joanne stops by to give Emilie a small present, knowing also that it is her last day. She has made some of her jewellery for Emilie: earrings, a necklace and bracelet. Emilie is overwhelmed by the generosity and love that the friends she has made here in Nairobi have shown her. It is touching. After lunch I head around to visit Helen and Kevin with Emilie. On the way, deciding not to brave the short-cut, we take the longer route along the main road of Dagoretti but even this is not without some action today. We're approached by a middle-aged man who is carrying a bucket of coals and ranting about something in Swahili. He is drunk and Emilie and I can't seem to shake him off. We walk a bit faster and chat to each other but he continues to follow. We run into one of the nearby shops and crouch down, hiding behind an aisle hoping he will pass by. Emilie rightfully calls it another Karibu Kenya moment in a growing list of experiences we've shared together. The young shop assistant sees us smiles at the sight of the two mzungu girls hiding behind a shelf. Obviously we still have some growing to do to be able to handle these situations like real Kenyan women. When the coast is clear, we head out again and are back en route to visit Helen and Kevin in Gatina.

Relieved to make it safely to Gatina, I realise how my perspective about being in a safe environment has changed over time. Whereas I once had my guard up when walking through these areas, the slums have now become familiar and safe to me, and the community that exists within them provides a sense of security that is stronger than I could have imagined. I have even managed to shake the hiking boots, comfortably walking around in my flip flops like a local through the dirt paths and littered streets. This shows me how far I've come!

Helen is doing well and manages to walk even farther again today as we help her outside onto her chair near the avocado tree. Kevin is also home and he tells us how he is looking forward to starting school again. He organised the paperwork immediately after Emilie arranged his sponsorship with the clinic. It's nice to see somebody appreciate so much the opportunity to finish his schooling. These are the people who deserve these chances. We spend some time talking with Helen and Kevin before being greeted by Patricia, one of the community health workers from AMKA. Having heard it is Emilie's last day, Patricia invites us into her home, which is not far from Helen's. I can't believe how many people we've run into today, realising how much we've integrated into this community here. It's a great feeling.

Patricia is our colleague who often helps out with the Friday morning food distribution at the clinic. What I didn't know before talking with her in her home today is that, at just 21 years old, Patricia is also HIV positive. She shares her story with us and I learn that she has two young children who live with her and are in school. Patricia explains it is a struggle to support them while living in this small shack in the slums. When we visit people in their homes it is often their turn to share their stories with us. It is also their chance to ask us for help, outside of the clinic where we work. These chances don't come around often, and having learned that Emilie is leaving it is Patricia's chance right now. There is always more to learn about the people we meet here; a sad story behind their happy and confident faces, or a hidden illness behind their apparent healthy bodies. Patricia is our girlfriend whom I've joked around with in the food shelter at the clinic when handing out the flour and getting it all over my clothes. Today I've learnt her story.

After saying goodbye to our friends in Gatina, Emilie and I head back to the Dagoretti clinic for a small gathering with the AMKA team to bid Emilie a final farewell. Sister Veronica has come to join us in this special occasion and she delivers a special speech before Oloo, Solphine, George, Annie, Emilie and me on how much Emilie has given to the AMKA project and how all the patients will miss her greatly. Especially her close friend Kevin. She presents Emilie with a kanga, as well as a personal card she has made with a photo of Kevin and Helen on the front. All of this attention and gratitude is enough to make Emilie shed some tears, wishing deeply that she could stay longer. We then take a seat around the table and Sister Veronica hands out some plates and chips and yoghurt drinks she has bought for the occasion. Watching the excitement in Oloo and Solphine, I can see that they don't celebrate like this very often. It really is a special occasion. The atmosphere is positive and filled with laughter as we drink our flavoured yoghurt drinks and share the chips around the table.

Once we've all finished and start to pack up, an old man who appears to be looking for something stumbles into the gates of the clinic. Oloo and George say they know this man, he lives in the community and is a resident drunk. Some of the slums brew their own beer which is more than likely how he's got himself in this state. Sister Veronica offers to drive us back in her car to Jamhuri to avoid any confrontation with the man on Emilie's last day. As he stumbles around the front entrance of the clinic we try and avoid him and I dive into the back seat of the car, with Emilie and Annie right behind me. We take off and are heading down the road when suddenly I see the old drunk man running up behind the car. He's chasing us down the main road of Dagoretti! We shriek from the back seat, telling Sister Veronica to put her foot on the accelerator. She does, and we speed away with a small yet fearless nun behind the wheel! It seems only fitting that on Emilie's last day there is yet another Karibu Kenya moment as we try to escape a crazy drunk man for the second time today in the slums. I will miss her.

Chapter 37 – Madaraka day

1st June 2006 – Nairobi, Kenya

Today is Madaraka day, a public holiday to recognise Kenya's path to independence. The clinic in Dagoretti will be closed to celebrate the day, so I've decide to spend the morning with Annie on a big walking tour in Kibera. After breakfast I pack my backpack and put on my boots and head into Kibera with Annie. Peter, our Kibera contact and friend, has agreed to meet us and show us around.

Our meeting place is Ushirika clinic and I'm delighted to return there and see all my friends again - Debra, Judson, David, Daniel, Ruth and Anna. They greet me warmly, asking as always if I've come back to work with them. I decline, regretfully, but reassure them that I will return at some stage. Peter arrives and we head off on into the interior of these enormous slums. Although I've already spent some time working here, I have hardly covered more than the surface of Kibera. Today Peter is going to take us into the depths of Kibera, to show us what it is really like in these impoverished slums. It will be Annie's first experience here in Kibera. It may be a public holiday, but for the people in the slums it's another day to feed their families, so work does not stop here. All the stalls have been up and running since early morning selling fruits, vegetables, clothes, electronics and so much more. There are hair dressing salons set up in the open air and large pots of ugali that are already brewing for lunch.

I start to think how I've become more accustomed to this environment now from all the community work I've been doing in the slums. These types of living conditions have become my work place at AMKA clinic and it has become less shocking now than in my first week. However there are still some things that you can never be completely prepared for - like what it is you're walking on, the smells, or the young boys we pass this morning who are cooking animal legs (which ones, I'm not sure) over a fire to make soup. Every day here *is still* an adventure. My lessons are ongoing. Peter takes Annie and me into one of the many orphanages in Kibera. The conditions here are appalling. We're shown into the rooms where the children are taught during the day and then up to

16 of these children sleep in this same one room at every night. It's a tiny room with just one single bed. There are two of these rooms in the orphanage to accommodate the children. There is no electricity, running water and minimal resources. The children are visibly in need of clothes, food, books and toiletries. This is one place I would really like to help, simply because I know that whatever small contribution I make would be a huge difference to them.

    I talk to Peter as we leave the orphanage and ask him about the worst areas of Kibera. How bad are the worst living conditions in these slums, because what we've seen so far has already been appalling? Does it get much worse? Peter agrees to take Annie and me into these parts of Kibera. We continue walking around the main street of Kibera then take a short cut and follow Peter up a set of very old and unstable wooden stairs. If there was a rail, I would be holding on tightly right now. But it's everyone for themselves as we make our way down. At the top there is a view overlooking this part of the slums. The tiny matchbox shacks that are these people's homes are incredibly tightly packed together. From above, all we can see are the timber roofs overlapping and heavily littered with the famous flying toilet bags. This highly condensed and populated area has no roads going in or out, just a number of tiny hidden pathways that weave in and around to access each family's shack. There is no electricity, running water and of course no sewage system.

    We follow Peter down into the slums to get a closer look inside the timber shacks. I have to crouch down and turn my head most of the time to avoid hitting the low timber roofs. These homes have been put together out of timber scraps and are at times only 10m^2 in size. Walking along the path, we pass many of the residents who are out washing clothes on their doorsteps, or just sitting outside watching their children play in the narrow paths polluted with running sewage and waste. The houses are too small and dark to stay inside so the locals live outside. These tiny narrow passageways are a labyrinth and provide a vivid insight into life here as we continue to walk through this congested part of the slum. It's unlike anywhere else I've been. I'm conscious of the lack of open air, since the space here is so confined and it smells. This seems to be the big difference between this part of Kibera and the slums I've visited on my home visits at AMKA. Here the space is so concentrated with people, housing and rubbish dumps that there is hardly any space left to move. It's horrifying.

Peter leads us into the house of somebody he knows. Her name is Joyce and she is standing outside the front door to one of these tiny shacks. Joyce invites us inside and it doesn't take long to glance around at all that there is inside this small room. Dirt floors, an old mattress to sleep on, a few kitchen utensils for cooking, some clothes inside a big bag, and that is about it. I later learn from Peter that Joyce is one of many prostitutes who live and work in Kibera. Joyce used to have a stable and respectable job as a receptionist but like many others has sadly turned to this work out of desperation and a need for money to survive. She has three young children who all live with her. With all of the people living in Kibera and the high rates of HIV that exist, prostitution is a concerning problem and one of the major contributors to the spread of HIV in this already poverty-stricken community.

We've been walking for almost three hours when Peter finally leads Annie and me back into the familiar gates of Ushirika clinic. It's exhausting physically but above all, emotionally, to process everything we've seen. I spot Daniel standing in the front yard at the clinic with his usual big smile and aura of positivity, and we decide to go and have a chapatti together for lunch. Just like the good old times. But during lunch I can't stop thinking about our morning's tour around the slums with Peter. As with everyday and every experience here, I am filled with thoughts about what I have seen and how we can help to change things for the better in Kibera - the under-resourced orphanage, the shocking reality of living conditions and the ongoing practice of prostitution. These experiences always leave me with so much to think about.

Chapter 38 – Beliefs

Change can either challenge or threaten you.
Your beliefs pave your way to success or block you
— Marsha Sinetar

Annie and I are on our way into Ngando for today's clinic. Once everybody has arrived, we open the clinic and one of our community health workers Rosalie asks me to accompany her on a home visit. She knows of some patients, a husband and wife, who are unwell in their home. They don't live too far away from the clinic and when we arrive we notice that there are already three other visitors inside the timber shack. The visitors are reading and preaching from their bibles. When we peer through and enter the front door they do not stop what they are doing, carrying on their recitals and deep conversation. Rosalie and I walk in hesitantly and take a seat inside the small room. Next to my seat a young man in his thirties is lying down with his thin long legs stretched out on the couch, covered with a blanket. This is James. Next to him his wife Grace is sitting up in a chair. The preaching continues.

'Jesus is the only one who can save you. It is he who can cure you.'

I'm immediately curious and sceptical about what is happening in this room. I've heard about some of the religious practices that take place within the slums that claim to be able to cure people of HIV and AIDS. There are churches that advise their followers to stop taking their ARVs and to leave their health in the hands of God. Other more alarming schemes involve the churches asking people to pay money, and for this fee, they will be prayed upon and then walk away from the church cured.

Suddenly I am included in this ritual, as the visitors ask me if I have been saved and if I want to be saved. I am completely unsure of what response would be the best in this situation. If I admit to not being saved, what will they think of me? If I say I want to be saved, what will that involve? I turn my head towards Rosalie hoping she can help me out but she seems to be just as uneasy as I am at this moment. My well thought out response is 'I don't know?!'

The visitors then turn towards James and Grace where they proceed to perform a ritual where a jug of water is held above their heads while they preach loudly. Another person arrives at the door. It is a pastor. He has come to join in the ritual and has the power to 'cure' James. At this point Rosalie and I decide that it is time for us to leave. We step outside of the house, away from the water jug, the hands, the pressure to be saved and the preaching.

I look at Rosalie and ask her what was happening in there. As some of the praying was in Swahili, she tells me that the visitors claimed to have felt a blockage in their prayers in the room. We both attribute this to our negative opinions of what they were practicing inside. Rosalie explains to me that their ritual claimed to cure the bedridden James of HIV. They claimed to be able to cure this man, who had not been able to walk for over one year, and that today he would walk on his own two feet into the church.

These are the types of challenges we are faced with in the community. They are so hard to overcome and these people's faith is so strong. It is often all they have to turn to and I completely support their religious beliefs. I think prayer is an incredible tool for helping those in need. But I also have a role to uphold in educating the community and ensuring these false beliefs about curing HIV that are causing people to pay money to a church and to stop their treatment, are dispelled. It can be a fine line to tread, to correct someone's beliefs without criticising their religion. I will have to return to James and Grace's place again soon to speak with them.

Upon returning to the clinic, I report back to George and Solphine about what we have witnessed. This is of course not new to them but it is concerning. Fighting the myths surrounding HIV and AIDS is an ongoing challenge for the clinic and the work of my colleagues. George and Solphine both agree that we must return to see James again soon when he is alone, so that we can establish how he is managing his health.

We break for our lunch of chai, bread and butter. As always there are many jokes shared around the table as we share this precious meal and time together. After lunch I help Rosalie and Solphine pack up the clinic by washing the dishes, mopping the floors, and returning all the furniture to its original place in the room. Then we all walk back through Ngando to the Dagoretti clinic.

Not long after we arrive back, Natalya walks into the clinic to see me. It is always a pleasure to see my dear friend who is forever smiling these days. She cannot stop herself from walking around everywhere now that she's back on her feet. I had promised Natalya that I would paint her nails for her. She has come to make sure I see my promise through.

We sit outside together on the wooden bench under the clinic's verandah and she gives me her hand and I paint her nails bright red. We giggle together like girlfriends, as I ask her what she has been doing, to which she responds nothing. Like many people in the slums this young woman with such potential has nothing to do with her days. She has no job, no money and no ambition or opportunity to get out of this situation. So she spends her time walking around. I ask her if she is feeling better, which she is.

The question of whether Natalya has been tested or not for HIV still concerns me, and I have mentioned it to George as something we should address now that she is getting her strength back. I ask Natalya about her young daughter who apparently stays with her mum but she doesn't say much. I finish her nails which look great. Natalya is delighted with them, holding them up to the light to better admire them. I tell her I'll come and visit her soon in her place. 'Hotel 46', she corrects me, and she laughs that beautiful Natalya laugh.

The afternoon, despite being quiet, does not pass without a little entertainment at the clinic. As we're closing, our resident drunk man returns. This time he is slightly more aggressive than last time. Solphine, Evelyn, Annie and I are the only ones left at the clinic. Evelyn tells him strongly to go away, that he is not allowed to come into the clinic. He wanders off. But shortly after, when I have my back turned and don't see him re-enter the clinic, he thumps me with his arm on my back. I scream out loud, in surprise and pain, to which Evelyn responds by turning around and throwing the drunken man into the bushes on the street. We grab our bags and run for the next bus out of Dagoretti Corner.

Besides the shock, I escape uninjured. More than anything I am impressed by Evelyn's display of power and control, and as we continue to run away we relive this moment of her pushing him into the bushes.

'Nobody messes with an African woman' she declares proudly, flexing her muscles for everyone to see. That's definitely true.

Chapter 39 – Masailand

I roamed the countryside searching for answers to things I did not understand – Leonardo Da Vinci

June 2006 – Masailand, Kenya

This weekend I've decided to get away from Nairobi for a few days. I've been feeling a mixture of emotions that a change of place will help me to work through. I'm heading into rural Masailand to stay with a Masai family and to see the famous Ngong hills. There are a number of volunteers who are placed out with families and who are working on local projects in this area. I take the bus into Nairobi city where I meet Eric at the volunteer office. He will accompany me on the bus into the town of Ngong. This town is the gateway to the Masailand and from here we will take another car to Veronica's Masai home.

Ngong is only 22km south west of Nairobi so it doesn't take long to arrive there once we are on the bus. Although it is not far from the city it is a dramatic change from Nairobi. The first thing I notice is the many Masai people walking around the streets. They are a beautiful sight, wrapped traditionally in their brightly coloured red, white, yellow and blue robes; accessorised with layers of similarly coloured beaded jewellery. The men are walking about the town with their wooden sticks in hand and wearing black rubber sandals. Many of the women are standing around in groups together with their young children and selling their foods or jewellery at their small shops. The Saturday morning markets are bustling. There are matatus that come and go in all directions. Ngong is the central town for the local Masai villages and many of the locals make the trip into Ngong weekly to get all their supplies before travelling back to their small isolated villages. It is new and exciting to be closer to the homeland of the Masai tribe.

Eric spots Veronica accompanied by four of the volunteers who are staying with her. They've travelled into Ngong for the day to get some supplies. Veronica is a beautiful Masai woman, aged in her thirties and dressed traditionally in a brightly coloured kanga with beaded jewellery and her short, shaved hair.

Eric introduces me to Veronica. She's very welcoming and speaks a good level of English which not all Masai people do. When she smiles Veronica displays a big gap between her front teeth which have been removed. She has her young baby daughter Purity strapped to her back in a sling, and she bends down to choose some vegetables at the small stall where we are standing. The other volunteers Veronica has staying with her are Maggie, Kim, Renee and Adrian. They all volunteer at the local school in Kimuka. I spend the rest of the morning looking around the markets with them, admiring the Masai jewellery, the kangas, selections of fruits and vegetables as well as buying all the necessities for the next few days. Like most Masai homes, there is no running water or electricity at Veronica's house. I'm looking forward to the experience of spending a weekend in a tribal family.

After the markets Veronica suggests we all go for lunch together at a small restaurant. We find a table together and order some rice, beans and cabbage. Prior to leaving the restaurant I decide to go and use the toilets before the ride to Veronica's place. Being in a rural Kenyan town, it has a pit toilet. It's not the first time I've used the pit (whole in a ground) toilet. They are everywhere in the slums and at work, but I am not yet the expert. I drop down my jeans, place my feet on either side of the pit and take my squat position. Somehow, and I don't know how, my technique completely fails me and I end up peeing all down my leg on my jeans! And, of course, these are the only pair of jeans that I've brought for the weekend. It's a complete disaster and despite fluffing about with my tissues, hand gel and anything else I can find, I realise the situation is hopeless. I zip myself up and rejoin Veronica and the others who are completely oblivious to my embarrassing accident. I am, after all, the white girl from the city.

We wait around a few hours in Ngong before finding a car that is going past Veronica's place. The taxi is actually a big pick-up truck, into which Veronica loads a wooden bed she has bought at the markets, her shopping and all of us volunteers. Everybody jumps into the back of the truck, next to the bed, ready for the ride back to Veronica's.

The drive is fascinating. I hold on to the side of the truck and feel an incredible sense of freedom as the wind blows my hair back and we travel through this stunning African setting. The road is bumpy and dusty and the views of Masailand are beautiful. It's a typical savannah with large open dry spaces and the occasional old acacia tree standing on its own. Then the breathtaking Ngong hills become visible. They are a chain of four green mountain peaks that form a brilliant contrast against the brown barren fields. We pass just a few timber houses, but each one is many kilometres from the next. In the distance I can spot the Masai people walking across their land, easily identified in their red cloaks and characteristically tall slim bodies. I feel alive in these incredible surroundings.

We arrive at Veronica's house shortly after. Set in front of the sunlit Ngong hills, her house is actually a house, not one of the tiny shacks I've become accustomed to in the slums of Nairobi. It is built of timber sheets with a few separate bedrooms, a wash room and a lounge room. Built separately outside is a small kitchen, and farther away again from the house is the small enclosed pit toilet. A thick fencing of thorny buses encloses the house. Out the front a separate small enclosure has been built to contain the family's cattle. Out here in Masailand space is unlimited. We are in the Kenyan countryside and already it feels incredible.

Veronica's children come out to meet me; her oldest daughter Priscilla, her son Tony and younger daughter Betty who is 4 years old. Veronica's children are delighted to have another visitor stay with them and they stand around watching me curiously. I take my bags inside where I am shown to my bed for the night in the same room as the other volunteers. I am then given a tour of the house and the other rooms. The floors are dirt and there are a few windows cut into the timber walls to illuminate the inside of her house. There is of course no electricity or running water. This is what I've come for; the real experience. Maggie informs me that they collect firewood for cooking and that everyday Priscilla walks to the dam with the big jerry cans to collect their water. This is the duty of the Masai woman.

I take a short walk around the property with Tony. Tony's job, as the son and a male Masai, is to look after the cattle. When he's not at school he spends his days out in the fields watching the twelve cows that they own. He's proud to show me his cows. Here in Masailand a family's wealth is determined by the number of cows they have. Already I can see many of these traditions present in Veronica's household.

Tony and I return to the house where Priscilla has prepared some chai for everybody. It is strong and the taste of fresh cow's milk is very different from what I've had in Nairobi. We all sit around together on the few couches inside the open living room. Veronica teaches me some of the Masai traditions, starting with how to greet visitors. The Masai have their own language, Maa, and there are different dialects too. I repeat: *'Supai'* and *'Ipa'*, for the formal greeting and reply. This also includes bowing the head as a sign of respect to any elder.

While we're taking our chai, Veronica has a number of visitors who come into the house to see her. They are other Masais who are dressed traditionally and have come to greet her. They speak Maa with Veronica and we all greet them formally. The Masai are a very social and welcoming tribe, stopping by to each other's homes quite regularly on their nomadic journeys.

Two of Veronica's family friends, Samuel and Samuel (whom I call 'The two Samuels' as they always travel about together) come by to visit Veronica's family and the other volunteers who they've come to know well. These two young men are aged in their early twenties and do not wear the traditional coloured robes or sandals. They are dressed in western clothing, jeans and t-shirts, and speak fluent English. The Samuels are an example of a newer generation of Masai. They have received a formal education and are integrated into the broader community outside of their homeland. They are still Masai men and proud of their tribe's culture and traditions. The Samuels announce that I must be given a Masai name, as they have done for all the other volunteers. They decide on *Naisula* as my Masai name which means 'winner'.

Samuel also adds that I am going to be his wife! Volunteer Maggie exclaims that she thought she was his chosen wife. Samuel clarifies that Maggie (who he calls by her Masai name *Namanyak*, meaning 'the lucky one') is the first wife and Naisula (me) is his second wife. The Masai are polygamous and it's obvious that this traditional is accepted in even the younger generations, whether they chose to lead the traditional tribal life or not. There is a long tradition for men to have multiple wives. I learn that Veronica is one of three wives. Her husband, Simon, lives with his youngest wife and their children. He usually comes by to visit her family once a week. For Veronica this is normal. While we're sitting down taking our tea, Veronica's husband arrives at their house and he comes inside. He's an older man, wearing a striped red and white robe that is draped around his slim figure and he carries his

Masai stick in his left hand. His long stretched earlobes hang down and he wears some bracelets and black sandals.

We're introduced to Simon and we all stand up one after the other to greet him, bowing our heads in respect before this Masai elder. He sits down briefly with Veronica and us but I oberve that he is a man of few words. One by one the children come into the room to greet their father. I observe that they too are shy and show a lot of respect towards their father. As is characteristic for Masai men, Simon shows little paternal love for his children. His visit is short and once he checks on his cattle outside with Tony, he heads off again.

It is so interesting to talk about the customs and traditions here in Masailand with Veronica. She explains that Simon is responsible for disciplining the children when they misbehave, having recently caned Tony several times for being lazy out in the field with the cattle. She talks openly about many of these topics, such as the practice of polygamy and male and female circumcision which are considered controversial practices but still take place amongst the Masai tribe today.

Later in the evening, as it gets dark, Veronica lights a number of small lanterns around the house. I go outside with the flashlight that I've brought with me from Nairobi and notice straight away that young Tony has his eye on it. A torch is a real luxury. I navigate my way in the dark to the kitchen where Priscilla is crouching down over a hot plate, rolling, flipping and cooking chapattis. She has been at it for a few hours now, in charge of cooking dinner for the family. I offer to help her but she says she has it under control. The kitchen is filled with a thick black smoke from the burning wood. I talk to Priscilla about school, living in Masailand and the city. She has been to Nairobi a few times, she tells me, but it still remains an exciting and unfamiliar place to her. She is 14 years old but has the maturity of a mother who has the responsibility of looking after her children.

It takes Priscilla another hour and a half to finish making the chapattis and cooking the cabbage and potatoes that we all share for dinner. It is very late by the time we eat but time is not a concern out here in Masailand. I sit blissfully on the couch in Veronica's living room sharing my dinner by candlelight with this amazing Masai family and my volunteer friends. After dinner there is not much else to do so we all go to bed. I walk outside with Maggie and Kim to admire the brightness of the thousands of starts decorating the night sky. It is so peaceful and despite being isolated, there is a strong feeling of security amongst the Masai people. I brush my teeth outside and then master the technique of using the pit toilet in the pitch black night before heading inside to my bed.

I wake up early in the morning to a few small cats that have fallen onto my mosquito net from the roof, causing it to collapse on top of me. The timber house made some interesting creaking noises during the night as it rattled with the evening wind. Young Purity is up and crying already and the sun is beaming through our small window. The day starts early in Masailand.

I wander into the living room where I find Veronica feeding Purity. She tells me that Priscilla is heating up some water for me to take a shower. The shower room is simply a small cubicle inside the house and Priscilla brings me a bucket of warm water to wash myself. Another new experience. I'm conscious of not using too much water knowing how long a walk it is for her to go to the dam everyday to collect it in the jerry cans and then bring it all the way back to the house. I'm also privileged, as a guest, to have a warm shower. That privilege is long gone for the other volunteers I learn later. After my shower I help out with all the dishes from the night before. We then eat breakfast which is half a banana each and half a chapatti that Priscilla has reheated from the previous night. We have to ration the food so there is enough to go around.

The two Samuels arrive early to have breakfast with us. They have offered to take us to see the giraffes this morning. Just the thought of giraffes being in our backyard is amazing. When everybody is ready, the two Samuels, Maggie, Kim, Adrian, Renee and I set off on our walk. I'm surprised to see both Samuels constantly checking their mobile phones as we walk along together. It's incredibe how in this extremely rural part of Kenya where running water and electricity are unheard of, there is a decent mobile phone network. The image of the traditional tribal Masai man carrying their spear in one hand and a mobile phone in the other is both surprising and fascinating. It's a typical example of the westernisation of their culture, where advancing technology meets the developing world.

No more than ten minutes from the house, Samuel points out a family of five giraffes. The sight is unbelievable. The giraffes are standing right in front of us, in their native environment with the stunning Ngong hills as a backdrop. There is no comparison to being on safari in a minivan amongst dozens of other tourists. This is the real Africa and I am so blessed to be having this experience. The two Samuels, like real Masai, know the countryside inside out and can predict when and where the animals are at almost any time. We don't get any closer than 100 metres, respecting the natural environment of these beautifully peaceful animals. After taking some pictures, the boys lead us on a long walk up into the hills, where we have spectacular views of the beauty of the Masailand down below. It is breathtaking, this vast open space that has been largely untouched. To be in the countryside like this is so refreshing. The image before me is just as I expected Kenya to be.

After a long walk we return to Veronica's place where she has brought out her collection of jewellery for everybody to see and to purchase, of course. She is quite the Masai business woman! Veronica also gives me some of her traditional Masai clothing to change into, as it is customary for volunteer visitors to have their photos taken with her, dressed up like a Masai. We have a lot of fun. I'm wearing the blue and red robe, the beaded headpiece and the layers of beautiful jewellery. It's so heavy! I have my photo taken with my 'husband' Samuel.

'My second wife, the white Masai!' he jokes. We all take lunch together inside the house which Priscilla has again prepared. It is ugali and cabbage. The time soon arrives for me to pack my bags and take a car back to Ngong and from there another bus into Nairobi. This weekend out of the city has been just what I needed. I have fallen in love with the Masai people, their environment, their kindness and hospitality and their captivating culture. I am certain to return here to visit Veronica and her family soon. I have loved the experience of being out in the country away from luxuries, electricity, running water and the busyness of city life. I can't wait to come back.

Chapter 40 - New battles

Obstacles are those frightful things you see when you take your eyes off your goal – Henry Ford

This morning I'm escorting Katie and another new volunteer in Jamhuri to Ushirika clinic where they will be met by Peter and shown to their projects at one of the orphanages in Kibera. It is a nice thought to know that I am now the expert with all of the right contacts and local knowledge, showing everybody around and running into familiar faces wherever I go.

After meeting up with Peter I head into work at the clinic in Dagoretti Corner where Sister Veronica and Annie are waiting for me. Today Helen has a check-up appointment at Riruta Health Clinic. This is a clinic that dispenses ARVs for HIV and AIDS and the doctors will assess Helen's overall health more closely. We're going to collect Helen from her home in Gatina and take her into the nearby clinic, since she is unable to get there any other way. I remember asking Kevin once about what he does when Sister Veronica is not around to help, and he said that once he had to take Helen on a bike with him to get to the clinic. I can only imagine how difficult this would have been, with Helen's weak heavy limbs unable to support her body weight.

We arrive in the car outside Helen's place, and with our help she manages to walk to the car, gaining confidence with each step. Kevin is not around today since he has started his new course at school which Emilie has sponsored. We manage to help Helen into the back seat of the car and arrive at Riruta Health Clinic. Annie and I help Helen walk into the clinic which is completely full of patients. They are all sitting squeezed in closely together on the small wooden benches, waiting patiently for their turn. There are even some patients waiting outside.

Inside the small clinic it is no different from Ushirika or the other clinics operating in the slums. There are posters on the walls for educating patients, a small yet congested waiting area and a number of separate consulting rooms. Staff in white lab coats constantly come in and out carrying patient folders.

Sister Veronica goes ahead to confirm Helen's appointment at the front desk with the staff. Annie, Helen and I then follow Sister Veronica as she walks on through to the Voluntary Counselling and Testing section of the clinic. Here there are even more people waiting. Some are squatting down in the corners and others stand lining the busy corridor. They are likely to have been waiting for hours. We draw a lot of attention as Annie and I, the two mzungus, walk Helen through the clinic. Fortunately Sister Veronica has managed to get Helen seen straight away.

The doctor talks to Helen and gives her a new supply of ARVs and multivitamins. The doctor is concerned about Helens' persistent cough, worried that it could be tuberculosis or pneumonia. She is referred for a chest x-ray to determine the diagnosis. There are no radiography facilities at this clinic so we are referred onto Melchzadik hospital for the chest x-ray to be taken. Sister Veronica, Annie and I help Helen back into the car and we drive to the hospital. Once there we are subjected to more waiting and forced to pay the fees for Helen to see the doctor. Sister Veronica does her best to have Helen seen quickly, as she is starting to look exhausted from the day's events.

Finally we receive Helen's x-ray report which indicates she has tuberculosis. This is not good news for Helen, having already battled TB in the past. TB is also one of the indicators that the HIV virus has progressed into AIDS. It is an opportunistic infection that often develops in HIV positive patients because their immune system has started to fail due to the dominance of the HIV virus. The day becomes even more long winded when we're told we must now return to Riruta clinic, where we started off the day, to get the TB medications for Helen. So we help her into the car, drive back to Riruta clinic and go in to see her doctor.

Walking down the corridor of the clinic I see a large rooster wandering amongst the queue of patients. Helen's medications are changed and a treatment regime to combat the TB is devised for her. As Helen has already had two bouts of TB she requires a different treatment from the conventional oral tablets. She will receive daily injections over 60 days that we hope her body will respond to. I'm worried for poor Helen. After all the progress she's made this is a big set-back for her. It will be devastating if her health starts to decline.

After more waiting around at the clinic, we finally head back to Gatina with Helen. The next dilemma is to arrange how Helen will have her daily injections administered. Sister Veronica knows of a community nurse in Gatina who lives near Helen whom she can ask to take on this role. This in itself proves to be another battle. A battle against Kenyan corruption. The lady meets with us but is insistent on being paid 100ksh per day to perform this duty. It's bribery! I cannot believe what I am seeing and hearing. Sitting in Sister Veronica's vehicle with poor Helen listening to the discussion about how much money one should pay to save a human life. It is absurd and sitting in the van Annie and I agree that we will pay the 50ksh for Helen to get her treatment and for this ridiculous conversation to end here and now.

So it's settled. The community nurse will be responsible for visiting Helen each morning to administer the TB injections. It's just another example of *corruption*, my *lesson number 11* in this journey. The government requests money to import medications, to have a patient treated, or the police will bribe visitors not carrying their passports for money. And unfortunately this mentality has now spread to some of the people working in the community. Sadly it's only natural that the people are learning from the bad examples being set by their leaders. We return to Helen's house and help her back into bed. She is exhausted from such a long day and worried by this new uphill battle.

Chapter 41 – Janet

Poverty is the worst form of violence – Mahatma Gandhi

I pack my bag after breakfast and lace up my boots as I head out the door to work with Annie. Today's clinic is in Gatina so as usual we walk through the main street of Jamhuri, passing our friends sitting and waiting on the corner and walk out onto Ngong road to take our matatu. We've become such experts now at this daily routine of hailing the matatu, climbing onboard, whether there is a seat free or not and signalling our stop. Except this morning we have a slightly different experience to normal.

Annie and I are seated in the very back seat of the matatu. Music, as usual, is blaring through the poor sound system and the driver swerves left and right, honking his horn in the usual manner as he negotiates the morning traffic. Annie and I are keeping our eyes on the road, as we always do, when we start to sense something strange happening up the front of the car. The driver is talking to his mate next to him in the passenger seat, whose job it is to collect the money from the passengers. Suddenly they call out, 'seat belt check!' to warn us that up ahead there's a police check and the word is passed back amongst the passengers to where we're seated in the back seat.

As I look down to check my seat belt, which is already secured, I see that the man next to me is trying to get into my satchel which is strapped over my shoulder. Annie has placed her backpack close to her on the seat and stops another young man from reaching into her bag. The seat belt check turns out to be a hoax, used to distract passengers from their bags as they frantically fasten their seat belts. Today there is no police check on the road. The young men appear to have planned this whole scam to try and catch us out. Fortunately for us we're no longer newbies in Kenya and have learnt from very early on that when travelling on these matatus you have to have your wits about you. We escape unscathed and hail the matatu to stop immediately and walk the rest of our journey into the clinic.

The morning clinic at Gatina is extremely busy today. We seem to be getting more and more patients recently from very difficult living situations and battling HIV. What is becoming more obvious is that these people's health problems often take a back seat to the desperation caused by their financial and social troubles. Many of our patients who are HIV positive manage to take care of their illness. Their biggest challenge is to help solve their rent problems, to find a source of income, to avoid the social stigma they experience in the community or to help enrol their children in a school. I was not prepared for this complexity in working at a HIV clinic or the reality of the poverty we're working in.

This morning I meet with a new patient, Janet. Janet is HIV positive and has started taking ARVs. She lives in the slums of Gatina, in a small shack, with her three children. The eldest has also recently given birth to a child. Janet tells me that they have not eaten for a few days. She has almost two months of rent outstanding and the landlord is now threatening to kick her out of her house. She has no source of income, her partner having left her three months ago. Where do I start with a case like this one?

I head out of the clinic on a home visit to Janet's place. When we arrive I meet her eldest daughter and her newborn baby whom she is nursing. I take a look inside her home which is a typical timber shack with one open room, dirt floors and a separated kitchen and sleeping space. It's a small space to house the five of them. I observe the empty pots and pans sitting in the corner, having not been used for some time. I can't help but think of this newborn baby, of the conditions that she has been born into and of her teenage mother who is not receiving the nutrition she needs to be breastfeeding her child.

Janet's case is one of many I encounter in my work where I don't know how I can help. And of course I desperately want to. Janet has approached me hoping I can resolve her rent problems. But it's not as easy as writing out a cheque to cover the last two months. What will she do for the next two months? These problems need to be addressed at the core so that patients can find a way to support themselves and not depend on hand outs. I promise her we'll look into her situation back at the clinic with the whole team. In the meantime she qualifies for the clinic's food distribution program. Janet returns to the clinic with me where we organise her food coupon and she receives rice, beans, and two lots of Nutrimix for her children who haven't been eating. It's a start. As is often the case, the path ahead will be a long one.

Annie and I visit Helen, to see how she is doing after such a long day at the clinic yesterday. She is pleased to see us; she's rested and regained her energy. We feel extremely close to Helen. We've shared so many moments with her, in and out of her house and constantly follow her battle with HIV. I take out my oil and give her feet and legs a massage. We're well aware of the importance of continuing our care for Helen once she starts her injections for TB which are extremely strong and could further weaken her system.

Soon it is lunch time and the clinic quietens down after all the food distributions have been completed. George, Oloo, Solphine, Annie and I go to our regular Thursday lunch spot at Moses' Fair Deal cafe where I order my usual chapatti and beans. After a busy morning at the clinic we enjoy sitting around the table together and sharing our lunch. George agrees that the clinic is getting a lot busier now and warns us that this is a trend they often see as the winter months approach. The cooler weather can often bring more challenges in people's lives in the community particularly to their health.

Chapter 42 – Home visits

Friday morning clinic starts busily in Dagoretti Corner. When we arrive at the clinic early in the morning there are already several women waiting patiently with their food tokens in hand. Annie and I spend the first part of the morning handing out the food. When we've finished I pay Natalya a home visit as I promised earlier in the week. My dear friend Natalya, having regained her strength and particularly her confidence, is becoming quite the cheeky 20 year old! Having asked for a massage I agree to come by and see her, realising it's important to keep up our contact with her since her recovery. After painting her nails for her during the week she asked if I could do them again. As a surprise during the week, I left the small bottle of nail polish in a plastic bag attached to the front door of her Hotel 46. This morning when I arrive she tells me she received the nail polish and shows me her brightly painted nails.

I haven't been inside her place since she was bedridden. As we walk inside many of the memories come back from my visits with Emilie of this dark time in Natalya's life. I'm surprised to see that today it's quite different inside. Natalya has cleaned up the shack. It is lighter and cleaner and hardly resembles the dark solemn place I'd come to know. She has decorated the timber sheet walls with posters of pop stars: Beyoncé and Nelly. The couch is covered in a crocheted rug and hung up all around the room are purple advertising banners of Cadbury Chocolate! On the tables there are empty containers of soda bottles and fruit juice that have been added for decoration. This is interior design Dagoretti style! It is great. I duck my head under the Cadbury's bunting and sit down on the couch next to Natalya, who is beaming with delight at showing me her new home. It is such a positive sign to see how she has turned this place around. Just another example of how she is trying to turn her life around and move on from her time of depression.

Back at the clinic it has also been a busy morning with new patients arriving as well as old ones returning. Oloo is busy organising many of the sponsored children's documentation. I notice that the brand new plastic wallet that Emilie and I gave him to help organise his paperwork has been left in the cupboard and he is back to his old technique of piles of papers and photos, and looking flustered as he searches for things. Some things you just can't change!

George, Annie and I set out on a walk to Ngando where a long-time patient, Faith, has expressed concerns over her son's health. His problems have been causing her a lot of stress and concern in her life, which has the potential to propagate into affecting her own health, living with HIV. It's a long walk through the middle of Ngando and off towards the outskirts where Faith leads us into her home. Inside her place, we're met by a drunken man who is her husband, and then we're introduced to her son. Faith's concerns are for his psychological state. We're invited to sit down and I observe her son who is 17 years old, as he eats his lunch and talks to himself rather aggressively in Swahili. He appears to be hallucinating and his eyes are not engaging properly. His violent body language and movements make me feel quite uncomfortable. I don't know what he is saying. I eventually choose to leave the room and wait for the others outside. It's too much for me.

Shortly after, Annie and George come out of Faith's place. George informs us that Faith's son needs to be admitted to hospital over the weekend to receive a psychiatric assessment. His symptoms seem to go beyond malaria hallucinations or substance abuse, such as marijuana which we had suspected. It is beyond our means to help him and yet we recognise the need to seek help. I think of Faith, who spends her days in this house with a drunken husband and a son who is obviously unwell and all of the stress and concern this is causing her in her life, on top of her own battles.

The afternoon is also a busy one. George, Annie and I travel all the way back to our Dagoretti Corner clinic and then head out again in the other direction towards Gatina to visit Helen in her home. We're going there to check on her and to see if the system we'd organised for her to receive her injections is working well.

When we get there we find Helen on her own in bed. She has not eaten anything since breakfast and did not receive her injection the previous day. This is exactly what we'd feared might happen, having negotiated a price with the community nurse to deliver the crucial injections to Helen as well as having paid her for the first week of injections. I feel so much sympathy for poor Helen. We have been doing our best to take care for her and guide her through this new course of treatment for her TB, and now I feel like we've failed and let her down. Helen looks worried today and helpless. The situation really concerns us and together George, Annie and I devise a plan for the weekend to make sure that Helen is looked after. Annie and I go and buy some food for her and when we get back we heat up some milk to make some chai. Kevin is at school. George agrees that for the weekend he will visit Helen in the mornings to deliver her injection until Monday when we will have to find out what happened to the community nurse.

On the walk back to the Dagoretti clinic we run into Kevin on the street. He is looking tired and withdrawn. We discover that he had not been to school that day and was in fact hiding outside so as not to disappoint his mother. It seems like he is feeling the stress of his mother's situation. George tells Kevin off, firstly for not attending school and secondly for leaving Helen at home without anything to eat. I can't help but feel for this poor young man who has so much resting on his shoulders right now. 'Life here is so hard' he once told me on a visit to see his mother. The telling off seems to make him even more withdrawn.

I'm keen to arrange a time to sit down and talk one on one with Kevin. Amongst all the setbacks with his mum's health, Kevin seems to be forgotten most of the time and yet he takes all the responsibility for this family. He looks so troubled and afraid for his mother. It's hard to leave him behind as we head back to the clinic knowing what he has to go home to.

Chapter 43 – Sunday Church

I'm excited this morning to go to a Sunday church service in the city. I've finally arranged to visit Daniel's church in Nairobi which he has been talking to me about since the first day we met at Ushirika. Daniel plays the keyboard in the church band which is an important role that he takes very seriously. He attends rehearsals during the week and performs every Sunday. Today he has invited Annie, Christine and me to the popular Sunday service.

We get dressed up in our best outfits at home. I choose one of my kangas to wear with a coloured blouse and the only alternative to my working boots, my flip-flops. However the morning in the house is unsettled. Lucy's bags are packed next to the door. The night before Lucy had whispered to me that she was leaving and asked me for my mobile number so we can keep in touch. 'What do you mean you're leaving? Where are you going? Why?' I asked her. She told me that Alice wanted her out of the house. I didn't understand at all.

This morning Alice tells us that Lucy is going because she hadn't been doing her job properly. Her reasons for sending Lucy back home were that she was lazy, that when we were all out working during the day Lucy was home talking with the neighbours and watching television when she should have been cooking and cleaning. We're all shocked and this news comes as such a surprise. It's a realisation for all of us that this is how the housemaids are sometimes treated here. Paid poorly and considered an inferior class. It's hard because we have always considered Lucy as one of us and are therefore sad and shocked to hear of her departure.

Annie, Christine and I take the City Hopper bus towards the city and get off at Nairobi Baptist Church. It is a large and modern establishment. Daniel spots our arrival and comes over to greet us happily out the front of the church with his younger sister Beth. He is dressed smartly in his black suit and blue tie and is grinning with excitement about our visit. He's proud and delighted to see us at his church where he will be performing and takes us on a personal tour inside. I ask him if he's prepared with his music, insisting he has a celebrity audience to perform before today. This makes Daniel smile even more. He says he's a celebrity himself, so today is just like any other day.

The church fills quickly. There are a lot of locals arriving and being seated on the long wooden benches that fill the large open space inside the church. In front of us is a big stage with a microphone and podium placed in the centre. In the middle of the stage is the church band. I spot Daniel's keyboard set up to the side. The service is divided into three parts: the youth service, the English service and the Swahili service. Each one delivers a similar message with lots of gospel singing, prayers and a sermon delivered by the pastor.

During the English service there are up to 1000 people seated in the hall and the pastor asks all new visitors to stand up. We are all welcomed into the church and we join in the dancing and singing to the songs and prayers. I watch Daniel, who is behind his keyboard on the stage, playing confidently and proudly. He continues to smile with enthusiasm. Almost four and a half hours later the service is over. Annie, Christine and I step outside of the church. It's been a marathon morning but well worth it! I feel uplifted to have taken part in something that is so precious to so many people. It's been particularly special to join Daniel in something that is so important to him. Meeting us outside and knowing how long the service can feel for the unaccustomed visitor, he says 'So, you didn't fall asleep?' Quite the contrary. We thank Daniel for his invitation. He graciously tells us that our visit today has made his day.

Annie and I stop at the supermarket on the way home to buy a few supplies for tonight's dinner. We've volunteered to cook in Lucy's absence and also because Alice has been studying hard for her final exams. Each night when she gets home from work she takes out her accounting books and studies for most of the night. She has just a few hours sleep before waking up early in the morning to study again.

When we get home I start the preparations. I'm making my first attempt at cooking chapatti on my own. I start by making the dough using the flour, oil and water. I then divide the dough into small portions, rolling them out and then swirling them into a circle. Then I roll them out flat before cooking each one on the hot chapatti plate which is a heavy, concave and circular plate. Alice looks over my shoulder. She sees me flinching when I turn the chapattis over on the hot plate, scared to burn my hands. I still have a long way to go before doing it as well as the African women! We enjoy a rare three course dinner tonight. Annie has bought some corn chips and prepared guacamole with avocados she bought at the markets. With the chapatti, I've cooked some beans. And for dessert we have fresh fruit and yoghurt. It's a real treat especially the yoghurt, since without a fridge we rarely have dairy products.

After dinner we sit down together to watch *Secreto de amor* with Alice. She takes a break from her studies to enjoy the one hour show with its entertaining, over-dramatic, soap opera storylines. In tonight's episode Andrea secretly hides her pregnancy from her protective family and another character Paulo discovers he has HIV and is dealing with accepting his illness. Maybe *Secreto de amor* is educational in Kenya after all!

Chapter 44 – Rose

Do not watch the petals fall from the rose with sadness, know that, like life, things sometimes must fade, before they can bloom again
– Unknown

Today we're off to our clinic in Ngando. Once we open the clinic with prayer and greet some of our regular patients who are already sitting outside the clinic, our team gathers inside to have a meeting. George, Oloo, Solphine, Annie, Rosalie, Joanne and I sit around one of the small desks to discuss the current situation with one of the clinic's patients, Rose. Rose has recently been discharged from hospital where she was admitted due to severe weight loss, dehydration and pain in her abdomen. She is HIV positive. Now she is being cared for by her family in her home but is refusing to eat or drink and has not taken her ARVs for a few months. She is despondent and weak and has mentally given up her battle. George arranges for some of us to pay Rose a home visit this morning to assess her situation. He fears she will have to have an IV drip attached soon if she continues to refuse any fluids. We need to report back to establish a plan for managing her care. So Annie, Solphine, Rosalie and I set off on our walk from the clinic to Rose's place.

Although sunny, it's another cold June morning. The winter is short in Kenya but the cooler weather is a big challenge for many of the people living in the slums. The locals are rugged up in beanies and their warmest jackets to fight the morning chill. With no insulation in the houses, the nights and mornings can get very cold. Walking out of the clinic we follow Rosalie to Rose's place. We pass the chickens wandering around the dirty streets, the stray dogs lying on the path and the women dressed in bright kangas walking back home with their heavy jerry cans of water. The market stands are up and running and children who are not in school are already out playing in the streets. It's just another day in Ngando.

At Rose's place, we let ourselves inside the small timber shack. Her family is not home, Rose is on her own. The dark, musty interior of her home is now becoming familiar to me on these home visits. A place lacking life and hope. As we approach the mattress on the floor, I strain to see her frail body curled up under the sheet. Rose is frighteningly skinny, almost skeletal. Her cheek bones protrude outwards and her eyes appear sunken back in their dark sockets. Her hair has been braided neatly back by her sister. Rose is a young woman in her early thirties, but right now appears to be carrying many more years on her troubled face.

We introduce ourselves and sit by her side around the mattress. On the small table next to her is an energy drink, which has been opened for her but not touched. Annie and I spend most of the morning by Rose's side. She is in need of support but refuses to help herself, turning her head each time we offer her the drink. She rolls over on the mattress, grabbing her stomach and screaming words in Swahili. She's in pain, *uchungu*, but there's nothing we can do to help her. It's so hard watching her in this state of agony. She curls her body up even tighter in the foetal position. Annie rubs Rose's stomach in an attempt to relieve her pain which seems to help.

Situations like these where back home a simple prescription of painkillers would help to alleviate Rose's pain are hard to witness. Once again we are limited in what we can do, which never seems to feel like enough. Annie and I agree with Solphine and Rosalie to visit Rose daily. For as long as she is refusing to cooperate and to return to the hospital her situation is critical. We pray that she will make it through the next few days.

At the end of the day Annie and I walk home to Jamhuri where we meet our new housemaid, Virginia. She is a friend of Alice's who will now be staying with us to replace Lucy. Virginia is forty five years old and has three children who live out of the city. She only speaks Swahili. She will work and sleep at Alice's during the week and has Sunday off to travel home to see her family. Tonight is Christine's last night with us before flying home to Sydney, so we enjoy another special family dinner together. Virginia has been busy preparing some French fries, scrubbing, peeling and cutting potatoes in the kitchen for over an hour, which she serves with some vegetables and beans. It's a great dinner and as always I feel spoiled to be fed so well. Virginia brings out the thermos filled with the warm sweet chai after dinner which we all share before bedtime.

Chapter 45 – Walking around

Don't walk behind me; I may not lead. Don't walk in front of me; I may not follow. Just walk beside me and be my friend – Albert Camus

Evelyn's women's group, Harvest, is meeting today and Annie and I are off to pay them a visit in Dagoretti. We arrive at Evelyn's house and when we walk in it's full of many familiar faces who are all excited to see us, as we are them. Today I see Natalya in the group of women. It really is great to see her interacting and finding her place with the other women in her community. The group seems to have been organising itself well. They have a secretary to take notes in their meetings and a treasurer calculating the money that is required for their projects. These women are inspiring in the way they come together to try and make a difference for themselves and for others in the community. At the same time, it is heartbreaking to listen to their stories and to realise how difficult life is for them living in these slums.

One lady, Nadia, describes the days when she has to go home at the end of the day with no money and tell her children there is no money for food that night. It's so important that we're here at this women's support group, to listen to these women's stories and dreams. They need to be heard and shared.

We follow our stop at Evelyn's with a long walk into Ngando to visit Rose. Annie and I are accompanied by Joanne and Carly, a new volunteer from California who has started work at the clinic with us. When we arrive at Rose's place we let ourselves in. Knowing how fragile her condition has been, I'm very aware of the possibility that Rose may no longer be there as we walk inside her tiny timber shack. I'm relieved to see Rose lying on the bed and breathing but she is still in severe pain and clutching the side of her abdomen. Annie and I try to make Rose drink something, and she manages a little before turning her head and refusing once again. The food, fluids and medications that she has been refusing are starting to make her delirious and psychologically affected. We stay by her side for some time before finally heading back to the clinic to report back to George. Rose's condition is not looking good at all and he says he wants to return later to insert an IV line to give her some much needed fluids.

Carly and I then set out on a walk through Dagoretti towards Gatina to see how Helen is doing. Already, Carly is noticing just how much walking we do each day as well as how much of our time is spent outside in the community around the slums. This is where the work is.

We find Helen doing alright when we arrive, but she has been very tired from the last few days of drugs. Since the weekend George has managed to resolve the problem with the community nurse who is now visiting daily to administer Helen's injections. Today Helen asks Carly and I if we could bathe her. It's the simple activities like these that somebody like Helen is also deprived of in her situation. We take some of the plastic buckets and warm up some water over the gas to give her a sponge bath. We can see the difference this makes to her. She tells us it has been about two weeks since her last bath. It really picks her up.

I notice that the plastic chair we use to sit Helen on outside has been tied up to her ceiling with rope, out of reach. When I ask Helen why the chair has been taken away, she tells me Jane did it. Jane is Helen's sister who lives and stays with her but we have never met her. She is always away working during the day. Until recently I had no idea that they had another family member in Nairobi. Helen and Kevin had never spoken of her because they do not get along. Helen explains that Jane punishes her and Kevin for being sick with AIDS. She earns an income but keeps everything and just cooks for herself. Jane has deliberately tied up the chairs so that Helen can no longer walk outside and sit in the sun by the avocado tree. She prefers her to stay locked up inside and miserable with her illness.

I am furious to learn that she has done this. Jane lives with them and yet every day we find Helen alone having not eaten and lacking family support. It's another challenge in the growing list of problems faced in this community.

Chapter 46 – Hospital

Life is pleasant. Death is peaceful. It's the transition that's troublesome. – Isaac Asimov

I've packed my bag this morning ready to return for a long weekend in Masailand. I'm so excited to return to this rural part of Kenya that I fell in love with while staying with Veronica's Masai family just a few weeks earlier.

It's an early start. First I head into Ngando clinic to visit Rose. We've become quite concerned at the clinic about her deteriorating health. George phoned Annie and me last night to say he was unable to insert an IV drip into her veins when he went to visit her later in the afternoon. He has asked us to check on her again first thing this morning.

Annie and I walk into the dark and sombre interior of Rose's place and once again we find her alone lying on the bed. Her condition and her pain are worsening and Rose seems to be more and more distressed. She is now too weak to drink from her bottle with a straw, and this leaves Annie and me wondering what to do next. It really is third world medicine with no access to modern equipment or most medicines. We walk to Sister Veronica's convent where our Ngando clinic is usually held. There is a dispensary there where we hope we will find some syringes that we can try and feed Rose by hand with. We see Sister Veronica who is aware of Rose's situation and is certain we will have to drive Rose back into the hospital today based on our reports. She shows us into the dispensary and we take a small number of supplies before walking back through the slums to Rose's.

Annie and I do our best to feed Rose some water directly into her mouth using the syringes. It is hard to know how much she is actually consuming as she is not voluntarily swallowing. I take a moment to take in everything around me in this desperate situation: the fleas all around us, the impoverished matchbox shack, the dirty mattress where Rose's skeletal body is curled up, and her eyes empty with defeat. These are the rawest and most difficult moments of our work.

Annie holds the water-filled syringe to Rose's mouth. We stay by Rose's side for a little longer, sitting in silence and feeling rather helpless about what else we can do to help her. Annie reaches out again to help rub Rose's abdomen, but this time it doesn't provide any relief, making her wince weakly with what little energy she has left. We ask Rose where her pain is. '*Wapi?*' It's everywhere. Her body is so frail, each rib is protruding from her chest and her hip bones form a concave surface with her flattened abdomen. She has not eaten in days. Sister Veronica suddenly arrives to see how we're going with the syringe feeding and checks on Rose, a long time patient at AMKA. She is shocked by her condition and deeply concerned for Rose. Sister Veronica insists we transport Rose immediately back to the hospital since she is refusing to help herself and we can't do much more. Rose is dying.

The task of transporting somebody to a clinic or hospital is extremely difficult in the slums. Without a car the only option is taking a taxi which many people cannot afford. And transferring an ill person without a wheelchair or stretcher often means carrying them in your arms, slumping them over a bicycle or using whatever other objects are around. It is sadly for this reason that many people in poor health pass away in their homes.

Fortunately for Rose, Sister Veronica has a car which she drives in as closely as she can to Rose's place. All these tiny shacks that are closely built together are often without direct access, so the closest she can park is around the side of the path to Rose's place. Sister Veronica has called Rose's younger brother Francis to explain Rose's situation and to inform him that we're taking her into the hospital. Another of our community health workers, Millicent, has also arrived at the house to help. When Francis arrives he helps to lift Rose with Sister Veronica and Annie supporting her on either side, and they carry her fragile body out of the shack towards the car. Although she is emaciated and weak, her body's weight is still difficult to carry as she is completely unable to help herself. I watch on in horror as Rose's body starts to sink towards the ground as they struggle to carry her out of her home.

As they come out the front door Rose's head catches on a part of the timber sheet door, which scrapes her forehead and she yells out in pain. It is just awful to witness. How much simpler things would be with a wheelchair right now. The team manages to push Rose's body into the car and I stand on the opposite side of the car helping lay her across the back seat. It is a real struggle and particularly traumatic for somebody like Rose whose state is already critical. Sister Veronica, Annie and Millicent accompany Rose to the hospital with her brother Francis who sits next to Rose on the back seat. I know how long the process is to admit somebody into the hospitals here, it can take hours to complete the forms and pay the fees before a bed is provided. I can only hope it goes quickly for Rose today.

I stay behind as our Gatina clinic is currently taking place and I have to take a matatu to go and help out the rest of our team there. When I arrive, I report back to George about Rose and the decision to take her into the hospital. He tells me it's also been a very busy morning at the clinic in Gatina and I catch up on some of the information concerning our patients. I pay Helen a quick visit in her home and she seems to be doing alright today. She's eaten the lunch that Kevin prepared her before going to school. I then return to the clinic where we finally break and take lunch at our regular Fair Deal cafe. What a morning it's been!

After lunch I farewell my colleagues who wish me a safe journey, *safari njema*. I head out to take the bus to Ngong for my weekend in Masailand. I once again have to learn to leave my work behind in Nairobi, which is not easy given the intensity of the work we've had going on lately. But I'm picked up by the thought of arriving in Masailand and rediscovering this incredible place and its people.

Chapter 47 – The Ngong Hills

I sit in the back of a pick-up truck with a dozen other people, the wind running against my face, the dusty roads around me and the approaching view of the beautiful Ngong hills. I know that I'm back in Masailand. I love every aspect of the countryside here. Crouching in the back of a pick-up truck, our local taxi, is a new experience. And it is these new experiences, completely out of my comfort zone, that I am coming to love about this part of Kenya.

I'm travelling back to Veronica's house with Maggie and Samuel, who have met me in Ngong and are excited to have a visitor for the weekend. It's a special weekend here in Masailand. The next four days are the annual Masai show. Since my last visit to Veronica's house a few weeks earlier, it's all everybody has been talking about. The show will involve traditional singing, dancing, performances, jewellery displays and so much more. It is a showcase of the Masai culture and the perfect opportunity for me to learn more about his fascinating tribe.

I meet Veronica at her house. Her children, Tony and Priscilla, have just returned from school and come out to greet me. I'm overwhelmed by their welcome and so excited to be back staying with their family. Veronica immediately puts me to work, helping to peel the potatoes for dinner. We catch up on the last few weeks and I tell her how I've been extremely busy at the clinic with patients.

Veronica is very open-minded and speaks honestly about the problems with HIV in the Masai tribe. The practice of polygamy and lack of sex education considerably increases the potential spread of HIV in these communities. Interestingly, there is a much lower incidence of HIV and AIDS recorded in these rural Masai communities compared with other tribal groups and especially urbanised areas such as Nairobi. Despite being polygamous, the Masai people have traditionally married exclusively within their own tribe, making them an endogamous ethnic group and potentially less exposed to HIV. However many cases do exist and once infiltrated into the tribe the virus has the potential to spread rapidly. Centres have been established in the rural towns to implement educational programs about the prevention and transmission of HIV. These are particularly targeted at the young generation of Masai children and adolescents who are nowadays better educated and starting to break away from some of the more traditional Masai customs.

Veronica then opens up to me about the practice of female circumcision in the Masai tribe. It's a topic that I'm interested to learn more about and commonly referred to as female genital mutilation in the outside world. Traditionally, Masai girls are circumcised at the age of puberty in a ritual that symbolises their coming of age. It represents their becoming as a woman and prepares them for marriage. In the Masai tribe female circumcision usually involves a clitorectomy. The procedure is performed by an older Masai woman and is done using a sharp blade (or knife, or piece of glass) with no painkillers and in unsanitary conditions. The girl must remain silent as it is considered a sign of weakness to cry out in pain.

Veronica tells me that she was circumcised when she was a young girl and that her daughter Priscilla will also be circumcised next year. I'm really surprised to hear this. Veronica is well educated and more western in her thinking about many of the traditional Masai practices. She tells me that she is against female circumcision, that it violates a woman's rights and is not a safe procedure. There are serious risks of infections and even death, as well as long term complications from the procedure affecting urination, sexual activity, childbirth and HIV transmission. However it is Veronica's husband's decision to have Priscilla circumcised. Veronica says she has no choice but to respect the Masai man, especially her husband's decision. Female circumcision is illegal in Kenya. However, as a deeply ingrained practice in the Masai culture, it continues to be performed within many communities.

It is late into the evening in Masailand by the time dinner has been prepared and Veronica, Priscilla, Tony, Maggie, Adrian, Renee and I sit around the table in the living room and share our meal of ugali, cabbage and potatoes. It's an incredible feeling to be living amongst a big family of Masais and volunteers, and to share simple activities such as conversation and eating dinner by candlelight together. It's even more special without certain aspects of city life, where such things as busy lifestyles and technology can get in the way of these precious moments together. We're joined by the two Samuels who have come to visit the family and to organise our plans for tomorrow. Tomorrow is the opening day of the Masai show and tonight Veronica's place is filled with excitement and anticipation for what the next few days will hold.

Chapter 48 – Traditions

Culture is the widening of the mind and of the spirit
– Jawaharlal Nehru

The sound of a baby crying and the radio playing loudly wake me up at the crack of dawn on this glorious morning in Masailand. Maggie and I have our breakfast of chai and a small sweet cake together before getting ready and going to the first day of the show. Given the effort it takes to walk down to the dam to fill up the big jerry cans of water and to cart them all the way back to Veronica's, we don't shower every day. This morning we happily go without.

The two Samuels arrive to collect Maggie, Adrian, Renee and me early in the morning. As true Masai they are always up well before sunrise and are out walking through the long open fields of Masailand. They come in to greet Veronica who is feeding her baby Purity. The Samuels are excited and ready to show us the way. Priscilla joins us after finishing her morning chores and together we all set off on our walk towards Priscilla's school which will be the grounds for the weekend show. She makes this same journey by foot to and from the school every day.

It's about an hour's walk each way. We don't pass a single person or house between Veronica's place and the school. The countryside is amazing as we walk along the dirt track together, one after the other in single file, under the bright blue African sky. The environment around us is in its most natural form, with sporadic acacia trees and aloe vera plants in this otherwise empty and grand savannah. The beautiful Ngong hills seem to follow us in the background, our constant guide and protector. I'm amazed by the Masai's natural sense of direction, knowing well that I would have been easily lost by now on my own in this vast open space. Samuel stops to pull out a piece of long grass that he starts to chew, informing me it is what the Masai use to brush their teeth. At one point we spot a giraffe not too far away from our path. This environment is incredible and I am constantly taking in things I'd never expected to see.

Eventually we arrive at the school. There are already a large group of locals who appear to have come from all around for this event. Many must have walked for hours to get here. Most of the other people I see are Masais, dressed beautifully in their traditional tribal clothing and colourful jewellery. Their stunning appearance and customs never cease to amaze me and I'm in awe looking around at all the local tribal people in their home environment. Maggie and I follow our guides, the two Samuels, who stop and introduce us to many of their friends. We greet them all politely remembering, 'Supai' and 'Ipa' and bowing our heads in respect to the Masai elders.

There are gatherings of Masai women setting up their stalls to sell their food for the day and the odours drifting over smell great. There are other women including Veronica, who I can see has arrived with Purity strapped to her back, who are selling their colourful collections of handmade Masai jewellery. Some of the women are accompanied by donkeys that have been used to carry their supplies for the day. In the distance there are some traditional Masai huts, the manyatta, that have been built especially for the show. There is just so much to see I don't know where to start!

On a nearby dusty football field a large group of school children are playing a soccer match. Maggie and I stand on the side lines of the field with all the excited supporters, and watch her school team play against another local school. Everybody is so involved in the match. The players' classmates are dancing on the side lines, watching every move and cheering their teammates on. The atmosphere is incredible.

As lunch time approaches, Maggie and I find ourselves in an interesting situation. We are invited by a Masai man to see a goat being slaughtered under a tree at the show. Just to the side of the football field, not even hidden, a man stands with his goat in one hand and a machete in the other. He reaches out to me with the machete offering me the opportunity to do the slaughtering myself. I politely refuse despite his encouragement. He wastes no time in slashing the goat's neck and holding a small bucket to collect the blood, which is kept to make a traditional Masai soup. The goat is left to die slowly. The man skins it and butchers its body for meat. Despite standing at a distance, Maggie notices that she's managed to catch a splash of blood on her trousers. Yet another first time experience in Kenya.

But it seems like these experiences just keep on coming in Masailand. While sitting down on the ground and watching the football match, we suddenly hear shouting. A few Masai men come running towards us, chasing a couple of their donkeys that have tried to run off and nearly run us down in the process. We manage to quickly scramble out of the way in another close escape!

The highlight of the day is the traditional singing and dancing performed by the school children in the afternoon. They have been rehearsing these performances for weeks and are dressed proudly in their traditional Masai clothing and jewellery. Priscilla is performing with her class and I see her all dressed up. She looks radiant and beautiful. Like all of Veronica's children and the two Samuels, Priscilla is usually dressed in casual clothes such as skirts and shirts, and the boys in street wear and proper shoes. This is the case for many of the children in the younger Masai generation. In many parts it has been forbidden to wear traditional clothing and jewellery to school. This has been in an effort to outlaw some ongoing customs that are still practised in Masailand, such as female and male circumcision.

Today Priscilla looks like a mature young Masai woman. Her group performs the fertility dance which is traditionally performed with the medicine man when a woman cannot fall pregnant. The young girls move their bodies about effortlessly, with their necks bobbing backwards and forwards and their legs dancing to a constant rhythm as they rotate around in a circular pattern on the dirt stage before us. Their voices are in pure harmony.

The girls are followed by the young Masai men. They are dressed in the traditional red Masai robes, with bare feet and each one of them carries a wooden stick. The men, unlike the women, do not sing. Instead they make a fascinating sound from their throats. They bob their heads up and down and jump vertically in rhythm with the music. These young boys instantly resemble Masai warriors as they chant and move about before us. In addition to the group dances and songs, children recite poems before the panel of judges and the many onlookers who have travelled to attend this Masai show. It means so much to them to be involved in this event and the judges award them their final places in the competition.

I see my first *moran*. A moran is a Masai warrior. It is a young Masai who has been through the traditional ritual of male circumcision that is a part in their transition into a warrior. This procedure, like that of female circumcision, is carried out using a sharp knife and no anaesthetic and is performed by a tribal elder.

The boys are usually at the age of fifteen when they are circumcised in a big ceremony, which can take several months of recovery. These young Masais usually spend several years in isolation and training where they learn about their culture and their roles in their tribe. Today this moran is identified by his unique headpiece which is worn in addition to the traditional red robe and Masai jewellery. The moran is young, in his twenties, and he walks around the show grounds with confidence and is treated with much respect. I see several visitors at the show approach him to ask for a photo of the tribal warrior but he declines. The opportunity to observe this Masai warrior is extraordinary.

It's an amazing and long day in the sun at the show and all the excitement of seeing and experiencing the Masai culture takes its toll. Maggie, Adrian, Renee, Priscilla, the two Samuels and I walk home along the same long path through the savannah. We finally make it back, exhausted and satisfied from the show's first day's activities. In addition to feeling tired, my stomach starts to feel uneasy, a sensation that I have become familiar with since being in Kenya. Out here in the country, the food and water is a lot different to being in the city. It could be the chai tea made from fresh cow's milk, our lunch at the show today or simply the lack of hygiene in never having water to properly wash our hands, or a combination of these factors that does not agree with a city girl's body! The night proves to be a long one of getting up and creeping outside of the house and up the pitch black path to the isolated pit toilet, with my flashlight in one hand and toilet paper in the other. At one point I stumble over a stray dog which frightens the life out of me, and probably him too.

I wake up feeling better and take a walk with Priscilla to the dam to fetch some water. It's about a 20 minute walk from the house. When we get there, the small sized dam is surprisingly full of water. Until recently this dam has been completely empty. Kenya is extremely prone to severe droughts and Masailand has been one of the worst affected areas. A lack of water leads to a lack of food and famine, which has recently affected many of these communities. Veronica has a back-up water pump at her house that she uses to pump water when the dam is empty, but even this only lasts so long. Just before my arrival in Kenya our volunteer organisation GVN ran a special program to address the severe drought. This involved many of the volunteers helping out with a special food drop to the worst affected areas. It helped ease an otherwise desperate situation.

As we walk down to the dam, I try to follow Priscilla's technique of rinsing out the jerry cans before filling them up again. But I struggle with even this part of the process as I seem to collect more sediment than water in the jerry can. Priscilla helps and teaches me the method for collecting the water. Once we've filled the cans, I carry the smaller five litre container on my back, walking behind young Priscilla and her 20 litre jerry can that she slings over her back, and straps the rope around her forehead, making it easier to carry. She's a true Masai woman. I have no idea how she does it. She laughs when she shows me how women can even carry the jerry cans on their heads. I don't even bother trying that one, sparing myself the embarrassment.

Once Priscilla and I return to Veronica's with our refilled jerry cans, we get ourselves ready and set off on the walk for the second day of the show. Samuel says he's taking us on a shortcut to the show today, and after my experience with shortcuts on my home visits around Nairobi, I'm sceptical about what this means. And rightfully so as it turns out the short cut through the bushes and off the beaten track is over an hour and a half walk into the school, even longer than the previous day. And we all make an effort to point this out to Samuel, our Masai guide! But the experience is none the less fascinating. I just continue to take in the beauty of this place.

At the show today there are many different sports taking place including football, volleyball and netball. Many of the Masai women from yesterday are here again with their stands set up next to each other, under the acacia trees, displaying all their handmade jewellery and decorations. I walk by the stalls to admire all of their work and meet some of Samuel's and Maggie's friends from the local community.

After lunch a group of volunteers organise a volleyball game between the mzungus and a local team. It's a friendly competition that attracts a lot of interest. I've decided to watch and cheer on Maggie and Adrian who've chosen to participate in the mzungu team. More and more people come and stop by to see what is going on. The friendly rivalry seems to be heating up between the two teams. Eventually the mzungus are forced to give in to the stronger Masai team, much to the Masai's delight! The soccer finals also finish today, with the hundreds of supporters running around the dusty football field under the glorious setting of the Ngong hills, singing and dancing as they celebrate their victory.

Once the festivities end, Adrian, Renee and I walk back home to Veronica's. We walk part of the way before deciding to try hitching a ride as we're feeling worn out from the heat and the day's activities. We don't seem to have any problem hailing a passing truck that is travelling along the dirt road. The driver is a young friendly man who welcomes us onboard. We squeeze into his lorry, with Renee sitting next to the driver and then me having to sit on Adrian's lap to fit into the last remaining space. The driver says he recognises us from the volleyball match at the show. The people around here are so friendly and trustworthy. He's delighted to give the few mzungus in Masailand a lift back to Veronica's, and is even more excited when we leave him a few of our energy bars from our bags that he'd tried to negotiate from us along the way. So we exchange the goods for the ride. It's a fun journey back and yet another first time experience hitching a ride in outback Africa.

That night, I receive a text message on my phone from Annie. She has written to say that Rose passed away last night at the hospital. It is so sad to receive this news. I can only think of poor Rose. She was in so much pain and seemed to have lost her desire to live. In our work we do everything we can but sometimes it is not enough. That is the reality of the fight against HIV and AIDS.

I step outside of Veronica's house into the darkness of the night and look up at the sky. It is painted with an abundance of brightly shining stars, incredibly beautiful and peaceful. I say a prayer for Rose hoping she's in a better place.

Chapter 49 – Branding

You know you are truly alive when you're living among lions
- Karen Blixen

It's my last day in Masailand before I have to take the afternoon bus back to Nairobi. The day starts out perfectly as I wake up and spot a giraffe from the front door of Veronica's house. I hear young Tony calling out, 'Giraffes, giraffes, bring camera!' to us mzungus, knowing how much we all like to see them. But there is no time for the camera, as I step outside the house to see three giraffes standing peacefully not far from the house! It is beautiful and I couldn't ask for a better start to the day out here in Masailand. There is no comparison between seeing these animals in a zoo or safari park to this experience of stepping outside the front door to find a giraffe right there in our backyard that is Kenya.

After breakfast, Maggie, Adrian, Renee and I set out on a walk to visit another volunteer staying in Masailand. Adam is staying with a Masai lady named Beryl and her family. Her place is about a thirty minute walk from Veronica's house. Beryl's house is similar to Veronica's, made of timber sheets with multiple rooms and furnished inside. She even has a small garden with some vegetables growing out the back. Next to her house Beryl has a traditional manyatta where Adam has been living the complete Masai experience.

We take a look inside the manyatta. There is a bed made of a lattice of sticks with a cow's hide laid out over the top. There is a small window letting in some light, but otherwise the manyatta is dark and dusty. Whereas usually the manyatta sleeps a whole family, Adam is lucky enough to have this space to himself.

Today a special Masai ritual has been organised at Beryl's place where volunteers Adam and Adrian will be 'branded' in a traditional ceremony performed by Masai warriors. This will involve having permanent marks burnt onto their shoulders, which identify the Masai tribe and is usually performed in a large important ceremony.

The branding initiation ceremony starts when Beryl's father Joseph arrives dressed traditionally in his red robe and wearing some jewellery in his stretched earlobes. As a respected Masai elder he is in charge of the proceedings. The boys are looking rather nervous about their decision to participate in this tradition. We go outside where Joseph spends some time looking around for appropriate tree branches that will be used to brand several small circular marks onto the skin on the upper arm.

He collects the branches and then sits down on a rock and starts to shape them with his machete. Another Masai elder arrives to assist him. Together they crouch down next to each other and rub the sticks together to produce some friction. It doesn't happen straight away but before long they have produced enough heat for a small fire and to light the stick for the branding. Adam chooses to go first. Sitting down next to the Masai elders they use the burning stick to mark six small circles onto his right shoulder in a triangular pattern. Despite our concerns Adam says it is not as painful as expected. Joseph then applies some aloe vera leaves from Beryl's garden onto the arm as a natural medicine to prevent infection. Many of the Masai elders are also herbal doctors, knowing the uses for many of the different plants found in their environment.

Following Adam and Adrian's Masai branding, we're all kindly invited to have lunch at Beryl's. She has prepared a delicious meal of chapatti and beans. For dessert she has some fresh pineapple and then also offers us some sour cow's milk, which has been stored and fermented in a traditional Masai wooden flask. Adam with his willingness to try anything Masai, tries some. Beryl then presents us all with some Masai jewellery to take home. She gives me a wedding tiara made of bright blue, red, yellow and white coloured beads and some matching earrings which is extremely generous.

Maggie, Renee, Adrian, Adam and I are then lead by Beryl's eldest son Joseph into a separate part of the house where he lives. He shows us where he stays, which Adam has labelled Joseph's bachelor pad in Masailand. He has decorated the interior of the room with posters of international pop and R&B musicians and the most remarkably installed sound system. We're out in the middle of Masailand in rural Kenya where there is no electricity or running water, and yet Joseph has the most sophisticated sound system in his bedroom. It's a solar panel setup that generates electricity which feeds back through a big car battery that then passes through the CD player and then through his speakers. Where there is a will there is a way!

I ask Joseph, the resident DJ, to choose a song for us to listen to. After a little bit of fiddling around, 2Pac's Changes eventually comes through his speakers in excellent quality. I sit happily listening to one of my favourite songs with an amazing group of people in this environment that is always full of surprises.

Eventually we have to go back to Veronica's place where I pack up my bag and wait for the car that is taking me back to Ngong. In usual fashion I wait another hour before the taxi arrives. Veronica and her family present me with a farewell gift of some Masai jewellery which is so kind of them and characteristic of their tribe's generosity. I really feel like a part of their close family and promise to return again soon. As the taxi drives me away from the house I look out the window at the Ngong hills, appreciating every small detail of this amazing place.

Chapter 50 - Water and Roses
We never know the worth of water till the well is dry - Thomas Fuller

I'm refreshed to return to work after my time away in Masailand. As always there is work that awaits me on my return to Nairobi. I've caught up with Annie on the weekend's events and the sad passing away of Rose. Annie spent all of the weekend by Rose's side at the hospital. She has a very special touch in caring for the terminally ill and I'm sure she made Rose's spiritual journey as comfortable as possible. These cases we're faced with require such strength and can be emotionally challenging to go through, and I can see how it has affected Annie. Despite this we are ready to head into the clinic to regroup with our colleagues and to continue helping the many others in need.

Annie and I spend the morning with Eunice. She is a community health worker whom we have started to work with to implement a project we've been designing for the community. Having fundraised some money before coming to Kenya, I've been considering how best I can put this money to use in my work here. At the forefront of my mind are the women at Evelyn's women's group, Harvest. I'm passionate about helping the people in the slums who have become my friends and Annie and I have sat down to discuss the possibility of installing a water tank in the Dagoretti Corner community. There is currently no water tank in this large slum. The locals travel daily by foot or by bike to the next slum to collect water, *maji*, from a big tank where it is sold. They usually pay about 5ksh to fill a big 20 litre jerry can.

Water is one of the basic and most important elements for staying healthy. Our project of installing a large community water tank incorporates a small business project where we hope to employ locals to look after and manage the project. It will be a self-sustainable project that will provide resources as well as employment in the community. Sister Veronica has recommended we work alongside Eunice who has the experience and local knowledge to help our project, and today we've prepared a list of questions to ask her. We meet in Dagoretti and take a walk around together, surveying the area for a good and viable location as well as getting some quotes on prices. It's an exciting prospect to think that this project might work to benefit the community.

We take lunch back at the clinic with the usual Tuesday crew: George, Oloo, Solphine, Eunice, Margaret, Immaculate, Annie and me. After the weekend I'm still cautious about what I eat and drink and today I find myself having to explain to everybody at least several times over lunch why I am not drinking chai. In Kenya nobody ever refuses food or tea and despite explaining myself, my colleagues just don't understand why I don't want to drink chai with them today!

After lunch Annie and I take the shortcut through to Gatina to visit Helen. She is doing well and we give her a massage and some stretches to exercise her legs. She has still been receiving her daily injections from the community nurse as arranged. Helen passes us a note that Kevin has written us. Now that he is in school we don't see each other anymore. I miss seeing my African brother. He's written to say hello and that he misses us, and he thanks us for coming to visit his mother. While Annie gives Helen her massage, I write Kevin a short note that we leave with Helen. It's special to have this contact with him.

Annie has brought a big bag of soft toys with her that was donated by friends in Australia. She has chosen to distribute them to the young children we see outside Helen's house every time we visit. Between 4 and 7 years old, they are always playing games out the front, running around, or peeping through the window to see what the mzungus are up to with Helen. Today Annie empties her bag and the children come running from everywhere, full of excitement as she hands out the toys. Helen, lying in her bed, holds one of the plush ponies saying she wants one for herself. We give her the pony to keep which makes her light up in a way we haven't seen for a long time. The children stand around with the biggest smiles, showing their toothless grins, as they cling to their new bright and clean toys against their dirty school clothes.

When I arrive home at Alice's in the evening, I feel excited at the thought of my plans for tomorrow, which will be my twenty-fourth birthday. I'm thrilled to spend this day in Kenya with my Kenyan family and friends. Even if birthdays are not a big celebration here I feel like it's a special day for me and I'm looking forward to it. I pass Leon out the front of his apartment. I haven't seen him for some time. He's busy with his studies and making friends in Nairobi. He's still, as always, interested in our household of volunteers and the different people he sees coming and going. I update Leon on the current living situation and activities.

Virginia makes us an amazing dinner at home: chapatti, beans and cabbage. When Annie comes home she is carrying a big bunch of pink roses which she has kindly bought for me. They're a beautiful surprise and I have no idea where she had to go to find these in Nairobi! After looking around the apartment for something resembling a vase, we end up settling on an old water bottle, cutting the top off, and placing the flowers inside. They look amazing and I can't wait for tomorrow!

Belinda Evans

Chapter 51- African Birthday Girl
May you live all the days of your life – Jonathan Swift

21st June 2006 – Nairobi, Kenya

I wake up with excitement and anticipation for the day ahead. Spending my birthday in Kenya is not about receiving gifts or special attention, it's an opportunity to stop and reflect on what I've accomplished so far and all of the amazing people I have around me to spend this day with. And it's also a time when I know I'll be speaking with my family and friends back home and I am especially excited at the thought of this. Annie surprises me again in the morning with a gift she's so generously bought and even wrapped for me. Again, I can see she's gone to an effort to find wrapping paper in Nairobi. I open it up to find a book all about the Masai people, as she knows how fascinated I am with this African tribe.

Going with the theme of an African birthday, I've decided to go to work in a traditional kanga and make more of an effort to look like an African woman. So for today the boots and the jeans have been put aside as I find some matching earrings and ask Virginia to help me fasten my kanga, still petrified that I will lose it halfway between home and the clinic. That would do nothing to help my transition into living like a local!

I take the matatu into Ngando clinic where I meet up with George, Oloo, Solphine and Joanne. They notice my kanga straight away and point out how I look like a real 'African Australian woman'. George insists that I should wear a kanga everyday from now on. Joanne, Solphine and I set out on a few home visit this morning to see some patients. This becomes a new challenge, walking through the knee high grass, mud and puddles of sewage in my kanga skirt and flip flops. I joke with Joanne about how nice this is of her to take us through these particular parts of the slums today, of all days! As always the others laugh and rejoice in my struggle of getting by in their home environment.

Back at the clinic for lunch, we set the table with the chai, bread and butter when Annie surprises us all and walks in with a big white box. Inside, she reveals a beautiful birthday cake with

'Happy Birthday Belinda' written in pink on top of the white icing. The others are just as excited as I am to have a cake brought in to share. It turns out that Annie has spent the whole morning on a three hour mission to collect this cake, which a friend of Alice's has made. Annie has made such an effort to ensure my African birthday is a special one. And it is nothing short of it.

Everybody sings happy birthday to me, which is followed by, 'How old are you now... how old are you now'... then they all proceed to chant, 'cutta cutta cutta' while clapping their hands in unison. I have never heard this custom before which Joanne tells me signifies the cutting of the cake. Sister Veronica cuts the first piece of cake and in keeping with tradition she has to feed it to me. The sponge cake is delicious and we share it around the table. Something so simple and out of routine has created an atmosphere of excitement and celebration, which is much needed and brings us all together.

In the afternoon I walk into Kibera to visit my friends whom I have not seen recently. At Ushirika, I am warmly greeted by Anna and Ruth, who ask me to do a twirl in my kanga so they can admire my skirt. I see Daniel, Judson and David, and it's so nice to catch up with them. As always we stand outside in the yard chatting with the sounds of the World Music shop in the background. Peter comes in to see us and says he has a present for me. He hands me a beautiful necklace that has been handmade and wrapped in tissue. I'm overwhelmed by the generosity of all of my friends. It's incredibly thoughtful coming from somebody who doesn't have a lot to give. I cherish these gifts so much.

I've organised to go out to an African restaurant for my birthday dinner, one which Alice has chosen for us. As we all get ready at home we share around the limited clothing and jewellery we have. Katie, Annie, Alice and I all sit down on the couch and Virginia attempts to take a photo of all of us with one of our digital cameras. Virginia has never used one before and it turns out to be quite a challenge. We laugh in hysterics as she rotates the camera around and back and forth. After finding the button she has to push and taking a few photos of herself, she eventually listens to Alice's directions in Swahili and gets a lovely one of the four of us before we go to dinner.

We board a matatu that takes us into the city where Alice leads us to the restaurant. In true African style, she insists the walk is not far as we continue on a 30 minute walk from the bus stop up a dark isolated path until we arrive at the restaurant. It is more of a pub with a few televisions inside broadcasting the World Cup, and enclosed inside the same restaurant is a butcher. Typically Kenyan! It's not the African restaurant we had imagined with live singing and dancing, as we listen to old American pop songs being played. But that doesn't matter at all; this is Africa and you never know what you're going to get which is what I love so much.

Irene joins us for dinner with a new volunteer Sarah from Texas who will be coming to stay with us at Alice's from tonight. I've also invited George who arrives with a friend of his, Duncan. For dinner we order some roast chicken, potatoes and spinach which is shared around the table. Alice and I indulge in a glass of red wine, my first since arriving in Nairobi over two months ago now. After dinner the others go home and Annie and I stay on with George and Duncan. I finally give into George's persistent invitation to dance, and we all head over to the empty dance floor, which is light up by a shiny silver disco ball, and we all dance the night away.

The time comes when we're all ready to go home. George, Duncan, Annie and I take a taxi together and Annie and I get dropped off first in Jamhuri at Alice's. I've had an incredible day at the clinic and night out with my friends. I receive a call on the way home in the taxi from my close friend Zoe, who is in Rome on her round-the-world trip. I'm taken back to where I was this time last year on my birthday, which was also in Rome. I had a picnic lunch by myself on the lawn near the coliseum and pasta carbonara for dinner near Piazza Navona, followed by a walk to The Spanish Steps and some gelati. That seems like a world away, another life even. I feel so at home in Kenya and tonight am surrounded by the many great people I've met here.

Chapter 52 – Making music

I wake up the next morning still filled with excitement from the night before. The day starts off well with a serving of Virginia's pancakes for breakfast and a warm mug of chai tea. One of my all time favourite breakfasts. Today my kanga has been put back in my drawer and I'm once again dressed in my jeans, shirt and hiking boots. It's back to work.

With my bag packed and boots laced up, I step outside of Alice's with Annie and we walk through Jamhuri towards the bus stop on Ngong road to take the matatu to Gatina. As we're sitting squashed up together in the noisy matatu, I hear the driver shout out to us, 'Seat belt check!' Annie and I look at each other and say we're not going to fall for that one again, knowing with certainty it's a scam to try and get into our bags. With no sign of a police check up ahead, we stay in our seats with our bags held closely in and are proud to have become such experienced matatu travellers and not to fall for the hoax. Eventually our stop comes up, I tap twice on the roof to signal our stop and we jump out of the moving matatu just in time as it pulls back out onto the road. Phew, another safe journey into work. We walk up the long path that leads into our Gatina clinic ready to get to work.

Annie and I visit Helen during the morning clinic. Once again we find that she has not eaten today. She looks weak and helpless lying on the bed on her own. The situation is frustrating for us to see, as we know that she receives food provisions through the clinic's program and that Helen's sister Jane is boarding with them. But Helen explains to us that Jane only cooks for herself, leaving nothing for Helen to take during the day until Kevin returns from school in the evenings. Jane does not wish to take care of Helen. It is so difficult to witness this, especially since we've become so close to Helen and Kevin over these past months. While Annie gives Helen some stretches and massages to her legs and arms, I wander into the slums to find a nearby shop to get something for Helen to eat. I find a lady selling chapattis for 10ksh and take one in a small plastic bag as well as some bananas.

Back at the clinic I spend some time sitting outside talking with the patients. I've formed some nice friendships and have become accustomed to seeing many of these patients every Thursday when our clinic comes to Gatina. As I sit outside on the bench, one of our patients Janet, whom I met and visited in her home two weeks ago arrives and hands me an envelope with my name on the front. She has been having difficulties meeting her rent and supporting her three children and newly born grandchild. I open the envelope. It's a letter stating that the rent for this property is now almost 10 weeks overdue and that *Belinda* is required to pay the 2800ksh on behalf of this tenant immediately'! Janet has seemingly given my name to her landlord who has now redirected her debt on her rent to me. I look at Janet and explain that I cannot help her with her rent payment. I explain that we can sit down together and look into ways that we might be able to support her with food assistance, school sponsorship or a small business support, but our clinic's programs unfortunately do not extent to covering patients' rent difficulties. I've already checked with Oloo and Solphine about this and the AMKA project just doesn't have the capacity to help out in this way.

    I really wish I could help Janet and all of our other patients who've approached me with similar financial problems. Janet says that the landlord has threatened to throw them out by the end of the week. They have nowhere else to go and no means of paying. Situations like these are so difficult. How can I ignore her problems that are so serious? And yet what can I do to help her? She has come to me with this letter in search of help. I agree to discuss her situation with Sister Veronica and the others to see what can be done.

    While I have been talking with Janet and some other patients this morning, Oloo and Annie have been finishing up the food distribution in the shelter next to the clinic. As it approaches lunch time, we close up the clinic and head around to Moses at Fair Deal cafe for our regular lunch together. I present Janet's situation to the others who know of her case. George suggests I work on making Janet a candidate for the income-generating activity project by encouraging her to start up a small business activity. It's a good idea.

    On my way home from the clinic I stop by a small stationary shop in Jamhuri called Judd Stationers. It's where I recently purchased some empty note books for some of the patients in the clinic's income-generating activity program. On my first visit here I had enjoyed the upbeat music being played from the computer in the shop. Judy, the young woman who runs the store, insisted I return sometime so she can show me some more of her songs. Most of these small shops on the main street of Jamhuri have electricity. The local internet cafe never ceases to amaze me with its slow but available internet connection. Sometimes when I head in to check my emails I find it hard to believe I'm conversing with my friends who lead such different lives on the other side of the world. Very different from this small room of computers along the main dirt road of Jamhuri, where goats, chickens and old bicycles carting boxes of fruits and vegetables frequently go past.

As I walk past the stationary shop this evening I see Judy sitting down at the counter next to her computer. She's a young woman with her hair neatly braided into a pony tail and dressed in jeans and a smart jacket. Judy sees me walking in and her face lights up with excitement. 'Hello Belinda!' she says. 'Come in! Come and listen to some music with me'. Judy's smile is radiant and welcoming. She gets up and brings a chair out for me to sit down on. We talk about music together and I describe the styles I've been introduced to since being in Kenya ranging from African gospel, to African pop music to reggae to tribal music. I've been looking to take some CDs back home with me with a selection of this music. Judy insists she'll teach me about the different styles of popular music, and says she will make me some CDs of the music on her computer. We sit down and Judy starts to play DJ from her little stationery shop. She plays track after track for me to hear and waits for me to say 'yes' or 'no' as to whether I like it or not. She plays some Egyptian gospel music, African pop tunes as well as Benga Beats, another form of Kenyan popular music that I really like.

Judy translates the lyrics of the songs in Swahili, stopping and starting the tunes so that I know the story. I can tell she loves her music. She then plays some video clips of some of the well known Swahili pop songs she has on her computer. They're mostly about the beautiful girl being cheated on by her mischievous boyfriend. I ask Judy why it always seems to be the same storyline and she responds 'because that's how African men are!' I spend almost two hours sitting in the little stationery shop listening to music with Judy before I realise it's getting dark and I must get home to Alice's. I agree to stop by to see her tomorrow to collect the music that she's putting onto some CDs for me. I can tell she's grateful for the company just as much as I am to have made a new friend.

Chapter 53 – Friday drinks

It's Friday already and I'm back in the food distribution shed at the Dagoretti clinic handing out rice, beans and Nutrimix to our patients with Annie. As always it feels good to be deep in our work, greeting our regular clients and helping them out.

After lunch Annie and I visit Helen. We want to check in on her again before the weekend. We take the longer, less arduous route today, not quite feeling up to the challenge of the adventurous shortcut. When we arrive Helen's place looks locked up which is different to normal. We manage to open the door and there she is lying all alone on her bed in the dark. When we ask Helen if she's eaten today, she says no. Again. Annie and I can't understand what is going on between Jane and Helen that is causing Jane to neglect her sick sister. We realise that we need to intervene in the situation and to try and sit down and meet Jane to talk out some of these big problems that are dividing the household and affecting Helen's health. Helen tells us that Kevin is not even sleeping at their home at the moment because he is not made to feel welcome when Jane is there. They do not seem to get along and yet Kevin is such an important carer for Helen.

Annie and I decide to organise a meeting with Solphine for a group counselling session with Jane and Helen together. In the meantime, Annie has decided to pull down the plastic chair that Jane has tied up securely to their roof so that Helen can sit out in the sun for a bit. I help Annie untie the ropes that are holding the chair up and we take it outside. After some stretching, we help Helen walk outside to sit in the fresh air. Just getting out of her bed and the darkness of the empty shack makes such a difference to her morale. We leave Helen sitting out by the avocado tree with her eyes peacefully closed and smiling under the sun's soft rays.

On my way home from the clinic I stop by to see Judy again at the stationery shop in Jamhuri. She sees me arriving and calls out, 'Belinda! I have a surprise for you!' Judy pulls out three disks which she tells me she has spent all the day compiling with a selection of her music. She has labelled the disks 'Belinda's Kenya Music'. I can't wait to listen to them!

'I will make you some more too', insists Judy. She's there today with her colleagues Avril and Mohammed who are also our age and share our same interests. We all sit down together inside her small shop talking together like we've known each other for a long time. I decide that, being Friday afternoon, we should have a drink together and offer to buy them all a soda at the small corner shop next door. I return with some Fantas and a packet of chips and we sit around in her stationery shop, chatting, joking and laughing together. We listen to some more of Judy's music. It's so relaxing to be sitting with new friends, away from the busyness of work and everything else.

It turns out to be a nice quiet evening at Alice's house. Sarah and Katie have left together for a weekend in Mombasa with some of the other volunteers. Alice's mother is visiting from the country and staying the night with us. She's in her fifties and dressed elegantly in a bright green and yellow traditional blouse and skirt. She lives outside of Nairobi but sometimes makes the journey to the city to see her children. It's interesting to observe the differences between Alice's very traditional Kikuyu mother and her daughters, Irene and Alice, who lead rather modern and western lifestyles here in the city. Although Alice's mother does not speak any English we enjoy each other's company with plenty of smiles.

Chapter 54 – Souvenirs

On Saturday morning, Annie and I take the bus into Nairobi city to do some souvenir shopping. Time has been flying by and this is Annie's last weekend in Kenya before heading back home to Adelaide next week. She has fallen in love with this country and its beautiful people and insists she is not ready to leave. She's already planning her next trip back. So we decide to go to the Masai Markets together, putting into practice our well developed bartering skills and ability to ignore the persistent salesmen.

I often think how this aspect of Kenyan life has hardened me, having learnt to ignore the constant hasslers and turn a cold shoulder to the sellers that follow us around the markets. Volunteers often talk about their transition into their lives back home and how their time away can change their behaviours and perspective. Reverse culture shock is a common experience encountered by volunteers upon returning home. Today, as Annie and I wonder about what it will be like to return to a modern city with wealthy families and classy shops, we laugh at how we would be perceived if we called out 'No!' rudely to the shop assistant kindly proposing something for us to buy, a response that has become ingrained in us here in the market culture.

After the markets, Annie and I head into a nearby fabric shop. There are giant rolls of different types of fabrics; from the cotton kanga material to stunning Indian silk. The colours and textures are all so beautiful and we both buy some to take back home.

While I'm in the city, I carry out some errands including collecting some mail from the post office. I'm always so excited to receive letters from my parents, my friends and my Grandma. It's only natural that I miss my family a lot and treasure every piece of news I have from home. I pop into the internet cafe to check my emails and to continue some research into my travel plans for Tanzania and Uganda, where I would like to get to before heading home.

I walk into one of the travel agencies in central Nairobi to get some information on their weekend safaris to Tanzania. As I am leaving and taking the stairs down the six flights of stairs, a man starts to follow me. He's calling out to me saying he can offer me a better deal on a safari and that he knows what I'm looking for. He must have followed me here into the travel agency to know what I was doing. I tell him no thank you as I head for the stairs but he persists. I start to take the stairs as quick as I can, feeling slightly claustrophobic in the stairwell and worried about this stranger trying to grab my attention. He continues to tell me to come into his shop just to see what they have to offer. I quicken my pace, taking the steps two at a time and whizzing around the staircase; I can't get out of the building quick enough! It's another African experience - being chased down the stairs by a crazy travel agent. I definitely feel so much safer and calmer out in open spaces than confined in the city's buildings and traffic.

I spend the evening quietly at home. Annie decides to order some pizza from the one pizza restaurant at the Junction shopping complex. It's a real treat, one that Alice and Virginia have never experienced before, and we gratefully indulge together in front of an episode of *Secreto de amor*. These really are the best evenings. I feel like a school girl on a sleepover with her best friends, giggling along with Alice and Annie to the cheesiness of this soap opera. Even Virginia, who doesn't understand a word of English, sits at the back of the room laughing along with us to the scenes between the handsome Venezuelan Carlos and his mistress in the hotel.

Chapter 55 – Goodbye, for now
We only part to meet again – John Gay

It's Annie's last day at the clinic and we start off our morning with a visit to Evelyn's house and her women's support group, Harvest. They have invited us around for a small farewell for Annie. Annie has bonded so well with all of these women during her time in Kenya and they are all so sad to see her leave. Evelyn presents us both with a woven bag which members of her support group have made by hand. They are beautiful. Annie's is purple with pink flowers woven into the bag and mine is orange and brown with small sea shells dangling down the sides. It is so thoughtful of the women, who tell us the bags have been personally made by members of the group as an example of one of their business ideas.

Evelyn then puts some Congolese music on and we once again see how it doesn't take long for African women to start dancing! Evelyn, Annie, Joanne and some of the other women move about together to the beats of this tribal music and everyone starts clapping along and joining in. I watch Annie, seeing just how much she loves this place, and knowing that a piece of her heart will always remain in Africa long after she's left.

Back at the clinic, many of our regular patients and community health workers drop by to see Annie on her last day. She's formed such close relationships with so many people in the time she's been working at the clinic. Natalya comes in to see us at the clinic. She is looking so beautiful these days, a confident woman. She's had her hair recently braided and her figure looks stronger and fuller. And above all, Natalya's joyful personality continues to shine through. I just think how far she has come from that sick girl we found in the shack. It makes me so happy to see her and I know Annie shares the same joy.

While talking to Natalya, she asks me to come and see a friend of hers today who is unwell. I agree and head out on my own with Natalya towards Ngando. Natalya takes me down along the back route from AMKA clinic and after we've been walking for awhile we enter into what looks like a small shared residence.

There seem to be a few timber shacks in the enclosed compound where there is a lady hanging out her clothes. Natalya leads me into the second of these residences where I meet a young woman, no older than Natalya, who is lying in bed. She introduces herself as Sylvia. She gets up from her bed to greet us but I can see she is in some pain. Natalya explains that Sylvia is in the same situation as she had been when we found her. She's apparently had an abortion performed in the slums a few weeks earlier and is now suffering from pelvic pain and severe weakness in her legs.

As was the case for Natalya, Sylvia's abortion was performed by a local in the slums and she now has an obvious infection and complications from this brutal procedure. Despite being weak she appears well nourished and talks openly with me about her situation. Above all, I'm relieved that Sylvia and Natalya have trusted me enough to confide in me and to disclose the details of their very personal situations. In the slums this is how our referral system often works. Many sick people can't afford to go to clinics, so through word of mouth within the community they seem to find out about AMKA or we find out about them. Fortunately for Sylvia, Natalya has come to me with her case today. I tell the girls that I will return tomorrow, *kesho*, with some medications from George and also some exercises to help her in her rehabilitation. Despite the seriousness of their situations, they laugh with each other like two young schoolgirls sitting at the end of Sylvia's bed.

After spending some time with Natalya and Sylvia, I return to the clinic where everybody is starting to set up for our lunch. It's a large group today, with many of our community health workers visiting to see Annie on her last day. There is Evelyn, Joanne, Rosalie, Margaret, Immaculate, Eunice, Grace, and all of our regular team of Oloo, Solphine, George and Sister Veronica. We're ready for the party to start.

The clinic has been decorated and a heart shaped cake is brought out by Sister Veronica, much to everybody's delight. In true traditional style everybody starts to sing the 'cutta cutta cutta' song, clapping their hands and singing out loudly, as Sister Veronica cuts up the cake to share with everybody. She explains the meaning behind this tradition to us today. The chant gives you the courage to cut the cake and to embrace the act of sharing it with your company.

Sister Veronica is the first to give a speech for Annie, thanking her for all the good work she has done at AMKA and describes to everyone how she has bonded so well with many of the patients. Then Oloo, George and Solphine each follow, praising Annie's work and pleading for her to return to her job here at AMKA as soon as she can. Annie receives many gifts from the patients at the clinic: earrings, kangas, bags and some personal hand-written letters.

We eat the cake, along with our normal lunch of bread and butter, and drink our chai together. Everybody is having such a good time, as we always do when we're all together like this in each other's company. Then some of the women start to get up and sing and dance inside the clinic. Others follow: Joanne, Immaculate, Margaret and Solphine. Annie joins in, dancing away to their singing. We have such a good time. Before long I'm up there dancing too with Sister Veronica and George.

Following an afternoon of singing, dancing and eating cake, the party comes to an end and Annie farewells everybody at AMKA clinic. It's a sad moment for her to say farewell to Sister Veronica, Solphine, Oloo, Joanne, Evelyn and many of our other friends that she's shared so many special moments with. The tears start to flow as Annie had earlier warned everybody would happen. We leave the clinic together walking around to see Helen for a check up and for Annie to say goodbye.

We arrive at Helen's where we find her looking weak and withdrawn. Poor Helen, it just seems like things are not getting better for her. I sit down next to Helen and she looks exhausted, both mentally and physically. She tells us she's tired of the TB injections and how they are making her feel. I encourage her to continue taking them, insisting that they are important for her health. It's so hard to see Helen living in an almost helpless situation and knowing there is such a long road ahead of her. Annie finally says her goodbyes to Helen and leaves a message for Kevin too, who is in school. We hope Helen hangs in there.

After our visit, I head back home to Alice's with Annie where she finishes packing her bags. Before we know it her taxi has arrived and Alice and I help Annie out the front of our Jamhuri home with her bags. I'm sad to see Annie leave. It has been a very special time sharing all of these incredible experiences with such a special friend. I know tomorrow will not be the same when I walk out of Jamhuri and into the clinic on my own. And we both know that home will be a different place for us after what we've experienced here.

I am certain that Annie will return to Kenya. There are still many more adventures waiting for her in this beautiful country.

Chapter 56 – Sylvia
'We live our lives in fear' – *Sylvia*

I head out of Alice's on my own today, on that familiar walk down through Jamhuri to the matatu stop. I'm off to the clinic in Ngando. Once there I help set up the clinic with George and Oloo who are kept busy working their way through a queue of patients in the morning. Sister Veronica arrives with her car and I accompany her on a few errands. We go to a meeting with a micro-finance specialist who has some good ideas for the clinic's income-generating activity project as well as the water tank project that I'm still looking into. Sister Veronica then drives into town where she has a few jobs to do, and I close my eyes as she is behind the wheel and taking on the hectic Nairobi traffic. It's amusing to see a nun get just as frustrated as everybody else, honking at the traffic as we dodge pedestrians and matatus.

While we're in the car, I have an interesting conversation with Sister Veronica about why she decided to join the convent and what this work means to her. She's so gentle and always smiling and a real inspiration to be around. I learn that Sister Veronica has a degree in social work. Since joining the convent she has been assigned the role of looking after the AMKA health project. While George, Oloo, Solphine, myself and the community health workers are out on a daily basis visiting patients and looking after the different clinic sites, Sister Veronica is busy with the managerial role of looking after the funding for the projects and has many links with local and overseas sponsors who contribute to the project. It's a big job making even bigger differences in the community.

All in all, these errands take some time and I stay in the car as Sister Veronica runs in and out of offices with her documents. At our last stop she comes back to the car with some lunch for us both: a soda and a goat meat pie. It turns out to be really good. It's been nice to spend this time with her, to appreciate the work that goes on behind the scenes. We drive back to the clinic where I catch up with the others and organise my work for the afternoon.

Belinda Evans

My priority this afternoon is to visit Sylvia again. I've seen George and he has given me some medications to take to her. I feel that during my last visit I was only able to touch on the surface of what is a complicated situation for Sylvia. I've organised for Natalya to come by the clinic again so we can go to Sylvia's together. I step inside Sylvia's place and she is lying in bed, happy to see us again. I sit on the cold cement floor of her house, listening to Sylvia's and Natalya's stories of how many girls of their age (Sylvia, 18 years old and Natalya, 20 years old) are forced to lead lives like theirs. It is heartbreaking to listen to the desperation in their voices, particularly Sylvia's.

She tells me that this is not her house; it is her older boyfriend's place. He has been financially supporting her, enabling her to have an education in return for her living here. This is how she became pregnant.

'So many young girls live with a man, Belinda,' she tells me. 'We don't even really like them, but it is our only way to survive, to have a home, food and an education. And when they want favours, you give them to them.' She says it so matter-of-factly and yet it is so serious. For somebody so young, she seems so mature and grown-up in her perspective and openness.

Sylvia is no longer in school, having had her sponsorship abruptly cut halfway through this semester. She is therefore spending her days with nothing to do in these slums. It is probably how she has found herself in this situation. I examine Sylvia and ask her where the pain, *uchungu,* is. I then give her the medication from George, along with the instructions for taking them to treat her infection. I can see she has been eating from the saucepan on the floor next to the bed. Sylvia invites me to stay and eat again with her.

'I'll make you a Kenyan speciality Belinda', she insists. 'Dried tilapia and ugali'. I don't have time today, but am pleased to see she is in otherwise good spirits. After giving Sylvia a massage and some stretches, Natalya and I return to Dagoretti together.

Chapter 57 – Lake Naivasha

Sarah and I have planned a trip together to Lake Naivasha this weekend. We wake up in the morning to an amazing breakfast that Virginia has prepared for Katie's last day: mandazis, eggs and pineapple. The breakfast gives us the much needed strength to pack our bags as Alice is moving apartments today. It's a short move up the street to a slightly larger apartment in Jamhuri. I'm amazed that in the time I've been here, I think I have accumulated just as many things as Alice owns in her entire apartment. I see Leon next door and he asks where we're going. 'Up the road' I explain, reassuring him I'm sure we'll still pass each other in Jamhuri. Sarah, Katie, Alice and I set off on our walk down the street to the new home with as many of our belongings as we can carry. Alice has organised a car to move her furniture later in the day.

The new apartment has a very similar layout to the previous one. This time we're on the first floor of a building containing four apartments. There's an open living room, a small kitchen and two bedrooms next to the bathroom. We choose our new bunk beds inside the volunteer bedroom and walk up to the rooftop terrace where some of the women who share the building are busily hanging up their washing. Looking out the front, there is a view over the main street of Jamhuri and to the back I can see into the ever-busy slums of Kibera, just a short walk away.

Once moved, Sarah and I load our backpacks onto our backs and take a bus into Nairobi from where we'll need to find another matatu headed for Lake Naivasha. When we arrive in downtown Nairobi, we take out our guidebooks in search of the matatu station for the buses leaving for Lake Naivasha. The city is busy, crowded and bustling with activity. With matatus and cars honking their horns and people walking about everywhere, there seems to be no organisation whatsoever. This is Nairobi.

We continue walking into the city streets and soon find ourselves on River Road, the guidebook's 'no-go' zone of central Nairobi. As Sarah goes in search of a public toilet, I wait outside and suddenly there is a big brigade of people who charge past me knocking me out of the way. I manage to stay clear of the stampede as they chase somebody through the city. This city is full of surprises! Finally, we're pointed in the right direction to a matatu leaving for Naivasha and Sarah and I jump on board. We're packed into this small matatu where there is absolutely no leg space because other passengers have packed boxes of food supplies up next to us. Once in our seats there is literally no room for movement, we are wedged in. When the driver has found more than the legal maximum number of passengers to squeeze into the van, we eventually take off.

As the matatu leaves Nairobi we drive through a thick fog that is sitting over the Rift Valley. Looking through the front windscreen from my backseat position, the road ahead is completely invisible. It is almost impossible to see any oncoming traffic or the bends in the road. Our driver still has his music cranked up and is speeding along matatu style. We can only hope we get there safely.

When we arrive in the small rural town of Naivasha, Sarah and I push our way off the matatu and board another matatu that is headed for Fisherman's Camp which is by the main lake. On this matatu, at one point I count twenty-one heads from my back seat position, on the small fourteen seater Nissan. It seems like the more rural we are, the less strict the rules.

The campsite is really nice at Lake Naivasha. There are a number of different options for accommodation ranging from small apartments to cabins and tents right up by this beautiful glistening clear lake. We notice the electric fences between the lake and the tents. These are to prevent the hippos from going beyond where they're welcome during the night. That's reassuring! The campsite is surrounded by thick green foliage provided by large trees and lake-side scrubland. It is so refreshing to be in the clean non-polluted air, in these peaceful and beautiful surroundings. We've left Nairobi behind and embrace the serenity of rural Kenya.

Sarah and I check into a camp that is perched up on the hill, a short walk back from the lake. It is a *banda*, a single cabin hut with not much more than two single beds inside. It has a nice view from its high position but is fairly isolated and we seem to be the only ones staying there. We're approached by a few friendly locals, including a young man named Marcus, who offers to be our guide here in Lake Naivasha for the weekend. Marcus is young, friendly and very chatty. He has short shoulder length braids and is dressed trendily in street jeans and a t-shirt. He offers to show us the hippos, the giraffes and the nearby Crater Lake. Sarah and I decide that a guide would be a good idea and we agree on a price with him.

We start off on a walk along Lake Naivasha where we see some of the locals washing their clothes by the lake's edge as well as some donkeys standing nearby loaded with jerry cans of water on their backs. The area around us is very pretty and mostly untouched. It is not touristy which is what gives it the charm of a small rural Kenyan village. For dinner, Marcus recommends a local pub, where we're advised to order our meals now to give the chef time to get the ingredients for the evening. Sarah and I walk around some more by the lakeside which is so picturesque and peaceful, before heading back up to our small hut before dinner time.

The World Cup is playing on the small television in the corner of the local pub when we return later for dinner. Sarah and I sit down and watch the game with the locals who are closely following the different matches with much interest. Our meals of rice, vegetables and chapatti are brought out to our table, which are delicious. After dinner Marcus, who has been waiting around at the pub, walks us both back up to our hut at the campsite in the dark. It is pitch black and so quiet up there on the hill that Sarah and I feel quite isolated on our own once Marcus leaves us. Fortunately I catch a glimpse of what looks to be a night watchman (a common practice in Kenya) standing out alone in the dark with his stick; at least I think that's what he's doing there!

It's a rough night, as I keep waking up to the different sounds in this unfamiliar and very remote location. I can hear a man's voice talking quite loudly which alarms me. I soon realise it's the sound of somebody preaching and this is followed by the playing of some gospel music. I'm relieved when daylight finally arrives and I can put my mind and the night noises to rest.

For breakfast, Sarah and I sit on our beds inside the small hut and take out the bread and butter from our backpacks that we've brought with us from Nairobi. We seem to have adopted this simple and inexpensive combination for our breakfast and lunch now! Sitting on our beds we empty out all of the remaining money we both have on us and count up the Kenyan shillings. Living off our bread and butter for the remainder of the weekend, we will have just enough money to take the matatu back to Nairobi.

After breakfast Marcus meets us at the campsite ready for our day's adventure on Lake Naivasha and a walk to Crater Lake. We start by taking a boat ride to see the hippos. Marcus leads us onto a small dinghy boat and Sarah and I are pleasantly surprised to be provided with a life jacket each. Once on the lake, we approach a large bloat of hippos just twenty metres from our small boat. Even with the security of a life jacket, I wouldn't want to be falling into these waters right now. There is also plenty of bird life in this undisturbed environment. We sail along in the boat. Marcus pulls the boat into the land at the other end of the lake where we climb out. We walk through a big open park which is completely undisturbed and all around us we spot giraffes, zebras and gazelles. It is incredible to be walking around on foot amongst these animals in their natural environment. I ask Marcus if he has seen leopards in these parks, as we continue on our walk through the thick scrub. 'Of course!' he says excitedly, not realising I was asking out of concern rather than anticipation.

We're lead up around another path and after walking for awhile we arrive at the beauty of Crater Lake. It is breathtaking. The lake is surrounded by a dense vegetation of tall trees and bushes that enclose this incredible lake which is a beautiful green colour from algae. Dozens of bright pink flamingos are sitting on the lake, creating an amazing contrast of colours. After doing a tour right around the lake we head back on the same walk through the park, my ears well tuned for any rustling noises in the bushes. After passing more giraffes and zebras up close and personal, we safely get back to the boat and sail back across the lake to the campsite.

Sitting by the lake, Sarah and I pull out our bread and butter again and have a picnic lunch on the grass looking over Lake Naivasha before the time comes to collect our bags and return to the city.

The journey home is not without some interesting matatu experiences. Our first matatu takes an unannounced detour through a few different villages, and then we have a change of driver which is then followed a little while later by a change of matatu. To top this off, on the last leg of the journey Sarah and I find ourselves sitting in the back seat of the matatu for thirty minutes with our heads permanently tilted to the side because the seat is too close to the roof of the van!

Once in Nairobi, we're relieved to take a bigger City Hopper bus back into Kibera where there is the luxury of leg room and head space. We relax knowing we've made it back into familiar territory. Sarah and I walk back to our new apartment. Alice has finished moving all of the furniture in and it already feels like home.

Chapter 58 – Concerns

Human suffering anywhere concerns men and women everywhere
– Elie Wiesel

This morning I'm going to AMKA clinic with Sarah, who will be spending some time following home visits around the community to get a feel for what we do in our project. Sarah has been working at Ushirika in Kibera and so we enjoy sharing stories about our friends Daniel, Ruth, David, Anna and Debra. We also have another newly arrived volunteer staying with us; Cat who is from Canada. As I've been showing more and more people around the clinic and explaining the different projects that we do, I realise just how long I've been here now and how familiar I've become with the project. I really do feel like a permanent member of the team and George has even given me the title of the 'Volunteer Coordinator' after seeing me show everybody around, which I gladly accept.

We have a big day ahead of us because today Helen has her check-up appointment at Riruta clinic. Sister Veronica has arranged to meet Sarah and me at Helen's place and to drive us all to the clinic. When we arrive at her place I find Helen in a very weak state. She's not doing well and I'm concerned for her. Once again she has not eaten. Helen is unable to sit up in her bed today and shows signs of the flu from this cold winter weather and lies wrapped up in her blanket. We make her chai to have for breakfast and she eats some bread with it to give her strength for today's trip to the clinic.

When Sister Veronica arrives with her car, she drives in as close as she can to Helen's place. In her state of weakness, Helen is unable to walk at all and Sarah and I use all of our strength to carry her to the car. It's a struggle. I wrap Helen's arms around my neck and try to support her upper body, and Sarah carries her legs. We just make it to the car where Helen sleeps on Sarah's lap in the back seat, which we have had to awkwardly push her onto through the back door.

Sister Veronica drives us to the clinic. Once we arrive, in the absence of wheelchairs, Sarah and I carry Helen, whose body is slim but heavy and limp, into the examination room. Just these small steps seem so harsh for somebody who is already in a very fragile and poor state.

Inside the examination room the doctor examines Helen. Her TB injections are helping to counteract the tuberculosis but her body is also weakening. The doctor gives Helen a new list of medications. Once again the nurse reiterates the importance of eating food when consuming such a long list of medications so that Helen stays strong. After the visit Sarah and I pick up Helen, with one of us taking her shoulders the other the legs. Her body starts to slip and sink down as we rush towards the car. Sister Veronica helps us to seat her in the car. The people waiting in and around the clinic stare at us. It's undignified, degrading and feels cruel for somebody feeling so poorly to be handled like this.

Eventually we get Helen home safely and back into her bed. It's been a big outing for her and I have never seen Helen this down and unwell. I hope she can overcome the flu and regain some of her strength. This weekend we are all going to be out of town. The staff members at the clinic will be undertaking a weekend retreat in Nanyuki and I will be departing tomorrow morning to spend the weekend in Tanzania. We just pray that Helen will make it through these next few days until we all return.

Chapter 59 – Safari from hell

Death may be the greatest of all human blessings – Socrates

July 2006 - Tanzania

I'm waiting nervously inside Alice's apartment with my bags packed and ready to go on my safari to Tanzania. I've ordered a taxi to pick me up at 6:30am to take me into the city where the shuttle bus is leaving at 7:00am. It is now 7:00am and there is no sign of my taxi on the streets of Jamhuri. Why does this not surprise me? After all, I'm in Kenya and even taxi drivers seem to operate on African time.

Alice has not yet left for work and she gives me the number of another local taxi driver she knows. When I call him, he tells me he'll be there straight away. And he is. I'm convinced that I will have missed my bus' departure. I jump in the car and look over the driver's shoulder eagerly from the back seat as he makes his way through the city traffic as quickly as he can, knowing I'm already late. As it turns out the concept of African time is consistent across all domains, and I arrive at the meeting spot to find that my shuttle bus has still not left. Lesson number two in African time has worked in my favour.

On the shuttle ride into Arusha, which is the stopover town for safaris and trekking in Tanzania, I meet a friendly couple from Toronto, Alisha and Chris. They've been travelling around the world since the start of the year and are preparing to climb Mt Kilimanjaro. It's the first time I've been with tourists rather than locals or volunteers in such a long time, and in the beginning I am a little thrown to be back in the company of foreigners in this environment. We've all been put onto the same shuttle bus headed towards Arusha, despite being booked on different tours in Tanzania. So far I seem to be the only one doing the three-day tour that I booked in Nairobi. The couple seated next to me ask me many questions about my work here and the projects I've been involved in. Being asked these questions and having all the answers makes me realise the scope of my experiences, as I see them through the eyes of somebody else.

'You came here all on your own? You're travelling to Tanzania by yourself? Isn't the work just too sad at times?' asks Alisha. We even exchange details as they tell me they'll be spending some time back in Nairobi when they return from their trek, and would love for me to show them through the slums, having heard about my work and knowing this is beyond where any tourist group goes. I agree enthusiastically, as a personal guide to the slums of Nairobi.

The drive to Arusha is interesting. The sealed bitumen roads are a better quality than around Kenya. The environment outside is typically African savannah; dry and bare, with acacia trees spaced apart. The wildlife is sparse. I see the occasional camel, donkey and also some Masais herding their cattle in the distance. We even pass some very traditional Masai villages with the manyatta huts and the men and women dressed in their traditional robes and kangas with colourful jewellery. The Masai are a very prominent tribe in these northern parts of Tanzania.

I experience my first border crossing as our bus pulls into the passport check-point. We're all instructed to get off the bus and to form a long queue where, one by one, an officer looks through our passports before stamping them to recognise our entry into Tanzania. Back on the bus, as we approach Arusha, we start to see a more mountainous backdrop. Mt Meru is the closest mountain to Arusha and this landscape is different to what I've seen in Kenya. In the distance, I see the giant Mt Kilimanjaro. It would be a dream to climb it; one which I had considered at the beginning of my Kenyan trip. But since becoming involved in my work at AMKA I've decided I could put that money to better use on the projects I've been involved with at the clinic such as the water tank project, the patients' income-generating activities and the Harvest women's group. My priorities have changed.

I get off the bus in Arusha and am met by a member of the tour company I've booked with. The young man stands in the parking area holding a piece of paper with my name on it. That's a good start, I think, relieved to find I'm not left on my own in this unfamiliar country. I grab my bags and follow my guide. He leads me to where his van is parked and I'm driven to the tour company's office. It is here that all my dramas seem to unfold.

I sit in the small office for some time before a man finally comes out to meet me. His name is Alan and he's the tour guide operator. He seems friendly. Alan informs me that at the moment there is nobody else listed to go on my three day Lake Manyara and Ngorongoro Crater Safari, so he has allocated me onto a two day tour instead. I'm not happy to be told this having organised all of my tour in Nairobi, paid my money in full and been guaranteed that the tour would be departing. I explain all of this to Alan, but he seems reluctant to make any changes. Eventually, after a long discussion, Alan organises for the driver to take me to the guesthouse, which is my accommodation included in the tour for the night. He says he will inform me when he gets home later that evening of our plans, trying to remain optimistic. I'm doubtful, however, that my safari will be leaving. I arrive at the guesthouse. There lies the second surprise.

We drive out of the centre of Arusha and into an outer suburb. The guesthouse turns out to be a private home and far from a hotel as promised. It's a house that the tour company must rent for its employees to stay in. The driver tells me that 'at the moment' they have no electricity in the house. He leads me inside where it is dark and feels empty. There are separate rooms, and I can hear some other male voices. I'm given a key to my room which has four dorm-like beds inside, each covered with a mosquito net that hangs from the ceiling. Across from the beds are a bathroom and a small table with a single candle sitting on it. The roof of the room seems to be caving in and plaster boards hang down precariously. I can't believe it!

I'm starting to feel very uneasy about this whole situation. I'm all alone in a country I don't even know and I'm beginning to doubt whether this company is a tour company at all and whether I can trust these people. Tanzania and Kenya are known for their black market tour companies that promise safaris but deliver far from it, taking innocent tourists' money and trust. I feel alone and frightened about spending the night in the guesthouse. I lock up my bags in the room and since it's still the afternoon I decide to get out of this eerie house and to take a walk around Arusha. I need to clear my head and to work out what to do.

I find myself walking through some fantastic fruit and vegetable markets in the centre of the town. The colours, smells and sights all around me are incredible. The markets are noisy and exciting, full of lovely spicy aromas, different to what I've come across in Kenya. The women are dressed immaculately in bright kangas, walking with big baskets on their heads filled with fruits and vegetables. The picture is amazing. I focus on taking in this positive environment and the people around me to lift me up, and it works. I immerse myself in this fascinating city trying to spend as much time as possible outside before the evening hours arrive. The thought of that guesthouse still worries me.

At the markets I watch the maize being sorted from the big trucks and sold by women sitting on the ground. And all around the air is brought alive by the sounds of beautiful African voices, from the men and women at the marketplace who are singing wonderful songs in Swahili.

The Swahili that is spoken in Tanzania is slightly different to what I'm used to in Kenya. Listening to the locals, who are all extremely friendly, I start to learn some of the familiar greetings and exchange words with them. 'Mambo? Poa!' *How are things? Cool!* The city is not completely new to the presence of tourists, being the gateway for various safari trips and trekking groups. I stop in at one of the shops and buy myself a box of matches, an essential item to get me through the night with the sole candle in the bedroom. Then I find somewhere to have a soda. It's not that I am particularly thirsty, but it's a means of filling in some time and to avoid going back to what I have now labelled my dungeon guesthouse.

Seated outside at a small cafe I find myself being stared at by a group of local Masai as I drink my soda. There are a lot of Masai in this town, dressed traditionally in their red robes, black rubber sandals and beaded jewellery. A local comes up to my table, pulls out a chair and just sits next to me. He doesn't start a conversation or do anything; he just wants to sit next to the mzungu. I am clearly the new person in town, and it feels strange to have everybody staring at me drinking my soda.

Deciding to buy myself some dinner, I walk inside to ask what they have to eat. The owner gives me a personal tour of the kitchen, the inside of the restaurant and the bar, before I choose something off the menu. Once again, when my food arrives I am the centre of attention in this small square in Arusha. I can feel the eyes on me from other people sitting at the nearby tables as I eat each mouthful of my dinner. It's uneasy yet flattering as I indulge in their local cuisine and culture.

The time comes for me to return to the dungeon. I enter my room straight away, locking it from the inside and discover that there is no longer any running water. In the final hours of daylight I sit down to read my book and prepare for darkness and the long night ahead. I light my lone candle and set it up next to the bed where I lie down.

Late into the night, well after sunset, I hear knocking at the door. Before this I have heard the voices of men speaking in Swahili who are obviously also staying in the house. I wonder who they are and why they are also sleeping here. It's unsettling. I don't think I've ever felt so unsafe in a foreign country than how I feel right now. The person at the door knocks again. Refusing to open the door I get up and ask who it is. My heart is beating quickly.

'It's Alan, Please open the door'.

'No,' I say. 'I can hear you from here.'

I ask him what he wants. He's come to update me on my tour for tomorrow. He tells me he has some good news. That now my three day tour will be leaving as originally planned and that I need to be ready early to be collected in the morning. I'm relieved to hear this. Finally I'm able to blow out my candle and to try and get some sleep.

During the night I'm woken up with a text message on my phone. It's a message from Annie who is now back in Australia. Her message tells me some extremely sad news. She has received the news from George that Helen has died in her home. They had been trying to get in touch with me but being in Tanzania I'd been out of reach. I'm devastated to hear this news. I'm so saddened to learn that one of my closest friends in Kenya has lost her battle with HIV. It's even more saddening to hear this news on my own in this dark and isolated room in a foreign place.

I feel stranded, so far from the rest of Helen's family. I suddenly think of Kevin. Poor young Kevin. All I want is to be back in Nairobi close to Kevin where I can be there for him when I know he has nobody else to turn to. Now he's lost both his parents. All these thoughts are running through my head as I sit alone on my bed, crying. I decide to light my candle and, unable to sleep, I sit there on my own thinking of poor Helen hoping she finds herself in a more peaceful place. I feel guilty for being on a safari in Tanzania when I should be in Nairobi. And yet I am stuck here sleeping in a dungeon with messed up travel plans, which makes me think that this safari was never meant to be.

I can't believe she is gone. Beautiful Helen. All those moments we have spent together. Her gracious smile, her gentle nature and appreciation for everything she has, especially her wonderful son Kevin. Annie's message ends with the Serenity Prayer:

> God grant me the serenity to accept the
> things I cannot change,
> Courage to change the things I can
> And wisdom to know the difference.

Belinda Evans

Chapter 60 – Chances
To worry about tomorrow is to be unhappy today – Anonymous

Sunrise comes in the morning but I have been up long before. It's been a rough night and I no longer feel like Tanzania is where I want to, or should be. And yet I am here. I tell myself I need to deal with the situation as best as I can. I pack my bag and am ready, as instructed by Alan, to be collected for departure. However to add yet another surprise, Alan appears at the guesthouse where he tells me that no safari will be happening today after all. He tells me I will now have to wait until tomorrow to leave. I can't believe it, feeling like this is the last straw. He'd lied to me the night before just to reassure me knowing the situation would not be any different this morning. I've decided I want my money back and that I really must have stumbled across a dicey operator when booking my tour in Nairobi. He refuses saying they can't even do this.

Eventually I realise that Alan is not going to change his mind and that no matter how much complaining I do, the safari will not be any more likely to depart. I realise I have to just deal with this situation however frustrating and wrong it is. I decide to see it out and to give Alan one final chance. He insists that there will be a two day safari departing tomorrow. Knowing with certainty that I could not possibly spend another night in the dungeon, I make the decision to pay for a room in one of the cheaper hotels in Arusha. If I am going to have to spend another twenty four hours in this city I at least want to feel more secure than the night before. It proves to be the best decision yet. I check into my room where there is a double bed, a small TV, a shower and a nice view of Mt Meru through the window. And, perhaps the most thrilling part, there is electricity and running water! This time it actually is a hotel.

I spend another day looking around this small town. I discover some bigger markets which are full of excitement, incredible exotic spice odours, colours and plenty of buzz. The women are working hard sorting out their vegetables and fruits; others are sitting at their manual sewing machines making garments. The sights are breathtaking and take my mind off everything else that has been going on. There really is a lot of culture to take in here.

I'm proud of myself in how I've dealt with the events that have unfolded over the last few days. I haven't let this series of surprises get to me and have accepted that it's out of my hands. *Hakuna Matata*, one of my first and most useful lessons in this journey. I can only wait and see what unfolds. I know that if tomorrow falls through like these last few days then I will be on the next bus back to Nairobi. I sit on my bed in the hotel room overlooking the stunning Tanzanian landscape and hope that I will get the chance to see more of this country. My fingers are crossed for tomorrow.

Chapter 61 – The Crater

Another surprise arrives on Sunday morning when, contrary to what I'm expecting, I *am* actually picked up from the hotel by a green safari jeep. The safari is going ahead! The guide who collects me from inside the hotel leads me out to his jeep where I throw my bags into the back of the car. I join the four other girls who are a similar age to me, and waiting inside the car. I'm so excited to see other travellers. I immediately offload my 'safari-from-hell' story to them wondering if they've had the same experience. No, it looks like it's just me. Well that's in the past now they reassure me. After all the changes I have no idea where we're going or for how many nights, but I'm just happy to be going somewhere!

Our driver Regan is a young friendly Tanzanian who tells me we're heading on a two day tour including the Ngorongoro Crater. This UNESCO world heritage listed site is one of Tanzania's most popular natural attractions. The large crater formed when a giant volcano exploded and collapsed three million years ago and is now home to a high concentration of African wildlife and unique vegetation. But today our first destination is Tarangire National Park which is known for its incredible baobab trees and elephants. And we see many of them! In the jeep there is Mora from Israel, Anna from Germany, Eloise from Manchester and Lucy from Brisbane. We get along well in the back of the jeep and the drive is quite smooth. The only downfall is our broken exhaust pipe which seems to pump strong exhaust fumes through the inside of the car. Well, that's Africa!

Our first stop inside the park is a large waterhole where there are many zebras and waterbucks crowding around. It is such an amazing sight. There are animals bathing together in the waterhole and others standing around under the old acacia trees. The vegetation is sparse, with the thorny acacia and beautifully old baobab trees amongst an otherwise dry and brown undergrowth. We're all standing up inside the car, poking our cameras outside of the open roof to get the best picture.

Regan drives us to an amazing picnic site for lunch. It overlooks a stream where a few groups of elephants are wandering around. Some are drinking water from the stream, others are protecting their young and others are bathing themselves. It's a mesmerizing picture, watching these animals going about their daily routine. Regan brings out our picnic lunch boxes. We each have a salad sandwich, yoghurt, sweets and apple juice. This lunch, our setting, watching the elephants in the savannah, turns the page on my weekend so far.

We continue with more game driving all afternoon. Regan knows where to go to get the best views of more elephants, zebras as well as some hyenas we catch scavenging under the isolated baobab trees. While in the Masai Mara I saw such a range of wildlife, I feel that the attraction in this park today is its environment as much as the animals we see. The typical dry sub-saharan African scrubland with the hundreds-of-years-old baobab trees under the hot African sun. It's breathtaking.

We eventually drive out of the park towards a town near the Ngorongoro Crater as our overnight stopover. We have a really nice dinner prepared for us by the cook, Richard, which we all eat together before watching the World Cup final on TV. I feel so relaxed to be out of Arusha and finally on this safari amongst a kind group of people. It's a fairly early night for all of us. Regan tells us to be up at 5am the next morning for another big day of safari driving.

Following a great breakfast of pancakes, eggs and fruits we head off in the van towards the Ngorongoro Crater. It's a short drive from our campsite and along the way we pass a big open field of sunflowers, something I hadn't expected to find in these parts of Africa. We arrive at the gates of the national park and as we descend into the crater, I catch glimpses inside the crater through the thick bushes. It's incredible and we're excited with the anticipation of what lies inside. Since it's still early there is a layer of fog that we drive through and it's extremely cold outside. As we descend and the fog clears, the view is magnificent. It looks like something from another planet. An enormous open crater enclosed by naturally formed walls that provide a habitat for a wide variety of African wildlife.

Here we don't need to go looking for the animals; they are everywhere in this natural and undisturbed environment. We pass hundreds of wildebeest moving about together in their herds in the large open plains. Watching them run around freely is incredible.

We pass a big waterhole with a dozen hippopotamuses inside, hyenas and wildcats scavenging under the trees and also spot a male lion in the distance. There are zebras, gazelles and elephants. Lucy, our Australian companion, is a wealth of information on all the species of animals that we encounter. She becomes our guide for the day in this huge crater which is bigger than 260m² inside. Even a whole day is not enough to see everything.

We stop for lunch by a lake with a flock of flamingos. We get out of the jeep and sit down for our picnic lunch. From a distance I suddenly see an eagle circling above us, having spotted some food from far above, and I'm the first to run back to the car and to jump back in. I'm not willing to take any more risks!

In the afternoon our surroundings change from the vast open grasslands to thicker foliage with lush green trees. This is the forest area where the leopards are found; the hardest of the Big Five animals to spot. Unfortunately Regan notices that we have a flat tyre. Of all places to get a flat tyre, I think to myself, we're in the leopard's backyard! We get out of the car to inspect the tyre and in true African style, Regan discovers that we don't have the right-sized jack in the car to change our wheel. Lucy helps out and as they try to pull the wheel off, the whole body of the jeep tips onto its side, onto the spare wheel. Great! The weekend just keeps getting better and better! By this stage, I just stand there with the others and laugh at the situation.

As other safari vans pass by, we stop them one by one to see if they have the jack we're after. Eventually, as we start to be surrounded by lots of small monkeys that are coming down from the trees and getting rather aggressive, one of the vans that passes has what we're looking for and pulls over to help us out. The thought of being stuck here in the crater overnight is daunting. I'm not sure what is worse, being stuck in the national park or back in the dungeon guesthouse in Arusha. Somehow I feel like I'm in better company here.

We don't get our leopard sighting but we do manage to exit the Ngorongoro Crater in the late afternoon, after a spectacular day of animal watching. Regan then sets out on the drive back to Arusha where our safari will come to an end. I have one last night at the guesthouse to endure before my return bus trip to Nairobi tomorrow.

I'm dropped off at the tour guide's office in Arusha where Alan arranges my return journey for tomorrow. Trying his best to make my last night better than the previous ones, he arranges for one of his tour guides, Belly, to take me out for a meal. Belly is a young and very friendly Tanzanian who works as a guide trekking the Mt Kilimanjaro almost every week. But his real passion is music. We eat at a nearby restaurant. Belly also stays at the guesthouse and he understands my uneasiness about spending time there. It's nice to have his company and I feel more relaxed and safe having met somebody there.

When we get back to the guesthouse, Belly wants to play me some of his music. He's recorded a few CDs in a local studio and I listen to some of his songs. They're really good. The type of music is *bongo flava*, he tells me, which is a Tanzanian hip-hop. We say goodnight as I return to my solitary room. I discover that there's even electricity in the house tonight which makes me feel better about getting through this last night. I've had a great time in Tanzania but with everything that has happened I long to be back in Nairobi tomorrow.

Chapter 62 – Coming home

There's nothing half so pleasant as coming home again – Margaret Elizabeth Sangster

I'm shifted from two buses before settling on one that is confirmed to be going to Nairobi. There is still one last surprise left in store before this Tanzanian adventure is over. At the border crossing back into Kenya, our driver drops us all off to pass through the border control office and instructs us to walk through to the next car park before hopping on board again. Once our passports have been checked, however, and we come out of the building, the bus is nowhere in sight. At this point it would not surprise me if the driver had decided not to wait for us at all, leaving us at an isolated border crossing somewhere between Kenya and Tanzania. Having already learnt that every day is an adventure out here it really would be possible. Fortunately, however, as I walk around the car park I spot our shuttle bus. We pass through the second passport-check line to re-enter Kenya and off we go again.

Finally we arrive back in Nairobi. I never thought I'd be so pleased to see Nairobi city. It's familiar to me and it's my home now. I head into the volunteer office where I see Irene, and Alice happens to be there too. I tell them all about my safari from hell and they're all pleased to hear I made it back safely. I'm so happy to see Alice in the office that I give her a big hug and tell her how much I've missed her. It's been four days but it feels like so much longer. I can't wait to be back home at Alice's, to have dinner together and to see all my friends again in Jamhuri and at the clinic.

Chapter 63 – Admissions

It's back to routine as I pack my bag, put my boots on and head out of the door with Cat and Sarah on our way to the Ngando clinic. Last night I met a new volunteer Jen who has just arrived from Chicago and will be staying with us at Alice's and volunteering at an orphanage in Kibera.

Once at AMKA, I'm so happy to see all of my colleagues again, after what seems like such a long time away. I share my stories from my Tanzanian experience, which they seem to find funny rather than concerning, knowing exactly how situations like this arise all the time here. Solphine, George and Oloo describe their retreat in Nanyuki which went extremely well. They had many prayer and team building sessions with Sister Veronica and the other community health workers and seem refreshed from their break.

The morning is fairly quiet at the clinic with fewer patients coming out on these colder July days. I decide that I'm going to visit James, a patient we have seen a few times now in his home in Ngando. I talk to Solphine about visiting him and she agrees to come with me. We walk to his place, where Solphine recognises his young daughter Joy running around out the front of their shack. The shack is one of several that are enclosed together in a small compound, with a communal yard out the front where some of the women are busy washing and hanging out their clothes.

We go inside where James is lying on the couch, his legs still thin and immobile. His face brightens up with a smile as he sees us, pleased to have some company. We sit down inside and talk with James for awhile. He's softly spoken and tells us how he hasn't walked for over 18 months. Before that he was very active in the community, working and helping support his wife Grace and daughter Joy.

I immediately see a need to help James. Some simple rehabilitation on his legs could help him regain his strength and muscles. I talk to him about this, saying we will come regularly to help rebuild his strength, and we start right away with a massage and some stretches. When I ask James what he thinks of our plans to visit him in his house, his response is that it's exactly what he's been waiting for. On that note Solphine and I agree that James will become a regular home visit and we will return to see him very soon. We leave him looking brighter and motivated, filled with hope after our visit. It feels good to help others.

In the afternoon Sister Veronica comes to collect me from the clinic to help her transfer one of our patients, Fidelis, to Mbagathi District hospital. She's HIV positive and her health has been on the decline in recent weeks, trying to fight off the flu and other infections. Fidelis lives in a very unsettled area in the slums. Sister Veronica tells me that her home is dysfunctional, and as I walk up to her isolated shack, everybody appears to be drunk and disorderly including her older teenage children. They wander around aimlessly and yell out abusively at each other across the open yard that surrounds their shabby looking home. It seems no surprise that Fidelis is being neglected and that her health is deteriorating.

The children help us carry Fidelis to Sister Veronica's car. When we arrive at the hospital we experience the long process of having Fidelis admitted, which involves waiting in line and paying for a registration card, then registering, then waiting again in line to be seen by a nurse. All of this happens alongside another fifty or so patients who seem to have been waiting outside on the cold wooden benches since the early morning. Many may not even be seen today and will return to try again tomorrow. These conditions are shocking and typical of a local hospital here.

Inside the hospital rooms that we pass, there are two or sometimes three patients to a bed, with their heads at opposite ends of the beds. The rooms are cold and empty, containing a bed, a small table and a window letting in the cold outside air. The patients are required to provide their own toiletries and family members bring in blankets and containers of food during the visiting hours as none of these essentials are provided. In some cases the family members spend the night sleeping under the beds. And despite these conditions the hospital beds are not free of charge, with patients forced to pay about 200ksh per night in many cases, which is unaffordable for the average Kenyan. Fortunately for Fidelis and many of AMKA's patients, the clinic manages to cover their hospital expenses when required. I learn that this is also why not every one of our patients can be taken into hospital.

Sister Veronica and I settle Fidelis into her room and leave her to rest peacefully. We head back to the clinic where I talk with

George, Oloo, Solphine and Sister Veronica about the sad news of Helen's death. They are all extremely saddened by the news, having known Helen as a patient for almost two years and they are also very close with Kevin too. George tells me that it was Kevin who called him over the weekend to tell him the news about Helen. He was with his mother when she died. When I ask George what happened, he says she just became so weak with the flu and the tuberculosis that was attacking her body. And with the cold weather, she could no longer fight it. We agree to go and visit Helen's home tomorrow when our clinic is in Gatina to see Kevin. I can't stop thinking about what he must be going through and long to see him.

Belinda Evans

Chapter 64 – Grief

When you are sorrowful look again in your heart, and you shall see that in truth you are weeping for that which has been your delight
– Kahlil Gibran

At Gatina clinic this morning, Cat and Sarah head off on some home visits with Nancy, one of the community health workers. I stay at the clinic to meet with some of the patients and then help out with the food distribution. Once we've finished, Solphine and I go to Helen's place. It's the first time any of us have been there since her passing away. It feels strange and sad to walk into her compound area, on that walk which has become so familiar to me over the last few months. But there is a different vibe there today. Our little friends are not running around playing and it seems quieter than usual. When we knock at the door Helen's sister, Jane, greets us and invites us in. Kevin is not home. Inside the hardest thing is for me to see Helen's empty bed. It is here that I have become so used to seeing Helen's warm and graceful smile on every visit. We offer our condolences to Jane. I notice that her neighbours, who I have also come to know from my regular home visits, are cooking for her and doing her washing outside. The local community is grieving together which is extremely moving.

It's hard being inside Helen's home. I have really become a part of this family in many ways. I remember Helen holding my hand and introducing me to people. 'This is Belinda, my friend', she would declare. On our way out of Helen's place Solphine and I pass Kevin. I stop in my tracks, so glad that I have the chance to see him, as he's all that's been on my mind since that horrible night when I received the news about Helen. I give him a big hug, my African brother. We stand outside his house for awhile talking and I have the chance to say everything I'd wanted him to know. I reassure Kevin that he is not alone and that we will all continue to support him. I encourage him to come into the clinic to see or to talk with us anytime, and make sure that he knows that whether or not he needs help, we'll be there. He agrees to come and visit me at the clinic tomorrow before he has to head upcountry for the funeral proceedings. I sense that he is as pleased to see Solphine and me, as we are to see him. I just care so much about this boy and wish things will work out for him because if anybody deserves some good luck and a chance in life, it's Kevin.

Belinda Evans

Chapter 65 – Listening
Listen to many, speak to a few – William Shakespeare

On Friday morning Cat and I get straight to work with the clinic's food distribution, bagging the maize and the beans, and checking off the patients as they come into the clinic. The one thing I'm looking forward to today is seeing Kevin again. And he comes in to see me during the morning. We sit down together inside the clinic and talk. Kevin opens up to me about how he is feeling and how difficult things are at the moment. He feels lost and really on his own. It's so hard to hear him say that he's been having nightmares about his mother's upcoming burial. He dreams of her death and is hardly sleeping. I do my best to reassure and to support him. I'm touched when Kevin tells me that I am like a sister to him. He had a sister who died the same year his father died. He says that if his father were alive he would be proud of me. I'm so moved by these words. Kevin is a brother to me; my African brother.

Our talk together seems to really cement our bond that is now very strong. It is sad and hard to see Kevin walk away from the clinic as this may be the last time we will meet, with my departure date quickly approaching and his need to return to his home village for Helen's burial, which can be a several week long process in rural areas. I just hope that he leaves knowing that he has people around him who still care immensely about him.

After having lunch with the team, Cat and I set off on another home visit in the afternoon to see Sylvia. We spend quite a long time listening to her stories about life as a young woman in the slums. What Sylvia shares with us is honest and shocking. Cat and I sit on the cold cement floor inside Sylvia's place and are touched by the intensity of her words and the desperation in her voice to help her out of her situation and to give her a better life. Sylvia describes the situation about her sponsorship and how she believes the local organisation is corrupt, and that they have taken the money the family has supposedly sent her to go to school. During the week she had gone into the organisation demanding to know where the money had gone and she tells us that the staff threatened to send the police after her if she continued to ask questions like this. So here she is, deprived of an education and just waiting in the slums for an opportunity to come along.

Sylvia is frank with us, telling us how depressing and helpless her life is, just sitting around with nothing at all to do. She's just 18 years old and yet there's no hope, she tells us. That's why so many young girls like herself find themselves with a man they don't love but who can take care of them. That's how they find themselves with an unwanted pregnancy as she did.

'We live our lives in fear' she says. Sylvia starts crying and begs us to find something for her to do.

'Take me to your country, please, to be a maid, to look after children, I will do anything!' she begs us.

Sitting on the floor, I am lost for words to reassure Sylvia. How can I reassure her when I know her situation, as for many others, is really grim? What role does optimism play when the reality is that she will probably never return to school or get out of these slums? I can hear the anger in her voice, about what it's like to live in her shoes as a young Kenyan woman, with a poor family and little to offer. She goes on to talk about how these circumstances have led her to stealing and are responsible for her abortion. I don't know what to say. Life really is unfair. Sylvia is an educated and well spoken young woman who has a better awareness and perspective on life and the world than many others. Cat and I both leave Sylvia's house concerned and deeply moved by the way Sylvia has opened up to us. What's difficult is that up until now Sylvia has received a good education. She is an intelligent and very mature young woman. She has touched me in a way that I have to do my best to help her.

I finish a busy day by visiting James in his home in Ngando. As Cat and I walk towards his shack, I find myself taking in all the sites of this amazing place. The slums are full of life and activities and I've come to know so many people here. On the walk I pass, Doreen, a patient who stops to greet me and then not long after, a young school girl dressed in her school uniform yells out my name. I don't recognise her but am moved that she knows me, and that I have found an important place in this community.

Once inside James' house, we're greeted by his lovely daughter Joy and his wife Grace. Grace is also HIV positive, like James, and is in good health since taking her ARVs. She manages to work during the days to support her family and is also involved in HIV awareness programs in the slums. I give James a massage and some more stretches. It already seems like he is progressing which is great to see. It's amazing what even a little attention can do to inspire somebody to help themselves. He's so grateful for our visit.

I return to the clinic in Dagoretti Corner where I bid farewell to my colleagues until the following week. Tomorrow I am travelling to Uganda for one week with Sarah. This will be my last trip away before returning to Nairobi for my final week in Africa. My own departure from Kenya is rapidly approaching. I stop in at The Junction shopping centre to buy some final supplies before heading home and packing my bag with Sarah for our Ugandan adventure.

Chapter 66 – Kampala

July 2006 – Kampala, Uganda

Our exciting journey to Uganda starts with our departure from Nairobi, where Sarah and I have planned to take the night bus to Kampala. Loaded with our big backpacks we board the City Hopper bus from Kibera into the city. We are forced to spend the entire trip sitting on the seats with our faces squashed up against our enormous packs that we've wedged onto our laps, unable to see anything. Already we're laughing at ourselves and the crazy situations you find yourself in like this!

The night bus journey to Kampala is 12 hours long. We've come prepared with snacks, books and our charged MP3 players. But of course as I've already learnt not everything can be planned to perfection. In the middle of the night our bus arrives at the Kenya Uganda border crossing. Outside it is pitch black and there is a small immigration office where we notice a number of armed soldiers standing around. It's a rather intimidating scene. We're all instructed to get off the bus and line up, one by one, to pass through the small Kenyan immigration office. Our passports are checked and we have to walk a distance in these dark surroundings to a second office which when we arrive is locked up. We all stand outside waiting in line for somebody to open the office. Other than being somewhere on the border of these two countries, we have absolutely no idea where we are.

Finally, after what feels like an eternity waiting in these uncomfortable circumstances, the office is opened. The officer commands Sarah and I to stand aside as we do not have our visas yet. They see everybody else in the queue before finally getting to us, the only two mzungus on the bus. We eventually get the visa and stamp in the passport to enter Uganda.

As morning arrives on the bumpy bus ride, sunlight starts to creep through the window drapes and I'm eager to see the first sights of Uganda. Outside it's very green with large banana plantations and palm trees. We pass some roadside markets where there are lots of fresh fruits and vegetables, including large piles of plantains. Young boys approach our bus trying to sell grilled meat on a stick. Through the window I see a man who is trying to perform a prayer ritual, repeatedly changing his position from being on his knees, to standing up and reaching for the skies with a piece of wood in his hand.

We finally arrive in Kampala. The first impressions are exciting. The air is warm with crystal blue skies and the city feels welcoming and not as chaotic as Nairobi. It is a lot less developed than Nairobi, which despite its extensive slums has a western influence with its city sky scrapers and middle-class neighbourhoods. Kampala, however, is in many ways a different city in a visibly developing country. There are many half finished or half destroyed buildings, littered streets and signs of poverty all around. The city only has electricity supplied every second day. Every other day is a 'black' day which is today.

The city is interesting. The roads are busy with many matatus and *boda-bodas*, the motor bike taxis that are everywhere. There are street markets all around selling second-hand clothes, fruits, vegetables and spices. There are also many beggars on the streets. The city lacks organisation and is littered in many parts but we like what we see. Everybody who we meet is very friendly and approachable which is what we'd been told before arriving here. Sarah and I find a Mexican restaurant called Antonio's for lunch and we eat fajitas but made with a tasty chapatti rather than a tortilla. Fajitas African style! We visit most parts of the city, walking around with our map and guidebook in hand.

After a long day exploring, we take a matatu back up to our campsite where we've rented a double tent on a hill that overlooks this fascinating city that we still know little about. We get to bed early, as tomorrow it will be an early start. Sarah and I have signed up to go white water rafting. We're going to take on the treacherous rapids of Jinja, the source of the river Nile.

Chapter 67 – To being alive
Adventure is not outside man; it is within – David Grayson

Going white water rafting is something I never thought I would do. I am not usually one for extreme adventure sports. Yet my time and experiences in Africa have been full of so many new adventures that I have this feeling of invincibility. Hence the decision to take on the grade five rapids along the source of the Nile in Jinja.

The bus collects Sarah and me from our hostel in Kampala and we meet some of the other people who are also heading out with us today. There are Alex and Sherin, a couple from London, and then a larger church group who all sing Christian songs together on the bus. I hope that they will be able to pray for me given what lies ahead of us! Then there are a group of volunteers who work with the Invisible Children program in Uganda, in the northern city of Gulu. They work in a centre where they are helping to protect and rehabilitate young child soldiers. These are young children who, under the force of the Lord's Resistance Army (LRA) have been kidnapped from their homes and turned into soldiers, trained to use heavy armoury and instructed to kill others, including their families. In these parts of Uganda the overnight commute of young children from their villages to places of refuge to avoid the LRA troops is well known. Meeting these volunteers from other projects continues to open my eyes to a whole different range of problems going on in Africa.

At the Jinja campsite our rafting group is briefed about the day's activities. We'll be taking on 31km of varying leves of rapids. We have an amazing view over the River Nile. The broad river is surrounded by rich fertile soil and native trees along its river banks. We get changed and are given our gear for the day: a safety jacket, helmet and paddles. We're then divided into groups of eight which will be our crew. Everybody's really excited to get started. I really have no idea what we're in for. Sarah and I stand with our crew and we're allocated our guide, Tutu. We all have our photo taken together before walking down to the rafts. I choose a spot in the middle of the raft, hoping to minimise my chance of getting thrown into the rapids while also avoiding the responsibilities of being up front.

We begin with some training exercises in the calm water: 'forward paddle', 'back paddle', 'hold-on', 'get-down' and 'STOP!' Then we practise getting back into the raft from the water, as well as how to get out from underneath the raft in case it flips over. Once all the safety aspects have been covered the rafting begins. We all raise our paddles into the air and decide on our team name, yelling out, 'Extreme!" before starting to paddle downstream.

We descend down the river, one raft after the other, guided all the way by Tutu. To begin with, there are some smaller rapids that we cruise down, practising the different commands and it is fun. As long as we don't get thrown in, it's fun. Our team consists of me, Sarah, Alex, Sherin, Jolene and David and an older retired man from New York City, Glen. From the first rapid of the day, Glen has this ongoing commentary at each rapid where he screams 'Weeee-Daddy! 'Here we go!' Secretly, I find myself urging him to concentrate a little harder on his paddling than the commentary, especially since he's right behind me and I'm becoming more and more paranoid about being thrown into the powerful rapids.

The rapids that we are taking on are huge. The water is so fierce and it crashes up against itself. They are bigger than I ever expected. I look ahead and see the next rapid we're taking on. 'It's a grade five!' Tutu yells out and everyone raises their paddles and yells out our team name, 'Extreme!' with enthusiasm. I'm slightly less excited. Horrified, actually, for what lies ahead of me. Suddenly fear hits me. Why on earth would I decide to come white water rafting? This is not something I would ever normally do. But in the middle of this raft heading down the River Nile in Uganda it's too late to turn back.

We're quickly approaching the rapid and Tutu is instructing us to 'Go forward!', 'Go forward!' and to take on the rapid with all we've got. I look at Sarah across from me who gives me a frightened smile. Here we go! As we approach the rapid, Tutu yells out 'Hold on', and we all stop, then 'Get down!' and I crouch down inside the raft, gripping onto the sides with all the strength I have. But it's not enough. Along with most of the other members of my crew, I'm thrown out of the raft into the powerful and swirling waters of the rapid as our raft is flipped on its side. Before I know it I'm being swept right under the current, completely unable to resist the strength of the water. It feels like I'm under there for a lifetime and I'm terrified. My survival instincts kick in and I forget about everything else except getting up for air. But I can't get up. I'm convinced that this is it for me. All I can hear under the water is the sound of silence which lasts for an eternity. I eventually make it up for just a second and gasp some air before being swept right under again. I catch sight of Glen whose head is bobbing in the water not far from me I wonder if he's alive or not.

Somehow, and only god knows how, I survive. Glen too. The rapids have pushed me farther down this enormous river as I finally reach some calmer water and I come up gasping for air. Looking around me I can see a series of pink and blue helmets, my crew members, who have been thrown out as well and are waiting to be rescued. Tutu approaches me in the raft and I'm pulled back on board. I look around, my face still frozen with fear and shock and I see Sarah. We exchange the look of 'Oh my god, I almost died, this is insane' before helping Tutu to pull our other crew members back on board too. It seems like nobody got off lightly. I see poor old Glen who seems to have run out of his humourless commentary for now and Alex has scraped his back against some rocks on the rapids. Worse still he's lost his board shorts in the current. Apparently a regular occurrence, Tutu pulls out a spare pair for Alex to wear. We have some rebuilding to do. And the worst news is there are still another several rapids to go before we break for lunch.

I continue to learn so much about myself on this trip and as somebody who doesn't like to have things out of control (such as being stuck under massive rapids of water) this rafting experience is definitely a challenge. I glance over at the other rafts that somehow survived the last rapid and they are screaming with excitement and adrenaline. We approach the next rapid and Tutu tells us to 'Get down!' I crouch down as close as I can to the inside of the raft, gripping on with all my strength to the sides. But, sure enough, despite all my will and power to hold on, I am thrown out of the boat. Again. This time I'm the only one in the water. I swallow my pride as Tutu holds out his paddle for me to pull myself back onto the raft. The next rapid is slightly smaller and I manage to stay on board. I scream with delight as I raise my paddle to high five the team after the rapid, relieved more than anything to get through at least one of them safely. The next rapid we bypass, it's a grade six. The noise itself is terrifying, the water crashing against the rocks and leaving massive amounts of white foam and spray. These grade six rapids are not raftable by beginners and it is incredibly frightening as we paddle around the outside of it.

Much to my delight we then approach a stretch of flat paddling which gives me the chance to take everything in for the first time. The surrounding river banks are rich in rare bird life and green with foliage and trees. We paddle our raft onto a small island for our lunch break. I've been hanging out for this since the very first rapid of the day! As we pull up I see a group of a dozen or so rafters lining up at the first aid stand to have their scratches, dislocations and various other injuries attended to. At one point I see more people in the safety boat, which is a larger more stable boat for anyone opting out or injured, than in their own rafts!

Lunch is a big feast of sandwiches, fruit and refreshingly cold drinks. Sarah and I sit down together and rehash the morning's events. I decide at this point that I can't put myself through another grade five rapid and opt out and take the safety boat for the remaining big rapids of the day. Before reaching the rapids again there is a long stretch of calm water where we all jump into the water and let our bodies slowly drift down the Nile. I take in the surroundings. It is extremely peaceful and serene as I float in the water.

Convinced by Tutu and my team to rejoin them in our raft for the next grade three rapid, I agree. They reassure me it's a small one and nobody falls out at this one. I, of course, manage to prove otherwise and am tossed out of the raft and back under the water. By this stage I'm completely over it, waiting there in the water to be rescued again and pulled back on board the raft. I finish off the last big waves of the day in the safety boat which at one point I'm not totally sure will make it through unscathed. But we do. And I watch as one by one all the other rafts take on the rapids, many being spun into the air, crew members thrown into the water. The usual headcount follows. Just one boat manages to make it through without flipping.

I have never been as relieved as when our raft approaches land at the end of the day. I eagerly hop out and back onto safe ground. I meet up with Sarah and the rest of my crew. We have a drink together by the river and look back over the day's events. Back at the campsite in Jinja, Sarah and I settle into our room for the night. It is a large dormitory-style room with sixteen beds. I have never seen bunk beds four beds high, and being on the second level I have to slide myself in horizontally to get into bed, only just avoiding touching my head against the bed above. Sarah and I have dinner at the hostel bar with Jolene, one of our crew members from the day, and we reminisce over the day's adventures. We order shots and make a toast to surviving this crazy day.

'To being alive!' toasts Sarah.

'To being alive!' we cheer together.

Belinda Evans

Chapter 68 – Quad bikes and boda-bodas

It is in the compelling zest of high adventure and of victory, and in creative action, that man finds his supreme joys
– Antoine de Saint-Exupery

After a night in Jinja, Sarah and I continue our week of adventure activities by signing up for some quad biking at Bujagali falls. The views of the rapids are incredible from where we stand high on the river banks. Looking down, we still cannot believe that was where we were white water rafting yesterday! We're given all the gear we need for the quad biking: overalls, gumboots, helmets and goggles. Our guide takes us on a practice ride. It feels less risky than the rafting and just being back on solid ground is reassuring. After doing a few laps of the practice track, our friendly guide, Herbert, takes us out on a two hour ride into the countryside and through the local village.

It's a lot of fun. We start off at a site that overlooks the river Nile and its spectacular surroundings. Then we ride along some back routes through some small villages with banana and maize plantations and many small traditional huts made of mud with straw roofs. The young children come running out to wave at us, the obvious mzungus dressed in overalls, gumboots and goggles on quad bikes riding through their otherwise calm village. We wave hello to them. Herbert and Sarah, who speed ahead, have to keep looking over their shoulders at me as I refuse to go faster than a granny speed, being extremely cautious with everything I do now!

We ride down the main road and pull into a small cafe where we drink a soda outside. Once again we attract a lot of attention from the locals and many small children come up and stand outside the cafe, just to stare at us. It's a beautiful place and Sarah and I just love this country. The people are so friendly and life in this remote village is relaxed. These regions have been undisturbed by western cultures (aside from the obvious mzungus doing quad biking!) and remain rich in culture and tradition. We head back on the bikes along another route where we pass more plantations, before arriving at the end of our tour. After a delicious lunch of mashed plantains with beans at the local cafe, Sarah and I have our first boda-boda experience back into Jinja. I hold on tightly to my driver as he speeds off up the dirt road on his motorbike taxi back to our hostel. There we grab our bags and board the shuttle bus back into Kampala.

The bus is supposed to arrive back in Kampala in the late afternoon but the journey turns out to be much longer as we're caught up in the heavy matatu traffic going back into the city. The streets are busy and blocked with vehicles converging on the same roads, and it takes us an extra few hours to get back. Our plans to book accommodation and buses for our next trips have to be put on hold as we arrive back well after sunset. We hop off the bus with our big packs and stand in the middle of the matatu station in central Kampala which is completely dark. It's clearly another black day with no street lighting and there are people walking around us in all directions. It's a strange feeling being in such a foreign city with no plans of where we're going or what our next move should be.

Sarah and I walk around with my guidebook in hand searching for a hotel for the night. We don't seem to have much luck as we approach the recommended addresses in my book only to find the hotels don't exist anymore. We find ourselves stuck in Kampala in the dark with no accommodation for the night. We wander around some very shady areas aware of people looking at us with our big packs on our backs. One lady even stops to warn us to pay attention to our pockets and our bags, saying she can see some pickpocketers looking at us. Except for a few lanterns lighting up the small shops that are still open for business, the city is in darkness.

Sarah and I decide go to the hostel we'd camped at on our arrival in Kampala. Only we cannot find a matatu that is heading in that direction. Or even a taxi for that matter. After wandering around for a long time and aware that it's getting later and later into the night, we decide that our only way of getting out of the city centre is to take a boda-boda. Notorious for their careless driving and lack of road safety, a boda-boda ride in the city can be a risky experience. Knowing this but realising we have no other choice, we each jump on the back of a motorbike boda-boda, with our huge backpacks weighing us and the boda-boda down.

Sarah and I cannot believe we are doing this. We take off, leaning forward as far as we can to counteract our weighty backpacks and I grip on tightly to the driver's waist. The boda-bodas drive us up the dark streets weaving in and out of the traffic. At one point my driver curves around onto the footpath so as to overtake a few cars and a matatu. I share another horrified look across at Sarah as she disappears ahead of me in and out of the busy evening traffic. We eventually pull into the backpacker's hostel and climb off the motorbikes with our packs. The adventures just seem to keep on coming on this journey!

Chapter 69 – The Ssese Islands

The larger the island of knowledge, the longer the shoreline of wonder –
James Madison

For our remaining few days in Uganda, Sarah and I arrange to visit the Ssese Islands. These islands, of which there are more than eighty, are located in Lake Victoria in the Kalangala district. We'll be visiting the largest one called Bugala Island. We leave early the next morning, taking a matatu from Kampala to the town of Entebbe and from there a taxi to the ferry port. We wait a few hours at the port before taking the ferry onto the island.

The ferry ride is comfortable and I step outside to see the views as we leave the port behind us. On the deck of the ferry I talk with a few Ugandans who are very friendly and interested in my visit to their country. Meanwhile Sarah has an 'African moment' when she overhears one of the crew members trying to sell a lifejacket to some of the passengers, saying there aren't enough to go around so in case of a problem it might be a good idea to have one! Even more interesting is the demonstration of how to use a lifejacket, which none of the crew members or the passengers appear to have ever seen before.

We arrive on Bugala Island and it is beautiful. The weather is hot and sunny and the island is surrounded by the crystal clear water from Lake Victoria. We can see the local village and the traditional houses surrounded by banana plantations. It's so peaceful and quiet. Not a matatu or boda-boda in sight. We check in at the Pearl Gardens campsite and a guide, Morris, shows us to our lake-side tent. It's so serene, the sounds of birds chirping and the waves gently moving along the lake. Morris asks us what we would like to order for dinner tonight so he can start preparing, and after leaving our bags in the tent Sarah and I take a walk along the lake.

In the evening our dinner is brought out to us. We sit on the grass next to the lake and watch the beautiful sunset. Our dinner is great. We're served goat's stew, rice, matoke, fried goat and chips. Morris informs us the goat is delicious as it has been freshly slaughtered for our dinner tonight. And with that image, we dig into our meal. A bonfire is set up by the lake a little farther along the island. Sarah and I lie down watching the abundance of stars in this clear night sky. It's a perfect setting for a relaxing stay.

Chapter 70 – Night dogs

Waking up to the gentle sound of waves on the lake and birds singing softly is a beautiful welcome to another day on the Ssese Islands. In the morning Sarah and I are taken on a canoe ride on the lake in an old wooden canoe boat. We explore some of the other parts of the island which are undisturbed and very beautiful. After lunch Morris organises to take us on a walk through the local village and into the forest.

Sarah, Morris and I start off walking through the small village where we pass the traditional mud houses and the local children come out to say hello. Most of them are naked or wearing a few pieces of scrappy clothing. One particular young girl, no more than four years old, catches my eye as she stands naked next to her house holding a machete which is almost as big as she is. We pass through some banana plantations and then Morris leads us into the forest. The vegetation is quite dense here with many varieties of trees and shrubs. It's interesting walking through the forest but slightly creepy at the same time as we're all alone out here on this island. It feels like the setting for a holiday island horror movie as we pass a crooked creaking sign for the 'Ssese Island beach resort' and trip over some big vines before walking through spider webs. Sarah just laughs at my paranoia.

We come out of the forest walk and are safely returned by Morris to our campsite where he takes our order for dinner. We really feel like he's become our personal assistant, organising all of our activities and meals on the island. Like all Ugandans we've met, Morris is extremely accommodating and kind. Sarah and I take one last walk along the lake as dusk falls before returning to the campsite for our dinner.

In the very early hours of the morning, while it's still dark, we're woken up abruptly but some alarming sounds outside our tent. I sit up suddenly, as does Sarah, to hear the ferocious barking of some dogs outside. The island has a number of stray and domestic dogs that wander about. It sounds like there are two dogs brawling right outside our tent. But it's not just the sound that is concerning. They are so close that I can feel the body of the dog against my feet through the tent. I'm worried that our tent will fall down on us if they continue like this. There is absolutely nobody around. I wish I could just call out to our personal guide, 'Morris, help!' to come and rescue us. Instead we're on our own here.

The dogs continue barking aggressively and Sarah and I just sit there, rigid, realising we can't do anything. We're worried about what will happen next. Eventually the barking stops, but one of the dogs must have decided to lie down next to our tent. Sarah can feel it breathing at her feet. Its body is leaning in on the front part of our tent which we can see has been pulled down with the weight. The dog's paw then rips through the tent and I'm convinced that it will try to come in and attack us.

'Hold up the tent!' I tell Sarah as the front starts to cave in.

I grab my big backpack and push it up against where the dog is lying and has torn the hole, trying to block the tear. Then I put Sarah's pack up against it too, doing my best to block the entrance and to protect the tent from collapsing. The dog seems to have fallen asleep where it is. It is still dark outside and we spend the next few hours until daylight arrives sitting up in the tent, worried for the dog, the hole it's made, the tent and of course, ourselves.

When it's light outside, I peer out of the small window of the tent to see a black and grey dog sitting still against the entrance. Even now, yelling out help would not do anything as our tent is so isolated. Sarah and I work out what we can do. We cannot spend the whole day barricaded in here. Eventually I brave it and push the dog's body with my feet. When I step outside of the tent it has gone. Sarah joins me outside, and we investigate the damage from the night before with a big tear in the front of the tent. The black dog is lurking around with its glassy eyes and looks injured from the brawl the night before. Suddenly it approaches us again and in fear, Sarah jumps up into the tree, toothbrush in hand, legs wrapped around the tree's trunk. It is a classic moment looking up at Sarah perched in the tree, as the dog turns around and decides to leave us alone.

Chapter 71 - On the road again

You can't get there by bus, only by hard work and risk and by not quite knowing what you're doing. What you'll discover will be wonderful. What you'll discover will be yourself- Alan Alda

After more than fourteen hours sitting on an old bumpy bus from Kampala, Sarah and I pull into Nairobi city bus terminal. It's been a long journey from the Ssese Islands on the ferry and spending one final night in Kampala before boarding the bus back to Kenya. For both Sarah and me, returning to Nairobi means one step closer to returning home. Sarah will be leaving tomorrow night and I'm leaving in just one week. Our long bus journeys have given us lots of time to reflect on our time in Africa. Quite simply, Uganda has been amazing. Backpacking independently around this country is something I never expected to have done, and to have travelled with Sarah has been great and never short of entertainment. We have shared so many exciting and terrifying moments. The country is beautiful and the people we have met have been so friendly and welcoming.

It's night time in Nairobi as we hop off the bus and suddenly feel back in our comfort zones as we navigate the familiar streets and matatu traffic back into Jamhuri. When we arrive at the apartment, Alice, Virginia and Jen give us all a big welcome home. We share all of our entertaining stories with them, from the near-death rafting experience, to the dog attack in the tents, to riding boda-bodas with our huge backpacks around Kampala. Alice is extremely amused by our stories and can't stop laughing. Sometimes I wonder if she's laughing with us at these experiences or at us, the mzungus taking on Africa. It's so nice to be home and there's even some leftover dinner which we dig into after our long journey. After staying up and talking with the others, I finally head to our room to go to bed. Ahhhh, a real bed. What a luxury!

Chapter 72 – Compliments
A compliment is like a kiss through a veil – Victor Hugo

The next day I spend the morning going through the laborious routine of hand washing all of my clothes that have come back extremely well worn and weathered from our trip in Uganda. Today is Sarah's last day in Kenya. We've organised to have lunch together with Jen and another volunteer, Brooke, at Java cafe. We've also invited Daniel to join us. He arrives looking dashing in his black suit, white shirt and polished shoes. Noticing he's having difficulty choosing something from the big American-style menu, we order him a Mexican burrito. His meal arrives and in true American style it's huge. Daniel's eyes light up at the size of it, not knowing where or how to start. He says he's never had the privilege of eating out at a cafe like this before.

'I won't need to eat for a few days after this!' he tells us.

After lunch, Sarah and I walk with Daniel back to Ushirika clinic to see all of our friends there and for Sarah to say a final goodbye. As soon as we walk through the gates, Anna greets us excitedly and Ruth comes out to see what is going on. David and Judson also join us as Sarah and I start to tell them about our exciting stories from Uganda. Judson and Anna tell us that we look well and happy from our trip. David adds, 'Yes, you're nice and fat now!' Sarah and I are both slightly surprised to be told we look fat. It's another first time experience for us! Contrary to our own culture, what David has told us is considered a real compliment here in Kenya. David explains that when we arrived we were skinny and white and now, after some months, we are starting to look like real African women! To be told we're looking fat implies we're looking good. We'll take it like that anyway!

After Sarah says all her goodbyes and I'm made to promise that I will return to Ushirika soon, we head back to Alice's for dinner. Once Sarah has packed her bags and is ready for her evening flight, we eat together and Alice switches on the TV for our favourite weekend routine of watching *Secreto de amor*. Alice, Virginia, Sarah, Jen and I all sit around laughing once more at the over-dramatic acting and entertaining dialogue between the characters we've now come to know well. These are some of the best moments we share together in the evenings. Finally Sarah's van comes to collect her and we all bid her farewell on her long flight back home. Next week it will be me and I'm not at all ready to say goodbye.

Belinda Evans

Chapter 73 – The final countdown

'You have given me hope' - James

It's my final week at work and I'm ready early, keen to see my colleagues and patients after a week away. On my walk out of Jamhuri, I stop at the stationery shop to see Judy, Avril and Mohammed who are keen to hear about my trip to Uganda. I share my stories with them and of course they laugh at the thought of me rafting down the Nile. Judy tells me she's glad I'm back safely and that Jamhuri is where I belong. I have to agree. After wishing them a good day, *siku njema*, I continue my walk to the clinic. I pass the women sitting on the corner waiting, as they do every day, and we exchange our regular wave and smile. I'm taking everything in now, knowing these days are not going to go on forever, despite how much I wish this was so.

Once at the clinic, I'm so happy to see Solphine, George and Oloo again. They tell me that I have been greatly missed during my time away and we catch up on everything that has been going on. I really am a part of the team here. First up, George wants me to accompany him on a home visit to Sylvia's place, since she has been my patient and I know all about her story. Sylvia's doing a lot better now. She's finished her medications and is walking around strongly and confidently. Physically she is well. Emotionally she is still troubled by the ongoing problems with her sponsorship and lack of hope for her future, which is difficult to witness every time I visit her. In my last week I vow to investigate her sponsorship situation, at least to uncover this organisation that appears to be corrupt and to help get Sylvia back into school.

It is a busy morning at the clinic. Many of our regular patients and community health workers know that I just have a few days left and are stopping by to greet me. There's Margaret and Immaculate (the terrible sisters as Annie used to say, from the way they're always up to something together!), Natalya, Evelyn and Joanne. We spend time sitting outside together and chatting. It's moments like these in Kenya when the work can wait. People don't turn away the opportunity to see good friends. I must be getting used to the African mentality, finally! Solphine starts warming up the chai with Millicent in the kitchen and we all have lunch together. The slices of bread are laid out on the table, the tub of butter is taken out of the cupboard and when the chai is ready, two large thermoses of tea are placed on the table. Lunch is ready. We pray and then eat together.

In the afternoon, Solphine and I walk around to visit James' house for his rehabilitation exercises. We walk through the main entrance to the compound where he lives and as we walk through, we're met by an incredible surprise. Standing at the front door is James! I'm so delighted at what I see before me, as is James, from the big smile on his face. It has been almost two years since he has walked. This is such a special moment to share with him. Solphine and I go inside his house and give him his regular massage and stretches. He has been improving for some time now regaining strength in his legs. But I did not expect to see him walking so soon.

I sit next to James and he talks about how happy he is feeling these days. He now has hope and a genuine desire to get stronger. He talks with Solphine in Swahili and tells her that it is thanks to our home visits that he has made this progress.

'You have given me hope' says James.

I can see the change in his face. His eyes are no longer withdrawn and distant as they were on our first visit. They have a sparkle back in them now, and as I take James through his leg stretches I don't even have to help him. He proudly extends and flexes his legs in and out on his own, going through the regular motions. Today I take Solphine through all of the steps of James' exercises. Knowing that I will be leaving shortly she has asked me to train her so that she can continue my role with many of the patients. Seeing James really has been uplifting; to literally see the life put back into somebody. And to know that I have had a small role in achieving that progress.

Chapter 74 – Donations

Education is the most powerful weapon which you can use to change the world – Nelson Mandela

I take the matatu number 111 in the direction of Ngando for our Wednesday clinic. As we pass the Pathway Hotel, the sign that signals my stop, I tap twice on the roof and jump off the matatu as the driver swerves onto the side of the road. This once scary routine has now become second nature for me on my journey into work. This morning when our whole team is gathered together at the clinic, Sister Veronica comes to greet us and says she has something she wants to show us all. We excitedly follow her out into the outside area of the convent where her car is parked. She opens the back doors to the vehicle and reveals the surprise. It's a brand new wheelchair.

'Belinda has donated this wheelchair to the project', she tells everybody gratefully. 'I'm sure we will get a lot of use out of it'.

Everybody claps with excitement, delighted at any new donation to the project, especially something so new and technical. After carrying Helen in my arms back and forth from the car to the clinic and watching Annie and Sister Veronica with Rose, I decided that donating a wheelchair to the clinic using my fundraising money would be a practical and much needed donation to the project. And Sister Veronica has finally received the wheelchair we ordered together.

Everybody gathers around the new wheelchair. George is the first to take a seat and to test it out. Then Solphine follows, then Oloo and everybody else gets their turn including Sister Veronica. We're like a group of children playing with a new toy. It never ceases to amaze me how grateful and excited my colleagues are by the slightest act of kindness or generosity. And it's for this reason that I know this gift will be treasured.

As I continue to tie up all the loose ends with my work at the clinic, the other ongoing project I've been working on is the water tank project in Dagoretti. I have been trying to organise as much as possible with this project before I leave, and have spoken with Sister Veronica over its management. It is not always easy to instigate something new. It takes time, African time, to bring people together and to implement ideas, especially for a sustainable project. A meeting I had planned with Evelyn's women's group recently about looking after the water tank business did not eventuate. I would like them to manage the site, having seen how capable and inspiring they are. But I need more time to see this project through. I've decided to leave all of my ideas and planning with Sister Veronica who will communicate with me about how the plans come along once I'm gone.

Another project that I've been talking to Sister Veronica about is my decision to sponsor Sylvia to finish her high school education. I've come to know this courageous and intelligent young woman on a very personal level and the challenges she's facing in her life. I've listened to the devastation in Sylvia's voice at not having the means to return to school, knowing how important it is for her future. I believe that she, like many others, should have the right to an education. Giving Sylvia this opportunity to return to school will provide her with a foundation to make a different life for herself.

With the help of the AMKA program I will be ensuring Sylvia can return to her same school where she has one and a half years of study to complete to receive her certificate. She will require a new school uniform, books, a few personal belongings, a bus fare and tuition fees to be paid. Delivering this news to Sylvia brings her such happiness, excitement and appreciation. She is delighted to have something to look forward to and a reason to leave her idle life in the slums. Sylvia now has some hope for her future.

That evening back home, as Jen and I complain about our lack of sleep from the mosquitoes that are in our room every night, we decide to do something about it. Not having anywhere to hang her mosquito net from the top bunk, Jen and I set about tying a piece of string from the window frame across to the light bulb on the ceiling. Then from the piece of string she has somewhere to attach her mosquito net. We're proud of our creativity and it calls for a photo so we call Alice into our room to take our picture. There I am beaming in the foreground and Jen looking like a ghost under her mosquito net in the background. The three of us are riddled with laughter in the bedroom. These are the moments that I will miss!

Giraffes in our backyard, Masailand

The Masai with the Ngong hills in the background, Masailand

Belinda and Annie on Belinda's Birthday, 21st June 2006

White water rafting, Uganda

The AMKA team with their donated wheelchair

Chapter 75 – A friendly stalker

At Gatina on Thursday, I'm met by a number of our regular patients as well as some new ones. It's a fairly steady morning. With the rains returning, the streets are once again becoming muddy and shacks difficult to access for home visits. I help Oloo in the shed with the food distribution. After the clinic is finished, I see Moses for the last time at the Fair Deal cafe. I take his photo standing out the front of his cafe on the main road of Gatina. As always the sign is falling down and he is wearing the same red polo t-shirt I have seen him in every Thursday for the past three months. I'll miss our visits here and my chapatti and beans.

After lunch, Solphine, George, Oloo and I walk back to the Dagoretti clinic through the famous shortcut. We weave our way through the maize plants, across the wooden plank over the sewage stream and slide across the cement embankment. I think of Kevin and the many trips he led Emilie and me on through this shortcut. How considerate he was to stop and wait for us at each step, holding our hand as we stepped over the stepping stones or holding back the branches of the palm tree for us to walk underneath. Each time I'm in Gatina, like today, I think of Helen and Kevin. Most of my visits to Gatina have been to see them. Kevin is still upcountry for his family's burial so I will not see him again before I leave. But I have left a letter for him with Sister Veronica for when he returns, telling him how much I will miss him and encouraging him to keep reaching for his dream of becoming a doctor one day.

In these last few days I have been writing letters to all of the special people I've had the pleasure of meeting and becoming friends with during my time in Kenya: my colleagues such as George, Oloo and Solphine, our regular patients such as Natalya, Kevin and Sylvia. And of course my friends in Jamhuri, Stanley and Judy. It's my way of saying thank you and goodbye.

On my way home from the clinic, I pass a familiar face that I'd met a few weeks ago, Paul. He's walking in the other direction so he doesn't see me today. I don't know much about Paul, but he must live in the area as I've started to pass him quite often. He's very friendly and talkative and now and then has accompanied me on my walk to the clinic. He's told me about his drama studies and hopes of becoming an actor. It seems he knows I am leaving shortly and these run-ins of ours, coincidental or not, have become more frequent. Like many friendly but persistent Kenyans, Paul's looking for an opportunity to change his life. Jen calls him my stalker. The watchman at Alice's apartment, Adam, informed me yesterday that Paul had come by asking for me. I'm a little concerned that he has found out where I live. But compared to when I first arrived in Jamhuri when this would have really alarmed me, I now take it in my stride. A Kenyan stalker? Well why not, that's something new in this ever surprising adventure.

Chapter 76 – Queen cakes

My last days in Kenya fly by so quickly. As promised, I head into Ushirika clinic this morning to work with my close colleagues for one last time. It is here that everything started for me on this journey in Nairobi. I remember walking in with Molly on my first day across the railway line, through the stands of women selling fruits and vegetables and past the wandering chickens. Today I am alone on this walk, Molly having long flown home. Yet I don't feel alone at all. I have never felt alone in Kibera. The sense of community is overwhelming in the slums and as I approach those familiar gates to Ushirika Clinic, I hear the morning sounds of the World Music store filling the air and I couldn't be more excited to return to work.

I greet Anna at the entrance and Ruth is already busy in her small kitchen preparing everything for the day ahead. David, Judson and Daniel are delighted to see me back and I have to insist that it's just for one day. They show me the brand new HIV outpatient's clinic that has finally been finished, trying to convince me now that I should stay on and that there is a job for me.

I spend the morning working in the baby immunisation clinic with Daniel where I record the weight of the babies and fill out their cards. Daniel is happy to have me back particularly because he can hand over the book-keeping duties to me again, which he knows I dislike as much as he does! At lunch I have my mug of chai with Ruth in her small kitchen. I take in the sounds and activities around me in Kibera and wait for Jen and Peter who come and meet Daniel and me. Peter is carrying a walkie-talkie in his hand today, apparently working on the set of a new movie being filmed in Kibera. The four of us go out for lunch to a small road-side stand where we order our chapatti and beans. There's nowhere else I'd rather be than eating lunch with these friends on the streets of the Kibera slum.

When I get back from lunch, Ruth tells me that somebody had stopped by to see me. Paul, my stalker friend. Fortunately I wasn't there to see him. I'm surprised to learn that he's managed to track me down on this one day I'm spending at Ushirika. After doing some more of Daniel's paperwork on reporting the monthly number of malaria cases, I bid farewell to my Ushirika family. It's been great spending this day with them all. Despite not having worked with them since the beginning of my stay here they have not forgotten me and treat me as one of them. They will all remain such good friends.

On the way home I stop by at the stationery shop to spend some final time with Judy and Avril. We buy some sodas from the shop next door and sit down and listen to some music together. I stay there for awhile before going home to Alice's for dinner. On my way home I buy some small queen cakes at the corner store. These have been a tradition since arriving in the house for special occasions. When Alice arrives home from work that evenig she too brings out a packet of queen cakes from her bag. We really do think like sisters! I think back over all of the times we've spent together drinking chai with queen cakes, from when Alice went through her exams, to volunteer farewells and my birthday celebrations. Tonight is another special occasion to share this symbolic dessert together; it's my last night at Alice's. We wish each other a special *lala salama* before going to sleep.

Chapter 77 – Parting gifts

Each day comes bearing its own gifts. Untie the ribbons.
— Ruth Ann Schabacker

August 2006 – Nairobi, Kenya

I wake up this morning knowing it will be my last day at AMKA clinic. I'm excited about my farewell celebrations and prepared for feelings of sadness as I come to the end of this journey. Mornings are my favourite time in the household and once again I have the privilege of waking up to a great breakfast. Today it's pancakes with cinnamon and banana. I put on my boots, carry my bag over my shoulder and head off up the main street of Jamhuri, where I glance over my shoulder and catch a glimpse of my stalker Paul out of the corner of my eye. Quickly I cross over to the other side of the road and avoid a friendly yet unwanted run-in with him.

I take everything in on this last walk into Dagoretti Corner, passing the usual chaos of matatus and cars and breathing in the copious amounts of diesel pollution. I also find myself being greeted by more people than usual, most of whom seem to know my name. It's a nice feeling to know I have a place in this community.

When I arrive at the clinic, I'm greeted by Oloo, Solphine and George, who all call me a real 'African Australian' woman today when they see my braids that I had done in a small salon in Kibera. Throughout the morning, many of the clinic's regular patients come to visit me on my last day. Grace comes by and her face lights up with a huge smile as I give her a photo of the two of us. Sylvia and her friend Jane also stop by. Then Natalya comes into the clinic. My sister Natalya. I ask Natalya if we can walk to her house so that I can take a small video of her shack, the famous Hotel 46 as I've come to know it with its timber scraps, Cadbury flyers and pop posters decorating the inside. I give her a bag of some of my belongings that I will not be taking back with me, a few t-shirts, my nail polish and shampoo. She's so excited as she looks through the bag. I can only wonder what lies in store for

Natalya in her life, having seen her already go through so much just in these past few months. Just to see her back on track is huge progress.

Back at the clinic more of our friends arrive for the afternoon's party: Evelyn, Josephine, Joanne, Millicent, Margaret and Immaculate. But there's still some work to do first. Solphine and I visit James in Ngando. We walk down the back street and when we approach a train line crossing we notice a gathering of people up ahead and the sounds of a woman's voice shouting. As we get closer we see a largely built Kenyan lady yelling at her husband in Swahili. She pushes him onto the ground and continues to rave at him, much to the amusement of all the onlookers who, like Solphine, are enjoying the domestic dispute. Solphine laughs and says that this lady is a good example of why you shouldn't mess with a Kenyan woman. It sounds like she's accusing her husband of being lazy and not helping out with the chores. The scene winds down and the onlookers continue with their day.

When we arrive we're greeted by James' daughter Joy. Today I sit back and watch Solphine give James a massage with her little helper, Joy, who holds the bottle of oil as Solphine's assistant, having watched me many times now. James continues to do well and it is nice to see him this one last time before leaving. As has been the case with other patients I've been regularly visiting, James has been concerned that my departure will also mean the end of his home visits. I reassure him that he will not be forgotten and that Solphine will be continuing his rehabilitation and more volunteers will be likely to arrive at the clinic soon.

When we walk back to the clinic Solphine and I find a big gathering of friends, patients and employees of AMKA clinic waiting for the party to start. Sister Veronica has even arrived and we all sit down inside the main clinic room which has been transformed into a party room with a few decorations for this afternoon. Sister Veronica brings out a big platter of all my favourite fruits: pineapple, banana, pawpaw and mango. It is so delicious. She explains the tradition and significance of sharing food with people, especially in times of celebration. The other important custom is having somebody feed the guest the first piece of food. So George does the honour of preparing me a plate of food and feeding me my first piece of pineapple. Everybody cheers before helping themselves to the small feast.

We're gathered around the small table in the middle of the clinic room. The room is filled with excitement and happy banter. Sister Veronica calls for everybody's attention for the speeches. She starts by thanking me for all of the hard work I've done at AMKA clinic. She describes the different projects I've been involved in during my time at AMKA and how I've helped the clinic and its patients. She then asks everybody, one by one, to say something about me. I'm extremely humbled by everybody's kind words, not one to like being the centre of attention. Sister Veronica presents me with a card on behalf of the staff at the clinic: from herself, George, Oloo, and Solphine as well as on behalf of some of the patients who I have had the pleasure of meeting but are no longer with us to say goodbye.

Sister Veronica then asks me to stand up. She explains to everybody that since I've arrived in Kenya I've done so much walking. There's no doubt that everybody at some point or other has seen my muddy walking boots. The mzungu's shoes. Sister Veronica continues and says that after all of my hard work I'm in need of some new shoes. Oloo bends down on his knees and starts to unlace my boots. I'm then presented with some beautifully beaded sandals, handmade in Kenya, to replace my old shoes.

The theme continues as Sister Veronica then describes how my clothes have become dirty from my work here in the slums. Solphine can't resist chipping in with 'especially with all of that flour in the food shelter!' She giggles cheekily and everybody laughs. Sister Veronica presents me with a beautiful African blouse made of cotton and a matching tailored skirt, which they help me put on over my clothes. The ensemble is a lovely green with orange and white stripes. Joanne also gives me some beautiful jewellery which she has made herself and some colourful purple and pink kangas all the way from Mombasa. She remembers how much I've admired the kangas on our home visits together. I'm feeling overwhelmed with my friends' generosity and tell everybody that I feel like a model, as they ask me to show off my new look by walking around the room dressed in my new sandals, kangas and jewellery.

After the speeches the dancing begins. Joanne starts singing and one by one the others join in and start moving their curvaceous bodies to the African music. It's a sight to see, with Margaret and Immaculate competing against each other with their hip shaking, Oloo and Alex display some retro dance moves and Sister Veronica dances with Solphine in the middle of the circle. It is so much fun. Joanne pushes me into the middle of the dance circle where I have to move through everybody, one by one, dancing in turn with each person.

Eventually our party comes to an end. We all help to tidy up the room which is followed by many goodbyes with all of my friends. I'm already certain that this will not be a final goodbye for me in Kenya and that I will be back one day. I'm blessed by all the kind words that everybody leaves me with, as they insist that we will all meet again someday and that it had been God's wish to bring us together in Africa. In true Kenyan style my colleagues tell me to greet my family and friends back home in Australia.

Sister Veronica kindly drives me home to Alice's apartment in Jamhuri, where I continue packing my bags. I share a final meal with Alice, Virginia and Jen at home where I present them each with the small gifts and letters I've made for them. We all sit around and share some queen cakes together for dessert and I take in this special moment in my Kenyan home.

I receive a message on my phone which I don't recognise at first, but then realise that it is from Kevin who has tried to call me. I am so excited to hear from him just before leaving and call him back immediately from the roof top of Alice's building, overlooking Jamhuri. As soon as I hear Kevin's voice on the phone I feel that special bond again that we share. He is doing well and sounds positive. He's still staying with his family upcountry after Helen's burial. I tell Kevin that I am leaving later tonight and he's sad to know we will not see each other. I let him know that I have left a letter for him with Sister Veronica to collect when he comes back to Nairobi. I am so happy to have been able to speak to my Kenyan brother.

My taxi arrives and I load my bags into the car outside our apartment. Virginia, Alice, Jen and Adam the watchman are all standing around the car. I cannot believe my eyes when I spot Paul, my stalker, approach the car as he sees that I'm leaving. My Kenyan adventure is full of surprises right up until the last minute! To avoid a confrontation, I jump into the front seat of the car, close the door and wave goodbye to my Jamhuri family. I see Alice and Jen giggling together at my desperation to avoid Paul. This journey has never been short of laughter at these many incredible experiences I've had.

As we head up the street, I ask the driver to make one last stop. We come to a halt out the front of the Jamhuri stationery shop as I see Judy, Avril and Mohammed run out to say goodbye to me in the car. They surprise me with a farewell present; it's a beautiful wooden carving of an African woman. Finally I'm driven away waving goodbye to my friends and my home in Jamhuri.

Chapter 78 – Flying high

There is nothing like returning to a place that remains unchanged to find the ways in which you yourself have altered – Nelson Mandela

Sitting inside Jomo Kenyatta Airport and waiting for my flight to board I receive a final call from Alice to wish me a safe flight back home. I miss her already. Glancing around the airport I feel a world away from Jamhuri and the slums, seeing the abundance of chocolates, perfumes and alcohols in the Duty Free shops. The transition back into a western culture will be a challenging one. My boss, when I left my job before coming to Kenya, may have been right after all. He said 'Belinda, you'll come back a different person'. I shrugged off his comments insisting I wouldn't change.

I believe this journey in Kenya *has* changed me. How can all of my experiences over the last four months not affect how I continue to live my life? It has changed my outlook and perspective on life and life's events. I have learnt to appreciate what we have, to make the most of everyday and not to worry about what we can't control. Deep down I do believe I am still the same person. I made a promise to my friends to never forget them and their stories. And I will carry that promise forward with me.

Right before I board the plane, I receive a final message on my phone. It's from Evelyn and she writes:

> *Thanks for being with us. God had a reason for sending you in Kenya. You are our guardian angel. Safe journey and we will always love you dear*

I board my flight and as we take off I look out the window at Nairobi, the slums and the Kenyan countryside as they disappear below me. I'm leaving this beautiful country and its people behind but I know that a part of it will stay with me forever.

Promise You Won't Forget Us

Belinda Evans

Epilogue

Be the change you want to see in the world – Ghandi

February 2013 – Adelaide, Australia

Since leaving behind my experiences in Kenya and returning to my life in Australia and beyond, I have never stopped looking back on this life-changing experience. Many people say that a piece of your heart always remains in Africa once you've spent any amount of time there. And that has been the case for me as well as my volunteer friends with whom I shared my journey in Kenya.

I returned to Kenya six months later, having kept in touch with many of my friends there including Alice, Irene, Daniel, Sister Veronica, George, Kevin and Sylvia. I was always certain that I would one day return, treasuring every email and hand written letter addressed to me that kept the link alive with my life in Nairobi. On this return visit, I resumed my work at AMKA clinic where I was reunited with Kevin, Sylvia and many of my other incredible friends. I also took on a different role as a teacher at a primary school in Kibera, working closely with the children from this slum that has always touched me with its severe poverty and enormous sense of community.

Six years have now passed since I took my first steps down the streets of Jamhuri and into those slums of Kibera. Not a day goes by when I don't think about my journey in Kenya; the people I met, the adventures I experienced and the many lessons I learnt. Many of the incredible people I volunteered with have been influenced in similar ways and have maintained strong links with their projects and continued the fight for progress in Kenya.

Annie returned to Nairobi later that same year, not long after I left, and has since returned at least once every year for the past six years. She is currently planning her seventh trip and is an inspiration in her fundraising activities and journeys back to Kenya. Annie continues to work closely with GVN and has established her own charity, *Caring for the children of Africa*, for which she conducts regular fundraising activities which have enabled her to provide ongoing support to some of the areas she's identified as most in need of help. These include providing beds, materials and food for under-resourced orphanages, building temporary houses for the thousands of displaced Kenyans living in Internally Displaced Person (IDP) camps following the violent 2008 political elections as well as establishing sustainable income-generating activities. Annie's efforts and kind-heartedness are inspirational and she is deeply loved by all the Kenyans she continues to help.

Emilie has sponsored Kevin's education for the last few years through the AMKA clinic. I still remember our walk up Mount Kenya together, where she told me about her dream to become a doctor and to return to Kenya one day. Following her time in Kenya, Emilie was accepted into medical school and she has now realised this dream by qualifying as a doctor in Canada.

Jen has also regularly returned to Kenya and is currently living there permanently in Kibera slum. Jen founded her own charity called *Uweza Aid Foundation* with another volunteer she met in her project working at an orphanage in Kibera. Uweza continues to grow bigger and stronger and is making many positive changes in Kibera and beyond, with such projects as a child sponsorship program, a community soccer team, a counselling program and most recently a successful fundraising campaign to buy a community centre for the youth of Kibera. The community centre is a safe space where the children can engage in after-school activities as well as a base for organising future projects within the slums.

Already Uweza has made a positive impact on the poverty-stricken community of Kibera. Jen's dedication and motivation to help Kibera is beyond incredible. From time to time she sends me an email during her trips to Kenya to tell me that a young man selling fruits in Jamhuri (Stanley) was asking about me, or that she ran into Alice who says to say hello. It makes my day to receive news like this. On one occasion about a year after I'd left, Jen spotted my Kenyan stalker Paul still lurking around Ushirika clinic looking for me! It's nice to know I'm still remembered, in whatever way that may be!

I still receive emails from my Kenyan friends. Debra, the super nurse from Ushirika, has been working as a nurse in western Kenya. She recently informed me she got married and had given birth to a baby girl. Daniel also got married and has a two year old daughter. He was working in a UNICEF project as a nutritionist for a few years before finding himself out of work for a long time and struggling to support his young family. In his latest email Daniel wrote that 'God has finally answered my prayers', receiving an appointment letter from the Ministry of Health and securing a three year contract as a nutritionist in the north eastern Islam region of Kenya working with the Somali tribe.

Although the situation is improving and the fight against poverty continues, times continue to be tough for many in Kenya. The battle against HIV and AIDS is ongoing. Sadly, Evelyn passed away within the year after my first visit to Kenya. James is still going strong in his battle with AIDS as is his wife Grace. George and Solphine are still working with the AMKA project and Joanne is still actively involved as a community health worker. Oloo retired from his position of social worker not long after I left. The AMKA project continues to do its best to help the community with its limited resources yet hardworking and compassionate team.

Sylvia has kept in touch with me since I left Kenya. I arranged with AMKA clinic to sponsor her education, determined to give her the chance to get her high school diploma after all the problems she had faced. She finished high school two years ago. From time to time Sylvia emails me with news of where she is and what she is doing. Today, Sylvia is one of many women in the slums of Nairobi who is still searching for work and looking for a way to change her life.

I lost contact with Kevin, despite knowing that Emilie continued to sponsor him through AMKA clinic. Of all of the people I met in Nairobi, it is often Kevin who I have wondered about the most. There is that sibling bond between us and I have always prayed that he is doing alright, wherever his journey has taken him.

Incredibly, during the process of writing this book and at a stage when I was immersed in Kevin and Helen's story and re-reading some of the hand-written letters I have kept from him, one day I received an email in my inbox. It was from Kevin. He wrote:

Hi sister, it's Kevin your brother i really miss you, i know have been silent but it was not i like it but my finance status. I do cherish every moment that we spend together, sister this is my email address, nice time and love alway.

And then...

Hi Naisula, Belinda things have not gone the way i thought they will go but living here have became harder than before. I am used in moving from one place to another that is way you brother life is. I remember we love chapatti but nowdays it has became a story me. I am going to sleep. Nice time

After exchanging a few short emails, it was easy to know that it really was Kevin. I knew it was him. After years of not hearing anything, it has filled my heart with joy to re-establish some contact with Kevin. I took it as a sign that I was meant to write this book and to share these stories with the world. Kevin is still in Kenya and struggling to get by. His emails that ensued requested money for food and for clothes to wear. Like many, his life is a constant battle to survive.

Many positive efforts are being made every day to overcome the problems of poverty and HIV that are still affecting Kenya. Progress is happening and changes are being made. The rates of HIV have decreased in the last 10 years. However despite this progress there is still a serious HIV and AIDS epidemic in Kenya and sub-Saharan Africa. National elections held in 2007 saw widespread violence and political unrest that resulted in over 1000 deaths and up to 600,000 Kenyans displaced from their homes and subjected to extreme violence. Many are still living in IDP camps around the country today. The problem of poverty is an ongoing battle.

In Kibera, the government started a relocation scheme in 2009 to relocate the millions of residents living in these slums into formal new housing blocks. It's a part of the UN Millennium Development Goals phasing out programs of informal settlements and was initiated by the unity government of Raide Odinga, a Kenyan MP from Kibera. The relocation project is estimated to take up to 9 years and cost over $1 billion, supported by the UN. Despite good intentions, the scheme has not gone ahead without controversy, with speculation over the cost of these new apartments for Kibera residents, security and long-term feasibility.

My volunteer journey to Kenya is just one of millions that take place every year around the world. A friend once asked me what difference one can really make by going and volunteering in Africa, suggesting the problems are too big for the hands of a few people. I responded that it's not only about what we can do, but it's also about what we can see for ourselves and take back to share with others. Our efforts do not end the day we return home. In many cases, it is just the beginning of another journey. The journey of sharing our stories, of raising awareness and initiating further actions.

Not everybody has the incredible opportunity I had to volunteer abroad but there are endless ways that someone can choose to make a difference and contribute their time, money, ideas and resources. Whether it is donating soft toys and toothbrushes, sponsoring a child, hosting or supporting a fundraising activity, or simply reading an article about the current famine in East Africa, everybody can help in some small way. The Chinese proverb states that *a journey of a thousand miles begins with one small step*. I believe that many small steps have the power to make great changes.

Handwritten letter from Sylvia

6th May 2006

Hi Belinda

How is the going? Hoping that all is quite well with you. Even us here we are quite okay except for the few ups and downs of life. I've missed you quite a lot for you impacted on my life immensely. You visited me while I was sick, attended to me as a mother would do for her daughter, massaged my aching body with the tender love of a sister would do to her other sibling and most importantly you gave me a listening ear as a dearest friend to one of her pals. Indeed I felt a person worthwhile when I could share my problems and inner secrets to you. I felt relaxed and free of stress when you were around because I could speak my whole heart out with trust and confidentiality.

Belinda, a good friend is more precious than rubies and all the things there is none you can compare to. You gave me hope, hope that sustains life especially in a country like ours which is a capitalist society which thrives on exploitation of the poor but favours the best sycophants like ministers and their class. The rich continues to get rich while the poor wallow in absect poverty.

Words cannot express my gratitude and sincere appreciation for your pledge to sponsor my education. That's a very important gift you can give me especially in this modern world. Knowledge is power and education will enlighten me making me literate on the technical know-how to this changing world. Armed with knowledge I will be able to face the challenges of this society of today, for one cannot run away from challenges but once acquired you face them as a woman and to reach a level where I can also offer a helping hand to the needy especially needy girls sailing in the same boat as mine.

You have a good heart and good heart indeed especially the case you took all the way from Australia to come and to look for the sick patients in Kenya. We appreciate very much the trouble you took as my guardian to write to the organisation that I was all I can say is a big THANKS. It's very humbling that people like you exist out there especially in this world filled with people with moral decaying and corruption.

All the people back here home conveyed their greeting to you. Live on my star and illuminate my path. Thanks very much.

I remain yours faithfully,

Sylvia Akoth Atieno.

Dedication – 1st Corinthians Chapter 13, verse 1-9

2nd Corinthians Chapter 9, verse 6, 11

Promise You Won't Forget Us

Email from Sylvia

Subject: Greetings
Date: 20/09/2007
From: Sylvia

Hi Belinda,

How is the going? I pray all is okay in France. Belinda sister advised me to change school due to poor hygienic conditions in my former school. We used to share beds especially I used to sleep with a student who had tuberculosis. The problem was aggravated by the fact that the sick students were usually given medication of headaches and stomach ache so most of the ailing students used to pass the diseases to other students because there was no proper medical attention given to us.

There are no access roads to the district hospital for the students to be taken to receive treatment and the administration performance is of lacklustre attitude where everybody is to carry his own cross and God for us all. As such this becomes a stumbling block to me especially the fact that I come from very far. Sister has looked for me a school and I hope God willing this week I will be admitted.

Belinda, I always appreciate your concerns in my day to day life. You are a wonderful person and you occupy the first place in my life. I thank God for making our paths meet and for bringing a person like you into my life. Once again thanks very much for stretching a helping hand to me and giving me a shoulder to lean on. Thank you for moulding me and giving me a shoulder to lean on. Thank you for moulding me into a person of dignity when despair threatened to tear me apart. Thanks very much for making a space in your life for me. Thanks for accepting responsibility of me. Belinda I always work very hard and I personally glance at the past to make the present tolerable and the future worth waiting for. Thanks my star shining and illuminating my paths when all had conspired against me. When life currents threatened to swallow me you swam me to safety. I will be eternally grateful for you coming into my life.

Indeed a faithful friend like a timely shelter and he who finds one has found a rare treasure.

Lots of love

Sylvia.

Belinda Evans

Handwritten letter from Kevin

Received 2007

    Dear Naisula,

    Get more greetings from me, I just hope you are fine sister. It has been awhile sister since I heard your voice, I real miss it. The voice that gives me courage. Even if I miss it, I still have your courage through your messages. I like your messages sis.

    It has been sometime since my sister left for home but I feel like it is ten years since you left, I real miss you sister. I just hope God will help me to reach on the top of my dream, I am sure one day we will see each other sis.

    I just have my first cut since I join the course, I would like you to know that I real appreciate all support and everything that you give me, for that I would like to tell you thank you sis.

    I would like you to know that in Kenya we are getting rains but even if it's raining we still get some of sun rays.

    I just want to remind you that I was born in 28th March 1988. I would like you to pass my message to mother Emilie, greet her and ask her if she got my letter. I would be grateful if you help me sis.

    Just greet your father, mother, sister and all my friends. You know that all your friends are my friends. Have a nice day sis,

Bye

    Bye

        Bye

            Your brother

                    Kevin Nelly Kidiga

Belinda Evans can be contacted via email on belinda-evans@hotmail.com

Thank you for supporting her work and for helping share her stories from Africa

Global Volunteer Network

http://www.globalvolunteernetwork.org/

Our vision is to connect people with communities in need, with a particular focus on vulnerable women and children. We do this by supporting the work of local community organizations in countries through the placement of international volunteers.

The Global Volunteer Network (GVN) was launched in December 2000 by Colin Salisbury, its Founder and Executive Director, after spending time volunteering in Ghana, West Africa. While he was there he saw the tremendous difference volunteers could make in helping local organizations achieve their goals. Upon returning to New Zealand he spent some time researching the different volunteer organizations around the world and was amazed at how expensive and limiting many programs were in terms of volunteer opportunities.

At GVN we align with the idea of 'local solutions to local problems', so we work with local community organizations in each country. We believe that local communities are in the best position to determine their needs, and we provide volunteers to help them achieve their goals.

GVN has volunteer opportunities in a number of countries through our partner organizations in Asia, South America and Africa. They also do regular fundraising hikes to allow an active role in raising funds for communities in need, to Mt. Everest Base Camp, Machu Picchu, and Mt. Kilimanjaro.

Caring for the children of Africa

http://www.caringforthechildrenofafrica.org/

Caring for the Children of Africa Inc is a registered non-profit charity with the main focus being to support people affected by political unrest, famine and disease. It began in November 2007 following the second visit by my close friend Annie Copley to the slums of Nairobi, Kenya, where she worked with me as a volunteer with GVN (Global Volunteer Network). Annie has a passion for the people of Africa which stems from this work in the HIV/AIDS programs, working with the poorest of the poor.

On returning to Australia after her first 3 months in Kenya in 2006, Annie felt the need to continue the work and with dear friend Lauro Martire organised their first fundraising dinner in his popular Café/Restaurant, ETC. in Adelaide - the evening was a huge success so it was decided to make this a yearly event. Annie returns to Kenya each year to personally work in the various projects throughout Nairobi and Nakuru where the money raised continues to give hope to the people of Kenya by providing food (incl. child porridge programs), access to clean water, medical and building supplies to IDPs (Internally Displaced Persons) to build huts, class-rooms, toilet blocks etc. Local orphanages and HIV/Aids Clinics are also supported by this work.

Uweza Aid Foundation

http://www.uweza.org/

Uweza is the Kiswahili word for ability and power. Uweza Aid Foundation aims to combat the cycle of poverty that persists in Kenya's Kibera slum by building upon and nurturing already existing resourcefulness and capabilities. All of our projects are community-based, developed and/or run by Kenyans, primarily residents of Kibera who are dedicated to the betterment of their community. Uweza was established by Jen Saprito, a volunteer friend of Belinda's from their first trip to Kenya in 2006.

Uweza is a 501(c)(3) organization registered in Illinois, USA and a registered NGO in Kenya. Current projects target youth aged 4 to 25 and include a soccer academy, journalism and art clubs, traditional dancing group, educational sponsorship, and life skills training. We hope to contribute to the betterment of the Kibera community by supporting education, developing talents, building life skills, and improving emotional and mental well-being.

Uweza was created because we observed the resiliency and ingenuity of Kenyans working to better their communities. By working alongside Kenyans and providing the funding and resources to implement their ideas, we believe that we can find solutions and evoke change in a way that is valued and sustainable.

74490